D1246717

Third Edition

biography
for
beginners

Presidents of the United States

Laurie Lanzen Harris,
Editor

Favorable Impressions

P.O. Box 69018 • Pleasant Ridge, Michigan 48069

Laurie Lanzen Harris, *Editor*
Dan Robert Harris, *Contributing Editor*

Library of Congress Cataloging-in-Publication Data

Presidents of the United States / Laurie Lanzen Harris, editor.—3rd ed.
    p. cm.—(Biography for beginners)
  Includes indexes.
  ISBN 978-1-931360-45-6 (alk. paper)
  1. Presidents—United States—Biography—Juvenile literature.
I. Harris, Laurie Lanzen.
  E176.1.B63 2009
  973.09'9–dc22

                                       2009008230

The information in this publication was compiled from the sources cited and from other sources considered reliable. While every possible effort has been made to ensure reliability, the publisher will not assume liability for damages caused by inaccuracies in the data, and makes no warranty, express or implied, on the accuracy of the information contained herein.

This book is printed on acid-free paper meeting the ANSI Z39.48 Standard. The infinity symbol that appears above indicate that the paper in this book meets that standard.

Printed in the United States

Contents

The Presidents of the United States

Preface

Welcome to *Biography for Beginners, Presidents of the United States, Third Edition*. Since beginning *Biography for Beginners* in 1995, we have received many requests from librarians and teachers for a series on the Presidents written for early readers. The first, and subsequent editions of the volume were prepared in response to those requests.

The Plan of the Work

Biography for Beginners, Presidents of the United States was especially created for young readers, ages 7 to 10, in a format they can read, understand, and use for assignments. The Presidents are arranged chronologically, from George Washington to Barack Obama. Each entry begins with a heading listing the President's name, birth and death dates, number and length of term, and nickname, if any. Boldfaced headings lead readers to information about birth, growing up, school, political and professional careers, marriage and family, presidential term, life at the White House, and retirement and death. Each entry ends with a list of historic sites and addresses of Presidential libraries or museums that students may contact for further information. In addition, World Wide Web addresses are given for helpful sites on each President. Each of these sites has been reviewed, and at press time, each of these addresses was available and working.

Each entry includes paintings, photos, and other illlustrations from the Presidents's lives. These illustrations are taken from the Library of Congress and the individual Presidential libraries and museums cited at the end of the volume.

Audience

This book is intended for young readers in grades 2 through 5 who are studying the Presidents for the first time. Most children will use this book to study one President at a time, usually as part of a class assignment. For this reason, standard information about the Presidency and the history of the U.S.—facts behind the Revolutionary War, the Civil War, World Wars I and II; the content and purpose of the Declaration of Independence, the Constitution, and the Bill of Rights; a description of the Executive, Judicial and Legislative Branches of government; how Presidential elections and the electoral college work—are repeated in the entries.

Some of these standard topics are also described and defined below, under the section title, "Basic Facts about the Presidency." These topics are also briefly defined in the "Glossary" section at the back of the volume. Glossary topics are bold-faced in the entries, as are the names of other Presidents, to refer readers to the Glossary or other entries in the volume.

Appendix

In the Appendix of the volume, there are three graphs that bring together information on the Presidents in an easy to use format. **The Presidents' Term of Office** includes political party, dates of term, age at inauguration, Vice President, popular vote, electoral vote, and runner-up: with electoral and popular vote. **The Presidents' Personal Lives** includes date and place of birth, wife (with birth and death dates), children (with birth and death dates), occupation before Presidential term and date and place of death. **The Presidents in Their Own Times** provides a timeline that lists major historical and political events for each President's term, including the births and deaths of other Presidents.

Index

The volume concludes with three Indexes. The Subject Index includes references to all the Presidents, First Ladies, and important terms and events discussed in the entries. The Places of Birth and Birthday Indexes give information on those aspects of the Presidents' lives.

Our Advisors

The first edition of *Biography for Beginners*: *Presidents of the United States* was reviewed by an Advisory Board comprising school librarians, public librarians, and reading specialists. Their thoughtful comments and suggestions have been invaluable in developing this publication. Any errors, however, are mine alone. The Advisory Board for the first edition of the *Presidents* have all retired now, but their spirit continues to inspire us as we prepare new editions of the work.

Your Comments Are Welcome

Our goal is to provide accurate, accessible biographical information for early readers. Please write or call me with your comments.

Acknowledgments

I would like to thank the Prints and Photographs Division of the Library of Congress for their help in obtaining illustrations. Special thanks are also due to the helpful staffs of the many Presidential libraries that provided pictures of the Presidents and their families. Thank you to Sans Serif for outstanding design and layout.

Laurie Harris, *Editor and Publisher*

Basic Facts about the Presidency

THE CONSTITUTION AND THE PRESIDENT

The Constitution outlines the requirements that a candidate must meet to run for President:

1. The candidate must be born a U.S. citizen.

2. The candidate must be at least 35 years old.

3. The candidate must have lived in the U.S. for at least 14 years.

The Constitution lists the duties of the President:

1. Acts as Commander-in-Chief of the armed forces

2. Makes treaties with other countries

3. Appoints judges and ambassadors

4. Reports on the "State of the Union" to the Congress

5. Meets with foreign leaders

6. Upholds all the laws of the nation

7. May grant pardons to those convicted of crimes against the U.S.

8. Meets with the leaders of foreign countries

ELECTIONS

Presidents are elected for a term of four years. They can only serve two terms in office, for a total of eight years. Every four years, in November, voters go the polls to vote for President.

THE ELECTORAL COLLEGE

Americans vote for President and Vice President in a different way than they do for any other elected official. The rules for the election of a President and Vice President are outlined in the Constitution.

The President and the Vice President are *not* elected by direct vote of the people. Instead, they are elected by members of the Electoral College. When a voter casts a vote for a presidential candidate, he or she is really voting for an "elector." That is someone who is pledged to vote for one of the presidential candidates. After the presidential election, the electors meet and cast their ballots for the candidates they are pledged to.

The number of electors is equal to the total number of U.S. Representatives and Senators. Right now, that number is 538. To win the election, the presidential candidate must get a majority of all the possible electoral votes. Today, that number is 270 (one more than half of 538). If one candidate cannot get a majority of votes from the electors, then the winner is determined by the House of Representatives.

Twice in U.S. history, the President has been chosen by the House of Representatives. In 1801, **Thomas Jefferson** was unable to get a majority of electoral votes, so his election was decided in the House. In 1825, **John Quincy Adams** was unable to get a majority of electoral votes, so he also became president when the majority of the members of the House voted for him.

Presidents
of the
United States

George Washington
1732-1799
First President of the United States (1789-1797)
"The Father of His Country"

GEORGE WASHINGTON WAS BORN February 22, 1732, in West-moreland County, Virginia. His father was Augustine Washington, and his mother was Mary Washington. Augustine was a planter, and Mary was a homemaker. George was the oldest of six children. He had two sisters, Elizabeth and Mildred, and three brothers, Samuel, John, and Charles. Augustine Washington also had children from an earlier marriage. His first wife, Jane Washington, died in 1728. George had two half-brothers, Lawrence and Augustine, from that first marriage.

GEORGE WASHINGTON GREW UP in Virginia on the family farm, called Ferry Farm. Augustine Washington owned a plantation that was worked by slaves. When George was seven, his family moved to a larger farm, called Mount Vernon. George loved the outdoors and especially riding his pony.

When George was just 11 years old, his father died. Soon after, his half-brother Lawrence married and became head of the plantation at Mount Vernon. George lived with his mother and sisters and brothers at Ferry Farm.

George spent a lot of time at Mount Vernon visiting Lawrence. Lawrence was in many ways like a father to George. He taught him to hunt and fish.

GEORGE WASHINGTON WENT TO SCHOOL at a local school. His teacher was a minister who taught George how to read, write, and add. George only went to school for a few years, and he never went to college. He almost joined the Navy when he was just 14. But his mother was against it. Instead, George began to work when he was 16.

BECOMING A SURVEYOR: George Washington's first job was as a surveyor. A surveyor measures land for governments and for land owners to determine the boundaries of properties. As a surveyor, Washington got a chance to travel and see the country.

Washington's first job was to survey land in the western part of Virginia. He enjoyed this work for several years. But his life changed again when he was 20 and his half-brother Lawrence died. He had been very close to Lawrence, and he felt his loss deeply. A year after Lawrence died, Washington decided to become a soldier.

Washington as a surveyor, at about 18.

LIFE AS A SOLDIER: When George Washington was growing up, the United States did not yet exist. Instead, several European countries controlled parts of what is now the U.S. In the 1750s, when Washington became a soldier, the British and French were fighting over who controlled areas in what is now Ohio and Pennsylvania.

As part of an army of volunteers from Virginia, George Washington fought for the British against the French. He was a brave man, especially in a battle in what is now Pittsburgh. Twice

First Lady Martha Washington.

his horse was shot out from under him. He found four holes in his coat where bullets had gone through the cloth.

LIFE AS A PLANTER: In the 1760s, Washington gave up his life as a soldier and returned to Virginia. He took over Mount Vernon and became a planter. He grew tobacco, corn, and wheat.

Washington's lands were worked by slaves. It is hard for us to imagine that **slavery** was acceptable to a man as great as Washington. But he did use slaves to farm his land. After he and his wife died, all of Washington's slaves were made free.

MARRIAGE AND FAMILY: George and Martha Washington married on January 6, 1759, after he had returned to Mount Vernon to become a planter. Martha had been married before, but her first husband died. She had two children named John and Martha.

George and Martha never had children of their own. Washington always loved his stepchildren. He treated Martha, whose nickname was Patsy, and John, whose nickname was Jackie, as if they were his own. Sadly, Patsy died when she was just a teenager. Jackie died while serving in the Revolutionary War. Despite their losses, George and Martha were a happy, loving couple.

THE REVOLUTIONARY WAR: In the 1770s, most of the area that is now the eastern United States was a colony of England. That means that the people were ruled by England. They paid taxes to the British government and were ruled by a king, George III.

Some of the colonists were happy being part of England. Some were not. They believed that the colonies should have their own government, a government that they controlled. The people who wanted a separate government began to talk about breaking away from England. These were the people who began the American **Revolutionary War**. They chose George Washington to be the leader of their army.

Washington didn't really want the job. He felt he was "unequal to the task," that he couldn't do it. But those who knew him thought he was the best choice. Washington served the new country and was loved by his soldiers and the public. He became General of the army, but insisted that he not be paid for his work.

The United States became a country on July 4, 1776. That is the day that the Continental Congress accepted the "**Declaration of Independence.**" It states that all men are born equal and free. They have the right to revolt against those who will not give them freedom. Those are the reasons that the Revolutionary War was fought.

Washington was named Commander in Chief of the Continental Army. That means that it was his job to put together an army and train soldiers. He had to ask the new government for food, guns, and clothing for his men. Often the men were poorly fed and sheltered. One winter, the army stayed in Valley Forge, Pennsylvania. The soldiers suffered greatly because of the cold and lack of food. Washington pled with the new government for more food and supplies. They came at last, and the troops were ready to fight again.

The battles of the Revolutionary War took place in many areas throughout the eastern U.S. They fought in Massachusetts, New

★ ★ ★

WASHINGTON'S TEETH: People have often joked about Washington's false teeth. Like most people of his time he had false teeth because there was not dental care at that time. Many people thought his false teeth were made of wood, but they were actually made of **hippopotamus teeth**.

His false teeth were very uncomfortable. He was wearing them the day he was painted for the picture that appears on our one dollar bill. Maybe that's why he looks so unhappy in that picture.

★ ★ ★

York, New Jersey, and Pennsylvania. The war went on for six years. Finally, the British surrendered in the final battle of the war, at Yorktown, Pennsylvania. The Continental Army, under General George Washington, had fought and won independence for a new nation.

A NEW NATION AND A NEW CONSTITUTION: The United States was now a free nation. But the citizens had to decide how their new government would work. A group of men met in Philadelphia to develop the **Constitution**. The Constitution is the plan for the national government.

The U.S. Constitution divides power between the three branches of government. The Executive Branch is made up of the President and his **Cabinet**. The Legislative branch is made up of the **House of Representatives** and the **Senate**. They make the laws for the country. The Judicial Branch is made up of the U.S. Court system, including the nine-member **Supreme Court**.

THE FIRST PRESIDENT OF THE UNITED STATES: Washington never wanted to be President. He said that he "had no wish but that of living and dying an honest man on my own farm." But, he ran for the office for the good of his country.

HOW IS A PRESIDENT ELECTED? Americans vote for President and Vice President in a different way than they do for any other elected official. The rules for the election of a President and Vice President are outlined in the Constitution.

This painting is called "The Prayer at Valley Forge."
During the Revolutionary War, Washington and his troops suffered
through a harsh winter in Valley Forge, Pennsylvania.

The President and the Vice President are *not* elected by direct vote of the people. Instead, they are elected by members of the **Electoral College**. When a voter casts a vote for a presidential candidate, he or she is really voting for an "elector." That is someone who is pledged to vote for one of the presidential candidates. After the presidential election, the electors meet and vote for the candidates they are pledged to.

In that first election, Washington received all the electoral votes — 69 — for President. **John Adams** received 34 votes to become Vice President.

THE NATION'S CAPITAL CHANGES LOCATION: At the time Washington became president, New York City was the capital of the nation. So as the first President, he served from New York City. The next year, Washington and his wife, Martha, moved to Philadelphia, the new capital of the nation. Wherever they lived, Martha was known as a warm and gracious First Lady.

THE EARLY YEARS OF THE NEW NATION: In the early years of the country, many problems had to be discussed and decisions had to be made. Some people were afraid that the new government would grow too strong. It would become too powerful and individuals would lose their rights.

The country was growing. There were 13 states originally, and by the time Washington left office there were 18. What should the governments of each state be like? France was at war. Should the U.S. get involved? These and many other problems had to be decided by the new government.

Washington gave his advice on these and many issues. He was always a man of honesty and people valued his thoughts. Washington also created the first "**Cabinet**." The Cabinet is the group of

Washington as President.

9

advisers who help the President make decisions. Washington chose great patriots like **Thomas Jefferson** to be in that first Cabinet.

In 1791, Congress established the District of Columbia as our nation's capital. It was named in honor of our first president: Washington, D.C. Washington laid the cornerstone for the U.S. Capitol building in 1793.

Presidents are elected to terms that last four years. At the end of his first term, Washington was ready to retire to Mount Vernon. But the country still wanted him as President. So, reluctantly, he ran again. He was reelected by an overwhelming majority of votes and stayed another four years. Finally, in 1797, Washington stepped down.

FAMOUS QUOTE: When he left office, Washington gave a Farewell Address to the nation. In it he said:

"Observe good faith and justice toward all nations. Cultivate peace and harmony with all."

RETIREMENT TO MOUNT VERNON: Washington was happy to retire from office. He was eager to return to Mount Vernon and to his life as a planter.

But his retirement lasted only two years. In December 1799, Washington went out on his farm on a cold, rainy day. He became very ill and couldn't swallow or breathe. Martha was at his side when he died on December 17, 1799.

The country mourned the death of their first President. General Henry Lee spoke to the Congress at Washington's death. He called

CHOPPING DOWN THE CHERRY TREE: One of the most famous stories about George Washington tells of him chopping down a cherry tree. It is probably not a true story. It was most likely made up by people who respected George Washington, especially his honesty.

This is the story: George was given a hatchet when he was six. With the hatchet, he chopped at a cherry tree. The tree nearly died, and George's father was very angry. When he asked George who had chopped at the tree, George said he had done it. "I cannot tell a lie," he supposedly said. His father wasn't mad then, just happy that his son would tell the truth.

This story became a legend and was told for generations. Probably it became so popular because people have always thought so much of the man who was our first President. He was a man of great honesty, and he was humble, too. So the story is a way of remembering him and honoring him.

him "First in war, first in peace, and first in the hearts of his countrymen." Martha lived on at Mount Vernon until her death in 1802.

WHAT DID HE LOOK LIKE? Washington was a very tall man for his time—6 feet 2 inches tall. One of his favorite foods was ice cream. One summer when he was President, he spent $200 on ice cream alone.

FOR MORE INFORMATION ON GEORGE WASHINGTON:

Historic Sites:

George Washington Birthplace National Monument
1732 Popes Creek Road
Washington's Birthplace, VA 22443-5115
Phone: 804-224-1732

Mount Vernon
P.O. Box 110
Mount Vernon, VA 22121
Phone: 703-780-2000

WORLD WIDE WEB ADDRESSES:

The White House offers young readers information on the U.S. government and the Presidents on a Web site called **"White House 101."** The address is:
http://www.whitehouse.gov/about/white_house_101/

The Internet Public Library has a site on the Presidents. The address is:
http://www.ipl.org/div/potus

American Memory is a site maintained by the Library of Congress that contains biographical and historical information on the Presidents. It also provides links to Presidential portraits.
For George Washington:
http://memory.loc.gov/ammem/today/feb22.html

George Washington Birthplace National Monument
http://www.nps.gov/gewa/index.htm

Mount Vernon
http://www.mountvernon.org

John Adams
1735-1826
Second President of the United States (1797-1801)
"The Atlas of Independence"

JOHN ADAMS WAS BORN on October 30, 1735, in Braintree, Massachusetts. (The city is now called Quincy.) His father, John Adams, was a farmer. His mother, Susanna Adams, was a homemaker. John was the oldest of three boys. His brothers were Peter and Elihu Adams.

JOHN ADAMS GREW UP in Quincy in a family that loved reading. "I was very early taught to read at home," John Adams remembered. He also helped out around the farm, chopping wood and milking cows.

JOHN ADAMS WENT TO SCHOOL at a local school. His teacher was named Mrs. Belcher. She "lived in the next house on the opposite side of the road," he remembered. Later, Adams went to the local public school. He worked hard in Greek, Latin, and math. He wanted to go to college, so he had to do well in those subjects.

When he was 15, Adams went to Harvard College. He graduated four years later. In his first job after college, he taught elementary school. He wanted to become a lawyer, so after teaching during the day he studied law at night.

BECOMING INVOLVED IN POLITICS: In 1758, Adams started to work as a lawyer. Around this time, he became interested in politics. In the 1750s, most of the area that is now the eastern United States was a colony of England. That means that the people were ruled by England. They paid taxes to the British government and were ruled by a king, George III.

Some of the colonists were happy being part of England. Some were not. They believed that the colonies should have their own government. They resented the fact that they had to pay taxes to a government they didn't create or control.

The Stamp Act was a British tax that angered Adams. It forced the colonists to pay an extra tax on things like newspapers and legal papers. It even taxed playing cards. Adams wrote articles in newspapers about the Stamp Act. He became known as an important thinker and writer in the cause of freedom.

The people who wanted a separate government began to talk about breaking away from England. These were the people who began the American **Revolutionary War**.

MARRIAGE AND FAMILY:
John Adams married Abigail Smith on October 25, 1764. They had five children: Abigail, John Quincy, Susanna, Charles, and Thomas. Susanna died when she was two. All the other children lived to be adults. John Quincy Adams became the sixth President of the United States. John and John Quincy Adams were the first father and son to be elected President. In the twentieth century, **George Bush** and

First Lady Abigail Adams.

George W. Bush became the second father and son elected to the presidency.

John and Abigail spent many years apart during their long marriage. They wrote each other many letters over those years. Their letters show how much they loved and cared for each other. They also show what an intelligent and witty woman Abigail was. As the founding fathers were writing the Declaration of Independence, Abigail wrote to John: "Don't forget the ladies!" Men were working hard to ensure their rights and freedoms in the new country. She wanted to make sure that women would enjoy the same rights and freedoms, also. She is remembered as one of the most intelligent, warm, and witty First Ladies.

JOHN ADAMS AND THE DECLARATION OF INDEPENDENCE:
John Adams was part of a group that wrote the **"Declaration of Independence."** It is a document that states that all men are born

The Signing of the Declaration of Independence. Among the five men standing at the center of the painting, Adams is the figure at the far left. Thomas Jefferson is second from the right. Next to Jefferson is Benjamin Franklin.

equal and free. It says that people have the right to revolt against those who will not give them freedom.

Before they began, Adams wrote a letter to **Thomas Jefferson**, one of the men chosen to write the Declaration. In it, Adams encouraged Jefferson to be the main author of the Declaration. Adams could be cantankerous, and he knew it. He told Jefferson that his milder manner and fine prose would help the country and the document. Jefferson was indeed the main author of the Declaration, but Adams also had a major role. The Declaration was approved and signed on July 4, 1776.

The day the Declaration was signed, John Adams wrote to Abigail. "Yesterday, the greatest question was decided which ever was debated in America, and a greater perhaps never was nor will be decided among men. A resolution was passed without one dissenting colony, "that these United Colonies are, and of right ought to be, free and independent States'."

THE REVOLUTIONARY WAR: The U.S. went to war with Britain. The new country formed an army and organized to fight for freedom.

Unlike **George Washington**, Adams was not a soldier or leader in the army during the **Revolutionary War**. Instead, he used his talents to write and speak in Europe on behalf of the new nation. So during the war, Adams went to France to try to find money and support for the new United States.

LIFE IN EUROPE DURING THE WAR: Adams lived first in France and then in the Netherlands during the war. He and other Americans, like Benjamin Franklin, worked on agreements with European leaders. These leaders agreed to support the new country and to lend it money.

In 1781, the Revolutionary War finally came to an end. The Continental Army of the U.S. had defeated the British. The United States was a free country. Adams signed the agreement between the U.S. and Britain that ended the war. For his travels on behalf of the new nation he earned the nickname, "The Atlas of Independence."

In 1785, Adams became the first minister to Britain from the U.S. He and his family lived in England for three years. Then, in 1788, he came home.

RETURNING HOME: By the time Adams returned to the U.S., the country had a new **Constitution**. The Constitution is the plan for the national government.

The U.S. Constitution divides power between three branches. The Executive Branch is made up of the President and his **Cabinet**. The Legislative branch contains the **House of Representatives** and the **Senate**, who make the laws of the country. The Judicial Branch includes the U.S. Court system. It is headed by the **Supreme Court**.

The Constitution outlines how the President will be elected. In the first election in 1788, George Washington was elected President and John Adams was elected Vice President. He served as Vice President for eight years, from 1789 to 1797.

FIRST VICE PRESIDENT OF THE UNITED STATES: Adams didn't like being Vice President. He didn't really have much to do. At that time, the only responsibility he had was to attend Senate meetings. He said, "I am Vice President. In this I am nothing, but I may be everything." He realized the job of Vice President had few responsibilities. But if Washington died, he would be responsible for "everything."

THE DEVELOPMENT OF POLITICAL PARTIES: Washington was President when the first political parties came into being. These groups shared similar ideas on how government should work. Washington and Adams were **"Federalists."** That means that they favored a strong central government. They were opposed by the **Democratic-Republicans,** led by Thomas Jefferson. Jefferson believed that a strong central government was a bad idea. He thought it limited the power of the states.

PRESIDENT OF THE UNITED STATES: In the election of 1796, Adams ran against Jefferson for President as a Federalist. Today, candidates for President and Vice President are from the same

President John Adams.

party. They share the same ideas, and they run together. In 1796, the candidates for President ran alone, without a Vice Presidential candidate. The candidate getting the most votes won the presidency, while the second-place finisher won the Vice Presidency. In 1796, Adams won the election and became President. Jefferson got the second highest number of votes. He became Vice President.

Since Adams and Jefferson were from different parties, they didn't agree on many of the major issues facing the young nation. Adams could be tough and stubborn. He didn't mind standing alone.

During the 1780s, England and France went to war. The Federalists wanted the U.S. to get involved on the part of the English. The Democratic-Republicans wanted the U.S. to support the French. Even though it was unpopular politically, Adams kept the U.S. out of the war. He was always a man who stood by what he believed. He did what he thought was best for the nation, and it cost him political support.

RUNNING FOR REELECTION: Adams decisions made him an unpopular President with politically powerful groups. When he ran for reelection in 1800, he was defeated by Jefferson.

FIRST RESIDENTS OF THE WHITE HOUSE: John and Abigail Adams were the first President and First Lady to live in the White House. It wasn't called the "White House" at the time. It was referred to then as the "President's House.

The Adams didn't like the President's House. It wasn't finished when they moved in, in November 1800. There wasn't even a staircase. The rooms were drafty and cold. Abigail used one room to hang laundry.

Birthplaces of John Adams (right) and John Quincy Adams (left).

Yet despite their discomfort, Adams wished that the new house be the home of honest people always. "I pray Heaven to bestow the best of blessings on this house and all that shall hereafter inhabit it. May none but honest and wise men ever rule under this roof," he wrote.

RETIREMENT TO QUINCY: Adams left Washington as Jefferson took office in 1801. He never ran for office again. Instead, he and Abigail returned to Quincy. There, Adams enjoyed reading and writing. In 1812 he began to write to Thomas Jefferson. "You and I ought not to die before we have explained ourselves to each other," wrote Adams to Jefferson. They renewed their friendship, and over the years wrote many letters to each other. In them, the two founding fathers discussed many aspects of human nature and politics.

John Adams lived a long, full life. Abigail Adams died before her husband, in 1818. John died on July 4, 1826, at his home in Quincy. The day he died was the 50th anniversary of the signing of the Declaration of Independence. It was the same day his political foe and eventual friend Thomas Jefferson died. He did not know of Jefferson's death when he died. Adams last words were: "Jefferson lives."

WHAT DID HE LOOK LIKE? John Adams was 5 feet 7 inches tall, heavy set, and bald.

FAMOUS QUOTE:
On July 2, 1776, Adams wrote to his wife about how he thought future Americans would celebrate the Declaration of Independence. It is surprising how it describes the ways we still celebrate the Fourth of July:

"I am apt to believe that it will be celebrated by succeeding generations as the great anniversary of a festival. It ought to be solemnized with pomp and parade, with shows, games, sports, guns, bells, bonfires, and illustrations, from one end of this continent to the other, from this time forward forevermore."

FOR MORE INFORMATION ON JOHN ADAMS:

Historic Site:

Adams National Historical Park
135 Adams St.
Quincy, MA 02169-1749
Phone: 617-770-1175

WORLD WIDE WEB ADDRESSES:

The White House offers young readers information on the U.S. government and the Presidents on a Web site called **"White House 101."** The address is:
http://www.whitehouse.gov/about/white_house_101/

The **Internet Public Library** has a site on the Presidents. The address is:
http://www.ipl.org/div/potus

American Memory is a site maintained by the Library of Congress that contains biographical and historical information on the Presidents. It also provides links to Presidential portraits.
For John Adams:
http://memory.loc.gov/ammem/today/oct25.html#adamsfamily

Adams National Historical Park
http://www.nps.gov/adam

Thomas Jefferson
1743-1826
Third President of the United States (1801-1809)
"The Father of the Declaration of Independence"

THOMAS JEFFERSON WAS BORN April 13, 1743, in Goochland, Virginia. He was born on his family's plantation, called Shadwell. His parents were Peter and Jane Jefferson. Peter was a planter, and Jane was a homemaker. Thomas was the third of ten children, with four boys and six girls. Only eight lived to be adults. His surviving sisters were named Jane, Mary, Elizabeth, Martha, Lucy, and Anna. His brother was named Randolph.

THOMAS JEFFERSON GREW UP on Shadwell. As a boy, he loved to hunt, fish, and ride horses. His family was wealthy, and their plantation was worked by slaves. Jefferson's father died when he was 14, and he inherited Shadwell.

THOMAS JEFFERSON WENT TO SCHOOL when he was nine. He attended a local boarding school. There, he studied Latin, Greek, and French. When he was 14, he went to a boarding school in Charlottesville.

Jefferson went to the College of William and Mary when he was 16. After two years, he began to study law. He became very close to his law teacher, George Wythe. He said Wythe was like a "second father."

Jefferson's learning wasn't limited to school. He was one of our most intelligent and artistic presidents. He was a man of spirit, energy, and many interests. Jefferson loved music, and he learned to play the violin when he was young. He loved architecture, and he designed his own home, Monticello (mon-tah-CHELL-oh). He loved nature, and he developed types of fruits and vegetables still planted today.

POLITICAL CAREER: Jefferson finished studying law in 1767. He began to practice law in Williamsburg, which was then the capital of Virginia. He became interested in politics and began to visit the legislature — called the House of Burgesses — to hear debates. In 1769, Jefferson was elected to the House of Burgesses in Virginia.

MARRIAGE AND FAMILY: Jefferson met his future wife, Martha, in 1770. She was a lively and charming woman and the two shared a love of music. They married in 1772.

Jefferson's daughter Patsy, who served as White House hostess.

Thomas and Martha Jefferson had six children, but only two, Martha (called Patsy) and Mary, lived to be adults. A son died soon after birth. Three daughters also died in infancy. Martha died shortly after the birth of their last child, in 1782. Jefferson never remarried.

THE REVOLUTIONARY WAR: In the 1770s, most of the area that is now the eastern United States was a colony of England. That means that the people were ruled by England. They paid taxes to the British government and were ruled by a king, George III.

Some of the colonists were happy being part of England. Some were not. They believed that the colonies should have their own government, a government that they controlled. The people who wanted a separate government began to talk about breaking away from England. These were the people who began the American **Revolutionary War**.

Thomas Jefferson entered politics just as this revolutionary feeling was sweeping the country. He believed that the colonies should be free to determine their own government. He was a great writer, and he used that skill to write one of the most important documents in U.S. history.

THE DECLARATION OF INDEPENDENCE: In 1775, Jefferson was a delegate to the Continental Congress. That was the elected political group that represented the colonies. They chose Jefferson, **John Adams**, and Ben Franklin to write the **Declaration of Independence**.

Jefferson wrote the first draft of the Declaration. In simple, powerful language, he described what the colonists thought about their rights as individuals and as citizens. The Declaration states that all men are born equal and free. They have the right to revolt against those who will not give them freedom. Those are the reasons that the Revolutionary War was fought.

On July 4, 1776, the Continental Congress accepted the Declaration of Independence. The United States was born. Now a war would be fought to determine whether the new nation would remain free.

During the Revolutionary War, Jefferson served in the Virginia legislature and as Governor of Virginia. As Governor, Jefferson worked on an issue very important to him. He wrote the Bill for Establishing Religious Freedom. It said that all people should be free to worship as they liked. He always thought that bill was one of his greatest achievements.

The U.S. defeated the British in 1781, and the war was over. Jefferson's life took a sad turn after the war. His beloved wife, Martha, died after the birth of their sixth child in 1782. Jefferson was terribly sad. His daughter Patsy remembered that her father paced the floors all night.

At the urging of his friends, Jefferson accepted the job as representative to the new U.S. **Congress** in 1783. He helped to develop the system of money used in the U.S. to this day. He also developed the system by which territories became states in the new nation.

The Declaration of Independence.

MINISTER TO FRANCE: In 1784, Jefferson went to France. The U.S. needed to form trading ties with other nations. Jefferson worked on trade agreements between the U.S. and countries in Europe. He spent five years in France. There, in addition to his work on trade, he enjoyed the art, architecture, and music of the country. He studied their farming and brought home ideas for his own crops and animals.

SECRETARY OF STATE: In 1789, **George Washington** was elected the first President of the United States. He formed his **Cabinet,** which is a group of the President's closest advisers. He chose Jefferson to be his Secretary of State.

As Secretary of State, Jefferson advised Washington on how to handle problems with other countries. He helped Washington with issues like trade. When war broke out between England and France, he advised Washington that the U.S. should not get involved.

Around this time, the first political parties began to form. These groups shared similar ideas on how government should work. Washington and Adams were "**Federalists.**" That means that they favored a strong central government. They were opposed by the Democratic-Republicans. Thomas Jefferson was a **Democratic-Republican**. He believed that a strong central government was a bad idea. He thought it limited the power of the states.

VICE PRESIDENT: After Washington served two terms, he retired from politics. In the election of 1796, Jefferson ran for President against John Adams. Today, candidates for President and Vice President are from the same party. They share the same ideas. In 1796, all candidates for President ran against each other, and the one getting the most votes became President, while the second-place finisher became Vice President. In 1796, Adams won the election and became President. Jefferson got the second highest number of votes. He became Vice President.

Jefferson and Adams were political opponents and rivals. In 1800, they ran against each other again for President. Adams lost to Jefferson, who became the third President of the United States.

THE ELECTORAL COLLEGE AND JEFFERSON'S ELECTION: Jefferson's election to the Presidency was determined by the **House of Representatives**. That is because Jefferson didn't get a majority of **electoral votes**.

Americans vote for President and Vice President in a different way than they do for any other elected official. The rules for the election of a President and Vice President are outlined in the **Constitution**.

The President and the Vice President are *not* elected by direct vote of the people. Instead, they are elected by members of the **Electoral College**. When a voter casts a vote for a presidential candidate, he or she is really voting for an "elector." That is someone who is pledged to vote for one of the presidential candidates. After the presidential election, the electors meet and cast their ballots for the candidates they are pledged to. If a candidate does not get a majority of the votes cast by the electors, the House of Representatives votes to decide who will be President. That's how Jefferson was elected.

Only twice in U.S. history has the House determined the Presidency. The first time was in 1801 for Jefferson, and the second was in 1825 for John Quincy Adams.

PRESIDENT OF THE UNITED STATES: As President, Jefferson worked to cut taxes and government spending. Throughout his two terms as President, Jefferson was very popular with the American

President Thomas Jefferson.

31

people. He is best remembered for the **Louisiana Purchase**, the addition of lands that doubled the size of the U.S.

THE LOUISIANA PURCHASE: In 1803, Jefferson organized the purchase of a huge amount of territory. It was called the Louisiana Purchase. The territory ranged from the Mississippi River to the Rocky Mountains, and from the Canadian border to Texas. The territory was owned by France. It cost the U.S. $15 million, about three cents an acre.

Jefferson hired Meriwether Lewis and William Clark to explore the land. They journeyed for two years through the territory, finally reaching the Pacific Ocean in 1805. They returned and reported to Jefferson on the vast new portion of the U.S.

Jefferson ran for President again in 1804. He won reelection by a wide majority of votes. He received 162 electoral votes. His closest opponent, Charles Pinckney, got 14 electoral votes. During his second term, England and France again went to war. During this war, British ships would sometimes stop American ships and force their sailors into the British Navy. This system, called "impressment," was like slavery. Jefferson fought to end it by stopping all trading with England and France. It was a very unpopular decision, and Jefferson later ended the trade stoppage, called an "embargo."

U.S. ships were also attacked by pirates along the Barbary Coast of North Africa. These pirates stole goods from American ships. The U.S. went to war against one of the North African countries, called Tripoli. The U.S. won the war, and the ships were safe once more.

LIFE IN THE WHITE HOUSE: Jefferson wasn't a formal man. He liked visitors at the White House. They were welcome anytime. He liked to entertain, especially to have people to dinner. Because his

Monticello, Jefferson's home.

wife had died, he had no First Lady to help him as hostess. Instead, his two daughters, Patsy and Mary, acted as hostesses at the White House. Dolley Madison, the wife of the fourth President, **James Madison**, also helped out as hostess during Jefferson's years in the White House.

Jefferson's daughters lived with him during most of his presidency. In fact, the first baby born in the White House was Jefferson's grandson, James Madison Randolph. He was Patsy's seventh child.

In 1802, a cheese maker from Massachusetts sent a gift to Jefferson at the White House. It was a 1,235-pound cheese. It was addressed: "The greatest cheese in America for the greatest man in America."

Jefferson had a pet mockingbird named Dick. He rode on Jefferson's shoulder as the President walked around the White House. He even followed Jefferson up the stairs, hopping up one step at a time.

WHAT DID HE LOOK LIKE? Thomas Jefferson was tall, with red hair and freckles. At 6 feet 2 inches tall, he was very tall for his times. One of his nicknames was "Long John."

RETIREMENT TO MONTICELLO: In 1808, after two terms as President, Jefferson retired to his beloved home, Monticello. "All my wishes end, where I hope my days will end, at Monticello," he said. His retirement was anything but quiet and relaxing. He continued to write about government, and he wrote thousands of letters. His letters to John Adams are especially important. The two former political rivals became friends again and wrote to each other often. They wrote about politics, science, and philosophy.

Jefferson's active mind was still fascinated by many things. He invented new farm tools and developed new plants. He was a great lover and collector of books. When the congressional library burned down during the War of 1812, he sold his library to the U.S. government. It became the core of what is now the Library of Congress.

In 1819, Jefferson founded the University of Virginia. He designed everything, from the buildings to the courses for the students. He also hired the teachers. The first 40 students began classes in 1825.

Like Washington's Mount Vernon, Jefferson's plantation was worked by slaves. It is difficult to imagine that Jefferson, a great man, kept slaves. Yet, while he thought **slavery** was wrong, he was a slave owner.

Jefferson lived a long and active life. He died on July 4, 1826, the 50th anniversary of the Declaration. His great friend, John Adams, died on the same day.

Jefferson wanted to be remembered for three things, which are engraved on his tombstone: "Author of the Declaration of Independence, of the Statute of Virginia for religious freedom, and father of the University of Virginia."

FAMOUS QUOTE: These words from the Declaration are some of the most memorable ever written:

"We hold these truths to be self-evident, that all men are created equal, that they are endowed by their Creator with certain inalienable rights, that among these are life, liberty, and the pursuit of happiness."

FOR MORE INFORMATION ON THOMAS JEFFERSON:

Historic Sites:

Shadwell (Jefferson birth site marker)
Charlottesville, VA 22902

Thomas Jefferson Memorial
The National Mall
900 Ohio Drive, S.W.
Washington, DC 20024-2000
Phone: 202-426-6841

Monticello
Box 316
Charlottesville, VA 22902
Phone: 434-984-9800

WORLD WIDE WEB ADDRESSES:

The White House offers young readers information on the U.S. government and the Presidents on a Web site called **"White House 101."** The address is:
http://www.whitehouse.gov/about/white_house_101/

The **Internet Public Library** has a site on the Presidents. The address is:
http://www.ipl.org/div/potus

American Memory is a site maintained by the Library of Congress that contains biographical and historical information on the Presidents. It also provides links to Presidential portraits.
For Thomas Jefferson:
http://memory.loc.gov/ammem/today/april13.html

Jefferson Memorial
http://www.nps.gov/thje

Monticello
http://www.monticello.org

James Madison
1751–1836
Fourth President of the United States (1809–1817)
"The Father of the Constitution"

JAMES MADISON WAS BORN March 16, 1751, in Port Conway, Virginia. His father, James Madison, was a planter. His mother, Nelly Rose Conway Madison, was a homemaker. James was the oldest of twelve children. Two children died in infancy. He had six brothers and four sisters who lived to be adults. His brothers were named Francis, Ambrose, Catlett, William, Reuben, and Eli. His sisters were named Nelly, Sarah, Elizabeth, and Frances.

JAMES MADISON GREW UP on the family plantation called Montpelier. His great-great-grandfather, a ship carpenter from England, settled in Virginia in 1653 and started a tobacco farm. His grandfather and father moved west into present-day Orange County, Virginia. They built the family plantation to 6,000 acres. The chief crops were grains and tobacco, which were farmed by slaves.

JAMES MADISON WENT TO SCHOOL at a boarding school 70 miles away from his home when he was 11 years old. Before that, he was taught to read and write by his mother and grandmother. At boarding school, he learned English, mathematics, French and Spanish. Later he studied Latin, philosophy and astronomy.

When he was 18, Madison went to the College of New Jersey (now Princeton University). He completed the four-year course in only two years and graduated in 1771. After graduation, he returned home and continued his studies, especially in law. He also taught his younger brothers and sisters.

THE REVOLUTIONARY WAR: In the 1770s, most of the area that is now the eastern United States was a colony of England. That means that the people were ruled by England. They paid taxes to the British government and were ruled by a king, George III.

Some of the colonists were happy being part of England. Some were not. They believed that the colonies should have their own government, a government they controlled. The people who wanted a separate government began to talk about breaking away from England. These were the people who began the American **Revolutionary War**. That document delcared that all men are born equal and free.

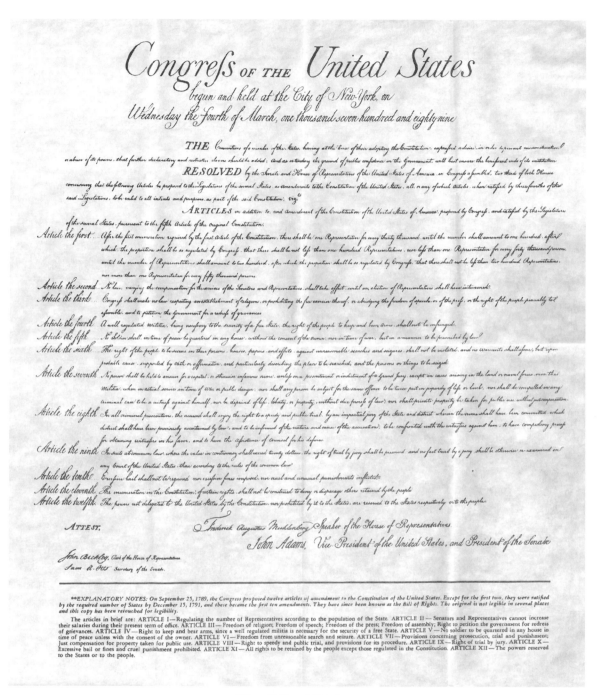

The Bill of Rights.

BECOMING INVOLVED IN POLITICS: As the Revolutionary War started, Madison enlisted in the military. Later, he had to drop out due to poor health. In 1776 Madison was elected as a delegate to the

Virginia Revolutionary Convention. He was 25 years old. He helped pass a resolution to issue the **Declaration of Independence**.

In 1779, Madison was elected to the Continental Congress. The Continental Congress was the government of the United States during the Revolutionary War. Even though he was one of its youngest members, he became its most effective legislator and debater.

WRITING THE CONSTITUTION: James Madison was the principal author of the U.S. **Constitution**. The Constitution is the plan for the national government.

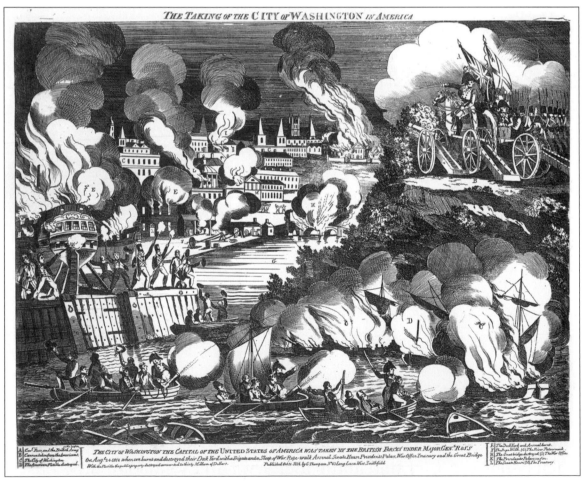

"The Taking of the City of Washington," during the War of 1812.

The U.S. Constitution divides power between three branches. The Executive Branch is made up of the President and his **Cabinet**. The Legislative branch is made up of the **House of Representatives** and the **Senate**. They make the laws of the country. The Judicial Branch is made up of the U.S. Court system, including the nine-member **Supreme Court**.

Madison wanted to convince the country to adopt the new Constitution. He wrote many articles, called the Federalist Papers. In his articles he tried to persuade people to vote for the new Constitution. He succeeded, and the Constitution was accepted by the American people.

THE BILL OF RIGHTS: Madison also wrote the first ten amendments, or additions, to the Constitution. These are known as the **Bill of Rights**. The Bill of Rights guarantees specific freedoms to all Americans. Some of the major rights we enjoy—like freedom of speech and religion—are outlined in the Bill of Rights.

SECRETARY OF STATE: In 1801 **President Thomas Jefferson** appointed James Madison Secretary of State. The Secretary of State helps the President solve problems with other countries.

In 1803, Jefferson organized the purchase of a huge amount of territory from France. It was called the **Louisiana Purchase**. The territory ranged from the Mississippi River to the Rocky Mountains, and from the Canadian border to Texas. As Secretary of State, Madison helped negotiate the purchase.

MARRIAGE AND FAMILY: Madison was still a bachelor at age 43. Then Senator Aaron Burr introduced him to Dolley Payne Todd. Dolley was 26 years old. She was a widow. Her husband and infant

First Lady Dolley Madison.

child had died of yellow fever. James and Dolley fell in love and were married on September 15, 1797. They did not have children.

PRESIDENT OF THE UNITED STATES: James Madison was a member of the **Democratic-Republican** Party. With the help of his friend, Thomas Jefferson, he was easily elected President in 1808. He defeated Charles C. Pinckney with 122 **electoral votes** to Pinckney's 47.

The years of Madison's Presidency were hard times for America. France and Great Britain were at war. America did not take sides in this war. This means that America was neutral. Even so, both Britain and France kept capturing American ships. Britain would force American sailors into their Navy. Finally, Madison asked Congress to declare war on Britain. This war is known as the **War of 1812.**

THE WAR OF 1812: As the war began in 1812, Madison ran for reelection and won, despite strong opposition from members of the Federalist Party. They did not want to go to war with Great Britain, and they didn't support Madison's stand.

At first, the war did not go well for the United States. In 1814 the British captured Washington, D.C., and set it on fire. Dolley

President James Madison.

"The White House," painted white after the War of 1812.

Madison barely escaped before the invaders. She took a wagon loaded with many belongings from the President's House, including a portrait of George Washington.

During the invasion of Washington, James Madison took command of the defending American army. He is the only President to ever personally command an army while in office. Later, the Americans won victories in Baltimore and New York. This forced the British to sign a peace treaty in 1814.

HOW THE WHITE HOUSE GOT ITS NAME: The Madisons had to live in another house, called the Octagon House, while the President's House was repaired after the fire. The President's House was painted white to cover over the scorch marks left from the fire. That's how the President's House came to be called the "White House."

REELECTION: Madison won reelection in 1813. He defeated De Witt Clinton, winning 128 electoral votes. Clinton received 89.

LIFE AT THE WHITE HOUSE: Dolley Madison was one of the most popular hostesses in Washington. She served pink ice cream at the White House. Known for her stylishness, she had a large collection of shoes and turbans. She set many fashion trends in Washington as the First Lady. When she bought a pet macaw — a kind of parrot — many fashionable ladies did so, too.

WHAT DID HE LOOK LIKE? James Madison was our smallest president. He was 5 feet, 4 inches tall, and weighed only 100 pounds. He had hay-colored hair, which he wore in bangs. Madison was the first president to wear trousers instead of the knee-britches that were common in his time.

RETIREMENT TO VIRGINIA: In 1817, after serving two terms as President, Madison returned to his family home at Montpelier. There he developed scientific farming methods that are still used. Although he was a slave-owner by inheritance, he opposed slavery. He worked hard to try to put an end to it.

Madison helped found the University of Virginia with Thomas Jefferson. He became its second president after Jefferson's death. He also continued to write articles on government until his death.

James Madison lived a long life. He died on June 28, 1836, at the age of 85. Dolley moved back to Washington, D.C., where she lived until her death in 1849.

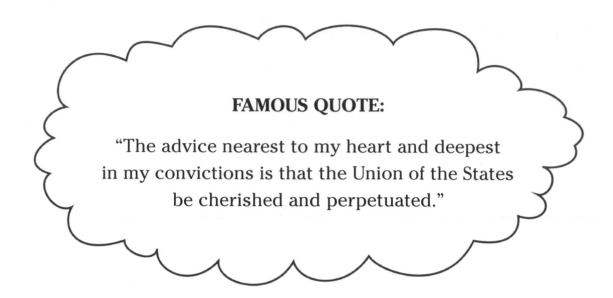

FAMOUS QUOTE:

"The advice nearest to my heart and deepest in my convictions is that the Union of the States be cherished and perpetuated."

FOR MORE INFORMATION ON JAMES MADISON:

Historic Sites:

Birth Site:
Belle Grove
Port Conway, VA

James Madison Museum
129 Caroline St.
Orange, VA 22960
Phone: 540-672-1776

Montpelier
P.O. Box 911
Montpelier Station, VA 22960
Phone: 540-672-2728

The Octagon House
1799 New York Ave., N.W.
Washington, DC 20006
Phone: 202-638-3105

WORLD WIDE WEB ADDRESSES:

The White House offers young readers information on the U.S. government and the Presidents on a Web site called **"White House 101."** The address is:
http://www.whitehouse.gov/about/white_house_101/

The Internet Public Library has a site on the Presidents. The address is:
http://www.ipl.org/div/potus

American Memory is a site maintained by the Library of Congress that contains biographical and historical information on the Presidents. It also provides links to Presidential portraits.
For James Madison:
http://memory.loc.gov/ammem/today/mar16.html

Montpelier
http://www.montpelier.org/

James Monroe
1758-1831
Fifth President of the United States (1817-1825)
"Last of the Cocked Hats"

JAMES MONROE WAS BORN April 28, 1758, in Westmoreland County, Virginia. His parents were Spence and Elizabeth Monroe. Spence was a planter, and Elizabeth was a homemaker. James was the oldest of five children. He had three brothers and one sister. His brothers' names were Andrew, Spence, and Joseph, and his sister's name was Elizabeth.

JAMES MONROE GREW UP in the country in Virginia. His father had a small farm, and James enjoyed playing in the fields.

JAMES MONROE WENT TO SCHOOL at a private school run by a man named Parson Campbell. James was an excellent student. He did especially well in Latin and math. When James was just 16, he went to the College of William and Mary. But his college years were cut short by the Revolutionary War.

THE REVOLUTIONARY WAR: In the 1770s, most of the area that is now the eastern United States was a colony of England. That means that the people were ruled by England. They paid taxes to the British government and were ruled by a king, George III.

Some of the colonists were happy being part of England. Some were not. They believed that the colonies should have their own government, a government that they controlled. The people who wanted a separate government began to talk about breaking away from England. These were the people who began the American **Revolutionary War**.

Monroe was just 18 when he left college and joined the army. He fought in several of the major battles in the war. In 1777, he was an aide to one of Washington's generals. Monroe was a brave soldier. In a battle in Trenton, New Jersey, he was seriously wounded. In 1778, he was given a group of soldiers to command. He was just 20 years old. He served in the army until 1780.

STUDENT OF THOMAS JEFFERSON: In 1780, Monroe began to study law with **Thomas Jefferson.** Jefferson thought his new pupil was very bright and able. He encouraged Monroe to enter politics. Monroe did, and he served his country in many different posts from 1781 to 1825.

ENTERING POLITICS: In 1781, the U.S. defeated the British and became a new, free nation. Monroe became a member of the Virginia legislature. Two years later, he was elected to the Congress of the Confederation. That was the political group that ran the country while the **Constitution** was being written.

MARRIAGE AND FAMILY: Monroe met his future wife, Elizabeth Kortright, in 1783, while he was working with

First Lady Elizabeth Monroe.

the Congress. They fell in love and married in March 1786. They had three children, two girls and a boy. Their daughters were named Eliza and Maria. Their son died when he was a baby.

From 1790 to 1794, Monroe served as the U.S. Senator from Virginia. In 1794, during the Presidency of **George Washington**, he was Minister to France. Two years later, he returned home. He was then elected Governor of Virginia, in 1799.

LIFE AS A DIPLOMAT: In 1803, Monroe's good friend Jefferson was President. Jefferson chose Monroe to go to France and work out the **Louisiana Purchase**. Monroe had worked in foreign countries before. Working with other heads of government, he developed his ability as a diplomat.

In the Louisiana Purchase, the U.S. bought from France a huge amount of land. The territory ranged from the Mississippi River to the Rocky Mountains, and from the Canadian border to Texas. The price was $15 million, less than three cents an acre.

Monroe was known as a skilled diplomat. He had done an excellent job for the U.S. The Louisiana Purchase doubled the size of the new country. It also showed Monroe as a man who was hard-working, intelligent, and able.

Jefferson next sent Monroe to England and Spain. There, he worked on treaties between the U.S. and those nations. In 1807, he returned to the U.S. Back in Virginia, he once again served in the legislature and as governor.

In 1811, **President James Madison** chose Monroe to be Secretary of State. As Secretary of State, Monroe advised Madison on how to handle problems with other countries. This was especially important during the **War of 1812**, when the U.S. went to war against England. England was the major naval power at that time. They would not allow U.S. ships to sail the oceans freely. As the war went on, Madison also made Monroe Secretary of War.

The U.S. won the war in 1814. Monroe, honored by his country as a man of honesty and dedicated service, accepted the urging of his friends and ran for President. In 1816, he was elected. He defeated his opponent, Rufus King, with 183 **electoral votes** to King's 34.

PRESIDENT OF THE UNITED STATES: President Monroe's first four years were known as the "Era of Good Feeling." It was a time of prosperity in the country.

Monroe had worked in government for a long time when he became President. He had helped form the **Democratic-Republican** party of Jefferson. But over the years, he had seen a lot of fighting between members of rival political parties. He saw how political rivalries could stop the progress of a nation. As President, he worked for more cooperation between the parties.

Monroe had excellent advisers in his **Cabinet. John Quincy Adams**, the son of the second President, was one of the finest. Adams was Monroe's Secretary of State. He worked with Great Britain to settle the border of Canada and the U.S. He signed a treaty with Spain that expanded the border of the southern U.S. He also worked out the purchase of Florida from Spain.

When Monroe ran for reelection in 1820, he won by one of the biggest margins in history. He ran unopposed and received 231 electoral votes. During his second term Monroe developed the policy for which he is best known, the **Monroe Doctrine**.

THE MONROE DOCTRINE: The Monroe Doctrine stated that the U.S. would not allow European countries to develop colonies in North or South America. The U.S. didn't want Spain, England, or other European nations interfering with the countries of the New World. The Monroe Doctrine was a declaration of freedom for the new nations of the Americas.

MONROVIA: Liberia was an African nation formed in the 1820s as a home for freed slaves. The people of Liberia named their capital, Monrovia, after James Monroe, in 1822.

LIFE IN THE WHITE HOUSE: James Monroe and his wife, Elizabeth, were more formal than Jefferson or Madison. They didn't like a lot of company at the White House. They enjoyed small, formal dinners with friends. Unlike Dolley Madison, Elizabeth Monroe didn't like making social calls. She was more reserved, and she didn't care much for Washington society.

President James Monroe.

The Monroes hosted the first White House wedding. Their daughter, Maria, was the first daughter of a President to be married in the White House. Maria married Samuel Gouveneur on March 9, 1820.

WHAT DID HE LOOK LIKE? Monroe was 6 feet tall and slim. He had fair hair and blue-grey eyes. He preferred to dress in an old-fashioned way, wearing knee breeches instead of long pants. For this, and for his close ties to the other heroes of early America, he gained the nickname "last of the cocked hats." A "cocked hat" was a three-cornered hat, the kind worn by soldiers during the Revolutionary War.

RETIREMENT FROM POLITICS: In 1825, Monroe retired from politics. After a lifetime given to public service, he returned to his farm in Virginia. There, he spent his last years writing. He had to sell much of his land after his retirement, because his political positions had not paid him very much.

Elizabeth Monroe died in 1830. Soon after, Monroe moved to New York to live with his daughter, Maria. He died there on July 4, 1831, at the age of 73. He shares the death date of July 4 with two other heroes of his era, **John Adams** and Thomas Jefferson.

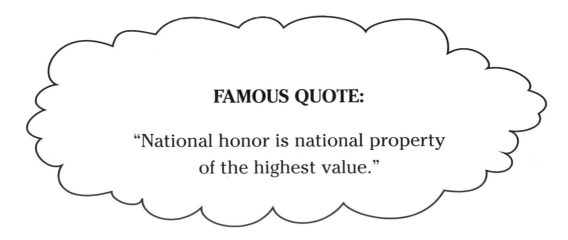

FAMOUS QUOTE:

"National honor is national property of the highest value."

FOR MORE INFORMATION ON JAMES MONROE:

Historic Sites:

Ash Lawn-Highland
1000 James Monroe Parkway
Charlottesville, VA 22902
Phone: 434-293-8000

James Monroe Museum and Memorial Library
908 Charles St.
Fredericksburg, VA 22401
Phone: 540-654-1043

WORLD WIDE WEB ADDRESSES:

The White House offers young readers information on the U.S. government and the Presidents on a Web site called **"White House 101."** The address is:
http://www.whitehouse.gov/about/white_house_101/

The Internet Public Library has a site on the Presidents. The address is:
http://www.ipl.org/div/potus

American Memory is a site maintained by the Library of Congress that contains biographical and historical information on the Presidents. It also provides links to Presidential portraits. For James Monroe:
http://memory.loc.gov/ammem/today/oct17.html

James Monroe Museum and Memorial Library
http://www.umw.edu/jamesmonroemuseum/history

Ash Lawn-Highland
http://www.ashlawnhighland.org/

John Quincy Adams

1767-1848
Sixth President of the United States (1825-1829)
"Old Man Eloquent"

JOHN QUINCY ADAMS WAS BORN July 11, 1767, in Braintree (now Quincy), Massachusetts. His father was **John Adams**, the second President of the United States. His mother was Abigail Adams. John Quincy was the second oldest of five children. One child died as an infant. He had one sister and two brothers who lived to be adults. His sister was named Abigail and his brothers were named Charles and Thomas.

JOHN QUINCY ADAMS GREW UP during the **Revolutionary War**. He was seven years old when the **Declaration of Independence** was signed. He watched the Battle of Bunker Hill—an important early battle of the Revolution—from his family's farm in Braintree, Massachusetts.

AN UNUSUAL CHILDHOOD: When John Quincy was ten years old, he went to France with his father. John Adams had been sent to France to win their support for the Revolutionary War. While in Europe, John Quincy learned French, Greek, Latin, and Dutch.

In 1781 John Quincy served as his father's interpreter and secretary on a mission to Russia. He was just 14 years old. He witnessed the signing of the Treaty of Paris in 1783, which ended the Revolutionary War.

After the war, John Quincy returned home and went to college at Harvard College. He graduated in 1787, and then became a lawyer.

MARRIAGE AND FAMILY: Adams met Louisa Catherine Johnson while he was on a diplomatic mission to England. She was the daughter of the American consul in London. They fell in love and were married in 1797. Louisa would become the only First Lady born outside of the United States.

John Quincy and Louisa had three sons and a daughter. The sons' names were George Washington, John, and Charles. Their daughter, named Louisa, died when she was a baby. They also raised three orphaned children of his wife's sister, Nancy Johnson Hellen.

EARLY DIPLOMATIC CAREER: A diplomat travels to other countries to speak for his government. In 1795, **President George**

Washington made John Quincy Adams the ambassador to the Netherlands. He was 28 years old.

President John Adams chose his son to be ambassador to Prussia (now part of Germany) in 1801. In 1809, **President James Madison** appointed John Quincy the first American ambassador to Russia. He was in Russia when the **War of 1812** started. That war, between England and the U.S., lasted for two years.

Adams worked on the peace treaty, known as the Treaty of Ghent, which ended the war in 1814. The next year he became the ambassador to Great Britain. He served in Britain until 1817.

SECRETARY OF STATE: President James Monroe made Adams his Secretary of State in 1817. The Secretary of State is part of the **Cabinet.** The Secretary of State advises the President on how to handle problems with other countries.

John Quincy Adams was one of the most important Secretaries of State in American history. He negotiated the Transcontinental Treaty with Spain in 1819. At that time Florida and most of western America belonged to Spain. Adams convinced Spain to turn over Florida and much of northwestern America to the United States. After the treaty was signed, the U.S. territory extended all the way to the Pacific Ocean.

THE MONROE DOCTRINE: Adams helped write the **Monroe Doctrine**. This doctrine was named after President James Monroe. It said that the United States would not allow any new European colonization in North or South America.

THE ELECTION OF 1824: Adams decided to run for President as a **Democratic-Republican** in 1824. The election of 1824 was unusual.

It was the second presidential election decided by the **House of Representatives.**

Four men ran for President that year. They were John Quincy Adams, **Andrew Jackson**, William H. Crawford, and Henry Clay. Andrew Jackson won most of the popular vote, but none of the candidates received a majority of votes in the **Electoral College.**

John Quincy Adams as a young boy.

THE ELECTORAL COLLEGE AND ADAMS'S ELECTION:

Americans vote for President in a different way than they do for any other elected official. The rules for the election of a President are outlined in the **Constitution.**

The President is *not* elected by direct vote of the people. Instead, they are elected by members of the Electoral College. When a voter casts a vote for a Presidential candidate, he or she is really voting for an "elector." That is someone who is pledged to vote for one of the presidential candidates. After the presidential election, the electors meet and cast their ballots for the candidates they are pledged to.

The number of electors is equal to the total number of U.S. Representatives and Senators. To win the election, the candidate must get a majority of all the possible electoral votes. If one candidate cannot get a majority of votes from the electors, then the winner of the Presidential race is determined by the House of Representatives.

In 1824, Henry Clay received the smallest number of votes in the regular election. He told his supporters in the House to vote for John Quincy Adams. Adams won the election by a narrow margin.

PRESIDENT OF THE UNITED STATES: After Adams was elected, he made Henry Clay his Secretary of State. Andrew Jackson's supporters called this an unfair deal. Because of this, they fought John Quincy's policies throughout his term.

Adams believed in a strong national government. He wanted the government to build more roads and canals. This would help the people settle the west. He also proposed a national university.

First Lady Louisa Adams.

Congress opposed most of his plans, and he had a difficult term. When Adams ran for a second term in 1828, Andrew Jackson beat him by a large majority.

LIFE AT THE WHITE HOUSE: Louisa Adams was a gracious hostess. She gave many elegant parties at the White House, even though John Quincy did not like to attend them. He described himself as a "cold" man, and he didn't like a lot of company.

John Quincy got up every morning at dawn. He read Greek, Latin, or the Bible before breakfast. Every day, weather permitting, he walked to the Potomac River, took off all his clothes, and went swimming.

Once, a female reporter tried to get an interview with Adams. He refused. She appeared one morning as he swam in the Potomac. She sat on his clothes until he agreed to talk to her. She got her interview.

HOUSE OF REPRESENTATIVES: John Quincy left office in 1829 and returned to his farm in Massachusetts. One year later he decided to run for office again. He was elected to the House of Representatives in 1830. He is the only President to be elected to the House after his Presidency. He served in the U.S. **Congress** for nine straight terms, from 1830 to 1848.

Adams soon became a leader in the fight against **slavery.** He especially opposed the expansion of slavery into the western territories. He got his nickname, "Old Man Eloquent," from the many speeches he made in Congress in defense of civil liberties for all Americans.

Adams also supported scientific activities. He led the movement to build the Smithsonian Institution in Washington, D.C. The Smithsonian Institution is one of our country's most important cultural centers.

In 1846, the U.S. went to war with Mexico. Adams opposed the war. He collapsed on the floor of the House of Representatives on February 21, 1848, while giving a speech against the war. He died two days later. Senator Thomas Hart Benton said, "Where could death have found him but at the post of duty?"

President John Quincy Adams.

WHAT DID HE LOOK LIKE? Adams was 5 feet 7 inches tall, and bald. He did not care much about his appearance and was known as a sloppy dresser. He wore the same hat for ten years.

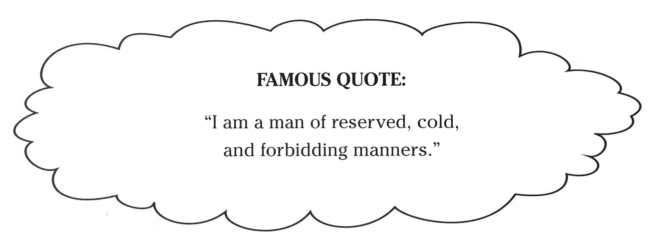

FAMOUS QUOTE:

"I am a man of reserved, cold, and forbidding manners."

FOR MORE INFORMATION ON JOHN QUINCY ADAMS:

Historic Site:

Birth Site:
Adams National Historical Park
135 Adams Street
Quincy, MA 02169-1749
Phone: 617-773-1177

WORLD WIDE WEB ADDRESSES:

The White House offers young readers information on the U.S. government and the Presidents on a Web site called **"White House 101."** The address is:
http://www.whitehouse.gov/about/white_house_101/

The Internet Public Library has a site on the Presidents. The address is:
http://www.ipl.org/div/potus

American Memory is a site maintained by the Library of Congress that contains biographical and historical information on the Presidents. It also provides links to Presidential portraits. For John Quincy Adams:
http://memory.loc.gov/ammem/today/oct25.html#adamsfamily

Adams National Site
http://www.nps.gov/adam/index.htm

Andrew Jackson

1767-1845
Seventh President of the United States (1829-1837)
"Old Hickory"

ANDREW JACKSON WAS BORN March 15, 1767, in Waxhaw, South Carolina. His father was Andrew Jackson, Sr., and his mother was Elizabeth Jackson. They were immigrants from Northern Ireland and had moved to South Carolina in 1765. Andrew Sr. died just a few days before young Andrew was born. Andrew was the youngest of three boys. His brothers' names were Hugh and Robert.

ANDREW JACKSON GREW UP on a poor farm in the frontier of South Carolina. He was the first President to be born in a log cabin.

As a boy, he lived a rough-and-tumble life. He was always known for being brave and stubborn. He never ran away from a fight, and he never quit.

ANDREW JACKSON WENT TO SCHOOL at the local school in the Waxhaw Settlement. Because of his chores on the farm, he could only attend school now and then. He learned reading, writing, and arithmetic, but he never was good at spelling or grammar.

YOUNG PATRIOT: In 1776, the American colonies declared their independence from Britain. The **Revolutionary War** began. In 1780, Andrew and his brother Robert joined the militia to fight the British. He was only 13 years old. The next year, the British captured them both after the Battle of Camden in South Carolina. A British officer ordered Andrew to clean his boots. When Andrew refused, the officer struck him with his saber. He bore the scar the rest of his life.

While in prison camp, both Andrew and Robert became sick with smallpox. Andrew barely survived the disease, but his brother died. After the war ended in 1781, his mother died of cholera. He was an orphan at age 14.

JACKSON MOVES WEST: In 1784, Jackson moved to Salisbury, North Carolina. He studied law and became a lawyer in 1787. The next year he moved west with the first group of pioneers to travel the Cumberland Trail—the route that most early settlers took to the western territories. He settled in Nashville, Tennessee, which at that time was only a group of log cabins.

Jackson's fortunes grew as the territory grew. His law practice prospered. What he lacked in formal education, he made up for with common sense. He also made a lot of money by buying and selling land. With his money, he began building his plantation, which he called the Hermitage.

MARRIAGE AND FAMILY: Jackson married Rachel Donelson Robards in 1791. Rachel had been married before, and both Jackson and Rachel thought that she had been divorced from her first husband when they got married. It turned out the divorce had not been granted when they were married. He and Rachel married again in 1794.

Rachel Jackson, who died just before her husband became President.

Jackson was devoted to Rachel. He resented any gossip about their marriage. In 1806, he fought a duel with Charles Dickinson, who had insulted Rachel. Jackson was wounded in this fight, and Dickinson was killed. The bullet in Jackson's wound struck next to his heart, where it stayed for the rest of his life.

Andrew and Rachel had no children of their own, but they took care of many homeless children. One of them was an Indian boy named Lincoyer. His mother and father had been killed during one of the Indian wars that Jackson fought. Jackson took him under his protection and raised him as his own son.

GETTING INVOLVED IN POLITICS: When Tennessee became a state in 1796, Jackson was elected its first representative to the

The Battle of New Orleans, where Jackson won a decisive victory over the British during the War of 1812.

U.S. **Congress**. A year later, he became a U.S. Senator. Jackson served in the **Senate** for just one year, then returned to Nashville to take care of business problems.

In 1798, Jackson was appointed a judge in the state court of Tennessee. In 1802 he was elected major general of the Tennessee militia. He returned to private life in 1804, devoting time to his plantation and raising racehorses.

THE WAR OF 1812: In 1812, France and Great Britain were at war. America did not take sides in this war. Even so, both Britain and France kept capturing American ships. Britain forced American sailors into the British Navy. Finally, **President James Madison**

asked Congress to declare war on Britain. This war is known as the **War of 1812**.

During the War of 1812, Jackson returned to military service. He was the only President to fight in both the Revolutionary War and the War of 1812. In 1813, he led a militia force against the Creek Indians.

Jackson defeated the Creeks at the Battle of Horseshoe Bend in 1814. His victory earned him a reputation as an able military leader. He was made a Major General in the U.S. Army. Next, he defended the port of New Orleans. In 1815, the American forces won an overwhelming victory at the Battle of New Orleans. The U.S. defeated the British, and Jackson became a national hero.

After the war Jackson returned to Tennessee. In 1817 he was called back to service to fight the Seminole Indians in Florida. Once again, he showed his bravery and ability in battle.

The United States bought Florida from Spain in 1819. Jackson was made the Governor of the territory in 1821.

PRESIDENTIAL CANDIDATE: After leaving Florida, Jackson returned again to his home, the Hermitage. But he didn't stay there very long. In 1823, he was elected again to the U.S. Senate. Then, in 1824, he became the **Democratic** candidate for President.

THE ELECTION OF 1824: Jackson was one of four candidates in 1824. He ran against **John Quincy Adams**, who was then Secretary of State under **James Monroe**; Henry Clay, and William Crawford. Jackson got the largest number of popular votes, but he did not get enough **electoral votes** to become President. The **House of Representatives** decided the election.

THE ELECTORAL COLLEGE: Americans vote for President and Vice President in a different way than they do for any other elected official. The rules for the election of a President and Vice President are outlined in the Constitution.

The President and the Vice President are *not* elected by direct vote of the people. Instead, members of the Electoral College elect them. When a voter casts a vote for a Presidential candidate, he or she is really voting for an "elector." That is someone who is pledged to vote for one of the Presidential candidates. After the election, the electors meet and cast their ballots for the candidates they are pledged to.

The number of electors is equal to the total number of U.S. Representatives and Senators. To win the election, the candidate must get a majority of all the possible electoral votes. If one candidate cannot get a majority of votes from the electors, then the House of Representatives determines the winner of the presidential race.

When the election of 1824 went into the House of Representatives, Henry Clay gave his support to John Quincy Adams. Adams was elected President by the House. Adams later made Clay his Secretary of State. Jackson's supporters called this a "corrupt bargain." They opposed Adams's administration throughout his presidency.

RUNNING AGAIN FOR PRESIDENT: Jackson ran again in 1828. He faced John Quincy Adams again. This time, Jackson won by a large majority. Jackson received 178 electoral votes, to Adam's 83.

LIFE IN THE WHITE HOUSE: For Jackson the joy of his victory was overshadowed by Rachel's death in December 1828, just one

Jackson's many supporters mobbed the White House at his inauguration in 1829.

month after his election. Their niece, Emily Donelson, was the White House hostess for much of Jackson's presidency.

Andrew Jackson was a man of the people. He was the first President who came from humble origins. He was also the first President from the western frontier. Because of this, he was very popular with the common people of America. Huge crowds of people came to Washington, D.C., to celebrate his inauguration. They mobbed the White House to shake his hand and wish him well.

PRESIDENT OF THE UNITED STATES: Jackson was the first President to call himself the elected representative of all the American people. He strengthened the power of the presidency. He vetoed — rejected — 12 bills during his administration. He used his vetoes to make his views and his powers clear to Congress.

President Andrew Jackson.

Although Jackson was always popular with the people, many of his policies as President were controversial. These included the policy of "rotation in office," the Indian Removal Act, and the Nullification Crisis.

He began the policy of "rotation in office." Before Jackson was elected, people who were appointed to run the day-to-day business of government tended to keep their jobs as long as they wanted. But Jackson believed that government should be "so plain and simple" that the offices could be rotated among qualified candidates. He thought it would make government more responsive to the will of the people. His opponents called this the "spoils system," based on the phrase "to the victor goes the spoils." They thought Jackson gave away jobs as rewards to political friends. It was a controversial way to appoint people to government jobs.

Jackson supported the Indian Removal Act of 1830. This forced all the Eastern Indian tribes to move to lands west of the Mississippi. The Indian removal opened up a lot of valuable land for settlement by white people. It also caused a great deal of suffering for the Indians.

THE NULLIFICATION CRISIS: Jackson was a supporter of states' rights. He believed that the power of the federal government should be limited, and that state governments should handle most of the affairs of the people. But even though he supported states' rights, he believed even more in the importance of federal law.

In 1832 the state of South Carolina, led by John Calhoun, declared the right to nullify (cancel) any federal laws that the state did not agree with. They declared that import taxes passed by the U.S. Congress were not valid in the state of South Carolina. South Carolina even threatened to secede (break away) from the U.S.

Jackson thought that Calhoun and South Carolina had gone too far. He called nullification treason, and prepared to send the army to South Carolina. Privately, he threatened to arrest Calhoun and hang him. Tensions were eased when Senator Henry Clay worked out a compromise, which gradually lowered the tax. The crisis was solved, and the **Union** was preserved.

REELECTION: Jackson was re-elected in 1832 by a large majority. He won 219 electoral votes, while his opponent, Henry Clay, got just 49.

Jackson lived up to his nickname, "Old Hickory." Like the tree, he was strong and unbending in the face of controversy. He influenced a generation of politicians with the force of his personality and was loved by the American people as the first "people's President."

RETIREMENT TO THE HERMITAGE: At the end of his second term, Jackson returned to his home at the Hermitage. He died on June 8, 1845. He was buried in the Hermitage garden, next to Rachel.

WHAT DID HE LOOK LIKE? Jackson was tall and thin. He was 6 feet 1 inch tall, and he weighed 140 pounds. He brushed his bushy hair high above his forehead.

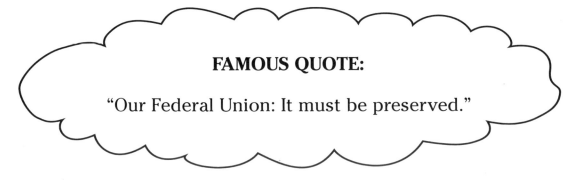

FAMOUS QUOTE:

"Our Federal Union: It must be preserved."

FOR MORE INFORMATION ON ANDREW JACKSON:

Historic Sites:

The Hermitage (home of Andrew Jackson)
4580 Rachel's Lane
Nashville, TN 37076
Phone: 615-889-2941

Andrew Jackson State Park
196 Andrew Jackson Park Road
Lancaster, SC 29720
Phone: 803-285-3344

WORLD WIDE WEB ADDRESSES:

The White House offers young readers information on the U.S. government and the Presidents on a Web site called "**White House 101**." The address is:
http://www.whitehouse.gov/about/white_house_101/

The **Internet Public Library** has a site on the Presidents. The address is:
http://www.ipl.org/div/potus

American Memory is a site maintained by the Library of Congress that contains biographical and historical information on the Presidents. It also provides links to Presidential portraits.
For Andrew Jackson:
http://memory.loc.gov/ammem/today/jan08.html

The Hermitage
http://www.thehermitage.com/

Andrew Jackson State Park
http://www.stateparks.com/andrew_jackson.html

Martin Van Buren
1782-1862
Eighth President of the United States (1837-1841)
"Old Kinderhook (O.K.)"

MARTIN VAN BUREN WAS BORN December 5, 1782, in Kinderhook, New York. His parents were Abraham and Maria Van Buren. Abraham was a farmer and tavern keeper. Maria was a homemaker. Martin was the third of five children. He had three brothers, Derrick, Lawrence, and Abraham, and one sister, Hannah.

FIRST PRESIDENT BORN A U.S. CITIZEN: Van Buren was born just one year after the Americans had won the **Revolutionary War**. That means that he was the first President who was born a U.S. citizen.

All the previous Presidents had been born when England still ruled the original colonies.

MARTIN VAN BUREN GREW UP in Kinderhook in an atmosphere of politics. His father's tavern was the place where people went to vote. In those days, judges sometimes heard court cases in taverns. The citizens of the town spent hours talking politics at the tavern. The young Martin Van Buren soaked up all the political news and loved it.

MARTIN VAN BUREN WENT TO SCHOOL at a private school called Kinderhook Academy. He left school at 14 to study law. At that time, law students didn't go to law school. Instead, they studied with a lawyer. Van Buren worked in the law firm of Francis Sylvester. He started out sweeping floors, then learned about the duties of lawyers.

FIRST JOBS: While still a teenager, Van Buren got the chance to handle his first case. He was in court with a lawyer who was arguing a case. Suddenly, he turned to Martin. "Here, Matt," he said. "Sum up. You might as well begin early." Although he felt unprepared, Van Buren gave it a try. He won the case. The lawyer paid him a silver half-dollar.

MARRIAGE AND FAMILY: Martin Van Buren married his wife, Hannah, on February 21, 1807. They had been childhood sweethearts and were distant cousins. They had four children, all boys. Their sons were named Abraham, Martin, John, and Smith. Hannah died in 1819 when she was 35. Van Buren never remarried.

GETTING STARTED IN POLITICS: In 1803, Van Buren began to practice law on his own. He was still interested in politics, though.

Van Buren as a young man.

In 1808, he managed the campaign of a friend named Daniel Tompkins, who was running for Governor. Tompkins won. He made Van Buren a judge.

After several years as a judge, Van Buren decided he wanted to run for office himself. In 1812, he ran for State Senator in New York and won. Next, he ran for the U.S. **Senate**. He won again, serving in the Senate from 1821 to 1828. Then he ran for Governor of New York, winning that election in 1828.

Van Buren only served as Governor for 10 weeks. The new President of the United States, **Andrew Jackson**, wanted him to be Secretary of State.

POLITICAL PARTIES: There were two major political parties at that time, the **Democrats**, headed by Andrew Jackson, and the **Whigs**. Van Buren was a Democrat. He and his party believed that the federal government should not be stronger than the state governments. They didn't like a lot of interference by the federal government in what happened in the rest of the country.

SECRETARY OF STATE: Van Buren served as Jackson's Secretary of State for three years. His job was to advise the President on matters dealing with foreign countries. He was also Jackson's political adviser.

Van Buren had a fine political mind. He loved the world of politics. He enjoyed working with different groups of people. Politicians must always compromise: they must try to get what they want done, while understanding the needs of others. Van Buren was good at that.

Van Buren became a powerful politician. Some people called him the "sly fox," suggesting he was perhaps more clever than fair. Yet he was always an honest man, and people trusted him. President Jackson said: "It is said that he is a great magician. I believe it, but his only wand is good common sense which he uses for the benefit of his country."

VICE PRESIDENT: When Jackson ran for reelection in 1832, Van Buren was his Vice Presidential candidate. They won that race, and Van Buren served as Vice President for four years.

Van Buren had wanted to be President for a long time when he ran in 1836. He called the office "the glittering prize."

"O.K." The expression "O.K." comes from the Presidential campaign of Martin Van Buren. He was from Kinderhook, New York, and his nickname was "Old

Hannah Van Buren, who died in 1819, before Van Buren became Preseident.

Kinderhook," shortened to "O.K." Most of the voters of 1836 thought Van Buren was "O.K." He won the election by a wide majority. He defeated his opponent, **William Henry Harrison**, with 170 **electoral votes** to Harrison's 73.

PRESIDENT OF THE UNITED STATES: Almost as soon as Van Buren became President, the country suffered a great financial crisis. It was called the "Panic of 1837." The banks failed, and people who had their money in banks lost all of it. Businesses were ruined, and many people lost their jobs.

Van Buren believed that there should be a separate treasury that would prevent another panic from happening. He helped develop what is now our U.S. Treasury. The economy got better, and people found jobs again. But Van Buren was an unpopular President because of the Panic. He ran for reelection in 1840 and lost.

Van Buren tried to be the Democrat's candidate in 1844, but didn't succeed. In 1848, he ran for President as candidate of the **Free Soil Party**. Once again, he was defeated.

LIFE AT THE WHITE HOUSE: Van Buren liked fine things. When he moved into the White House, he had it redecorated. His wife had died before he won the Presidency, so he had no First Lady to be hostess. As she had for other Presidents, Dolley Madison found a hostess for Van Buren. She introduced her niece, Angelica, to Van Buren's son Abraham. Angelica and Abraham fell in love and married. During Van Buren's years in the White House, Angelica served as hostess.

RETIREMENT TO LINDENWALD: After he lost the 1848 election, Van Buren toured Europe with his son Smith for two years. Then he retired to his estate in New York, called "Lindenwald." He lived

President Martin Van Buren.

Van Buren's home, Lindenwald.

there in his final years, writing his autobiography. Martin Van Buren died on July 24, 1862, at the age of 79.

WHAT DID HE LOOK LIKE? Van Buren was 5 feet 6 inches tall and slender. He had grey hair. He was considered to be an elegant dresser.

FAMOUS QUOTE: As eager as he was to be President, Van Buren was also happy to leave the job behind.

"As to the Presidency, the two happiest days of my life were those of my entrance upon the office and my surrender of it."

FOR MORE INFORMATION ON MARTIN VAN BUREN:

Historic Sites:

Birth Site:
46 Hudson St.
Kinderhook, NY 12106

Martin Van Buren National Historic Site
Lindenwald Residence:
1013 Old Post Road
P.O. Box 545
Kinderhook, NY 12106
Phone: 518-758-9689

WORLD WIDE WEB ADDRESSES:

The White House offers young readers information on the U.S. government and the Presidents on a Web site called **"White House 101."** The address is:
http://www.whitehouse.gov/about/white_house_101/

The Internet Public Library has a site on the Presidents. The address is:
http://www.ipl.org/div/potus

American Memory is a site maintained by the Library of Congress that contains biographical and historical information on the Presidents. It also provides links to Presidential portraits.
For Martin Van Buren:
http://memory.loc.gov/ammem/today/dec05.html

Martin Van Buren National Historic Site
http://www.nps.gov.mava

William Henry Harrison
1773-1841
Ninth President of the United States (1841)
"Old Tippecanoe"

WILLIAM HENRY HARRISON WAS BORN February 9, 1773, in Charles City County, Virginia. He was born on the family plantation, called Berkeley. His father, Benjamin, was a planter and statesman. Benjamin was a major figure during the **Revolutionary War** and a signer of the **Declaration of Independence**. Later, he was Governor of Virginia. William's mother, Elizabeth, was a homemaker. William was the youngest of seven children. He had four sisters and two brothers. His sisters were Elizabeth, Ann, Lucy, and Sarah, and his brothers were Benjamin and Carter.

WILLIAM HENRY HARRISON GREW UP on the plantation. He loved growing up in the country. He especially liked to hunt and fish.

WILLIAM HENRY HARRISON WENT TO SCHOOL at home until he was 14. He had a tutor who taught him all his subjects. When he was 14, he began college at Hampden-Sydney College in Virginia. His father wanted him to be a doctor. So after three years of college, William went to medical school briefly.

LIFE AS A SOLDIER: When Harrison's father died in 1791, he stopped studying medicine. He decided he would rather be a soldier than a doctor.

At the age of 18, Harrison began his career as a soldier. He started out at Fort Washington, near what is now Cincinnati. At that time, it was wilderness. Harrison fought in battles against Ohio Indian tribes. He served as a soldier for seven years.

MARRIAGE AND FAMILY: Harrison met his wife, Ann Symmes, in 1795. He was captain of Fort Washington at the time. Ann thought her father, a well-known judge, wouldn't approve of Harrison as a husband. So the couple ran away to get married on November 25, 1795. Harrison and Ann's father eventually became great friends.

William Henry and Ann Harrison had 10 children, six boys and four girls. Their daughters were named Elizabeth, Lucy, Mary, and Anna. Their sons were named John, William, John, Benjamin, Carter, and James. One of their grandchildren, **Benjamin Harrison**, became the 23rd president of the United States.

Poster showing W. H. Harrison as a war hero.

GETTING INVOLVED IN POLITICS: In 1798 Harrison left the army. That same year, he was chosen by **President John Adams** to be secretary of the Northwest Territory. Later, he represented the territory in the U.S. **Congress**.

While Harrison was in Congress, the former Northwest Territory was divided into the Ohio and Indiana Territories. The areas were growing, with more settlers moving in. After his term in Congress, Harrison became Governor of Indiana Territory. That area covered what is now Indiana, Michigan, Minnesota, Illinois, and Wisconsin. He served as Governor for 12 years.

RETURNING TO THE ARMY AND THE BATTLE OF TIPPECANOE:
Harrison returned to the army after his years as Governor. He became a war hero for a battle he led in 1811. It was known as the Battle of Tippecanoe. In this fight, he led the U.S. forces against the Shawnee Indians. Although he and his men were outnumbered, they won the battle.

In the **War of 1812**, the U.S. and the British were once again at war. Harrison served in the war as a general in charge of the Army of the Northwest. He fought against the British in Michigan and Canada. He led the forces that recaptured Detroit from the British in 1813. That same year, his armies fought and defeated the British at a battle in Ontario.

BACK IN POLITICS: In 1816, Harrison won election to the U.S. Congress from Ohio. He served for three years. Next, he was elected to the Ohio Senate. Harrison's next political move took him back to Washington. He was elected Senator from his state in 1825, and he served for three years.

RUNNING FOR PRESIDENT: Harrison first ran for President in 1836 as a member of the **Whig Party.** There were two major political parties at that time, the Whigs and the **Democrats.** The Whigs favored high **tariffs**, or taxes on imports to the U.S. They thought it would help the American economy. The Democrats at that time were followers of Andrew Jackson. They didn't believe the power of the federal government should be as strong as that of the individual states.

Harrison campaigned throughout the U.S. in 1836. Although he lost to **Martin Van Buren**, he was a popular candidate. In 1840, the Whig Party again chose Harrison as their Presidential candidate.

In the campaign of 1840, Harrison gave many public speeches. That was very unusual for the time. Most Presidential candidates didn't travel and meet voters. But Harrison did, and the people loved him. He was a war hero, known as "Old Tippecanoe" for his bravery in that earlier battle. Even though he was a wealthy man from a privileged background, he ran as a humble, simple man. That was very appealing to the voters. His running mate was John Tyler. Together, they were known as "Tippecanoe and Tyler, Too."

Harrison was elected in 1840 by a huge majority. He beat his opponent, President Martin Van Buren, with 234 **electoral votes.** Van Buren only received 60 electoral votes.

PRESIDENT OF THE UNITED STATES: Harrison became President at age 68. At the time, he was the oldest man to be elected President. Sadly, he also served the shortest term of any President, just one month.

FIRST PRESIDENT TO DIE IN OFFICE: On March 4, 1841, Harrison gave a long speech at his inauguration in very cold weather. He caught pneumonia and died one month later, on April 4, 1841. He was the first President to die in office.

President William Henry Harrison.

John Tyler, Harrison's Vice President, became President in April 1841.

LIFE AT THE WHITE HOUSE: When Harrison was elected President, his wife, Ann, was too ill to move to Washington. So Harrison's daughter-in-law, Jane Harrison, served as White House hostess for his one-month term.

After Harrison's death, Ann Harrison lived on at the family home in Ohio. She died in 1864, at the age of 88.

First Lady Ann Harrison.

WHAT DID HE LOOK LIKE? Harrison was 5 feet, 8 inches tall, and had a long, thin face.

FAMOUS QUOTE:
Harrison's last words were:

"I wish you to understand the true principles of government. I wish them carried out. I ask nothing more."

FOR MORE INFORMATION ABOUT WILLIAM HENRY HARRISON:

Historic Sites:

Birth Site:
Berkeley Plantation
12602 Harrison Landing Rd.
Charles City, VA 23030
Phone: 804-829-6018

Grouseland
3 West Scott St.
Vincennes, IN 47591
Phone: 812-882-2096

WORLD WIDE WEB ADDRESSES:

The White House offers young readers information on the U.S. government and the Presidents on a Web site called **"White House 101."** The address is:
http://www.whitehouse.gov/about/white_house_101/

The Internet Public Library has a site on the Presidents. The address is:
http://www.ipl.org/div/potus

American Memory is a site maintained by the Library of Congress that contains biographical and historical information on the Presidents. It also provides links to Presidential portraits.
For William Henry Harrison:
http://memory.loc.gov/ammem/today/may09.html

John Tyler
1790-1862
Tenth President of the United States (1841-1845)
"The Accidental President"

JOHN TYLER WAS BORN March 29, 1790, in Charles City County, Virginia. He was born on his family's plantation, called Greenway. His parents were John Tyler and Mary Marot Armistead Tyler. His father was a respected judge and was Governor of Virginia from 1808 to 1811. His mother was a homemaker.

John was the sixth of eight children. His two brothers were named Wat and William. His five sisters were named Anne, Elizabeth, Martha, Maria, and Christianna.

JOHN TYLER GREW UP in Greenway. His mother died when he was only seven years old. As a boy, John was thin and frail, and never in good health.

JOHN TYLER WENT TO SCHOOL at a local school. He was an excellent student. Legend has it that when he was ten he led a classroom revolt against the teacher, Mr. McMurdoo. John and his classmates thought Mr. McMurdoo was too strict. They tied him up and left him in the classroom. A passerby who heard his cries for help rescued him. McMurdoo complained to Tyler's father. He wanted him to punish John. Instead, the judge reminded the angry teacher of Virginia's state motto: *Sic Semper Tyrannis* (Thus Always to Tyrants). This means that tyrants should expect to be treated the same way they treat others.

John went to the College of William and Mary when he was just 12 years old. He graduated in 1807 at the age of 17. After college he studied law with his father and became a lawyer in 1809.

EARLY POLITICAL CAREER: Tyler's political career began when he was only 21 years old. He was elected to the Virginia House of Delegates (Virginia's state government) in 1811 as a **Democrat**. He went on to serve in almost every office open to a politician. He served in the U.S. **House of Representatives** from 1816 to 1821. In 1825, he was elected Governor of Virginia. He entered the U.S. **Senate** in 1827.

MARRIAGE AND FAMILY: Tyler was married twice. He met Letitia Christian when he was in his teens. She was the daughter of a Virginia plantation owner. After a long courtship, they were married in 1813. They had five daughters and three sons. One of the daughters, Anne, died in infancy. Their surviving children were

Letitia Tyler, John Tyler's first wife, died while he was President, in 1842.

Mary, Robert, John, Letitia, Elizabeth, Alice, and Tazewell. Letitia suffered a stroke in the late 1830s and was an invalid for the rest of her life. She died in 1842.

In 1844, Tyler married Julia Gardiner. They had seven children. Their names were David, John Alexander, Julia, Lachlan, Lyon, Robert Fitzwalter, and Pearl. All together, Tyler had fifteen children, the most of any U.S. President.

TYLER'S POLITICAL BELIEFS: Tyler was a member of the "Virginia Aristocracy," a group of rich and powerful plantation owners. His ancestors came to Virginia in the 1650s. His privileged life influenced his political principles. He thought that each state should run its own affairs. He believed that the federal government should have limited powers. Like most Southerners of the time, he supported low tariffs—taxes—on imported goods.

Tyler owned a plantation in Virginia called Sherwood Forest. As a plantation owner, he owned slaves. He personally believed that **slavery** was wrong, but thought that ending slavery right away would damage Southern society. He favored doing away with slavery gradually.

In 1836 Tyler resigned from the Senate and left the Democratic Party. He thought that many of the political actions of **President**

Andrew Jackson were unconstitutional. Tyler joined the **Whig Party** because they opposed Jackson, even though he disagreed with many of the party's principles. The Whigs generally favored high tariffs and spending federal money on local projects. They also were against the expansion of slavery into the new western territories.

VICE PRESIDENT: In 1839 the Whigs nominated **William Henry Harrison** for President. John Tyler was nominated for Vice President. Although Tyler disagreed with the Whigs, the party leaders thought he would win Southern voters. Harrison was a popular military hero, who had won the battle of Tippecanoe in 1811. Their campaign was famous for the slogan "Tippecanoe and Tyler, Too."

Harrison won the Presidential election 1840. However, he caught pneumonia at his inauguration and died after only one month in office. Tyler became President on April 6, 1841. This was the first time in American history that the Vice President took over the office after the death of the President.

PRESIDENT OF THE UNITED STATES: Although Tyler was elected into office as a Whig, he disagreed with most of the policies favored by the Whig leaders in Congress. He vetoed (canceled) bill after bill, including one for a national bank. Tyler stubbornly held on to his principles. He believed he was

Julia Gardiner Tyler was Tyler's second wife. They married in 1844, during his term as President.

acting in the best interests of the whole country. The Whig leaders angrily threw him out of the Party while he was President.

Tyler's administration had more success in foreign policy. He signed a treaty with Great Britain, which settled the boundary between Maine and Canada. He also opened trade with China for the first time.

Tyler worked to bring Texas into the Union. At that time, Texas was an independent country. He signed the law that made Texas a state in March 1845, just before he left office.

LIFE IN THE WHITE HOUSE: Tyler's first wife, Letitia, was very ill when she and John moved into the White House. Her only public appearance was for her daughter Elizabeth's wedding. This was the second wedding ever held at the White House. Letitia died in September 1842.

Shortly afterward, Tyler met Julia Gardiner, a young lady from a prominent New York family. They fell in love and were married on June 26, 1844. Tyler was the first President to be married while in office. He was 54 years old and Julia was only 24. She gained a reputation for being one of the most gracious hostesses in Washington. She began the tradition of playing the march "Hail to the Chief" whenever the President appears in public.

RETIREMENT TO VIRGINIA: Tyler served only one term as President. His party refused to nominate him for a second term because of his political differences with party leaders.

Tyler returned to his plantation, Sherwood Forest, in Virginia. Life at Sherwood Forest was filled with dinners, dances, and fox-hunts. Tyler actively managed the plantation and was an excellent farmer.

President John Tyler.

THE CIVIL WAR: The events leading up to the **Civil War** brought Tyler out of retirement. At the age of 70, he agreed to serve as President of the Peace Conference held in Washington, D.C., on February 4, 1861. Tyler's goal was to work out a compromise between the North and South that would avoid civil war. When the talks failed, he returned to Virginia and supported that state's secession—leaving the Union. He believed that Virginia's entry into the **Confederacy** might still prevent war.

Virginia left the Union on April 17, 1861. Tyler was elected to the House of Representatives of the Confederate Provisional Congress. He was the only U.S. President to hold office in the Confederate government. While serving in the Confederate Congress, he suffered a stroke. Tyler died on January 18, 1862, at the age of 71. Julia lived on at Sherwood Forest until her death in 1889.

WHAT DID HE LOOK LIKE? Tyler was six feet tall and thin. He had light brown hair, blue eyes, and a high-bridged nose.

FAMOUS QUOTE:

"Take care that the laws be faithfully executed."

FOR MORE INFORMATION ON JOHN TYLER:

Historic Site:

Sherwood Forest Plantation
14501 John Tyler Memorial Highway
Charles City, VA 23030
Phone: 804-829-5377

WORLD WIDE WEB ADDRESSES:

The White House offers young readers information on the U.S. government and the Presidents on a Web site called **"White House 101."** The address is:
http://www.whitehouse.gov/about/white_house_101/

The **Internet Public Library** has a site on the Presidents. The address is:
http://www.ipl.org/div/potus

American Memory is a site maintained by the Library of Congress that contains biographical and historical information on the Presidents. It also provides links to Presidential portraits.
For John Tyler:
http://memory.loc.gov/learn/

Sherwood Forest Plantation
http://www.sherwoodforest.org

James K. Polk

1795-1849
11th President of the United States (1845-1849)
"Young Hickory"

JAMES K. POLK WAS BORN November 2, 1795, in Mecklenburg County, North Carolina. His full name was James Knox Polk. His parents were Samuel and Jane Knox Polk. Samuel was a farmer, and Jane was a homemaker. James was the oldest of ten children. He had four sisters and five brothers. His sisters' names were Jane, Lydia, Naomi, and Ophelia. His brothers' names were Franklin, Marshall, John, William, and Samuel. James was the great-grand-nephew of the famous Presbyterian reformer John Knox.

JAMES K. POLK GREW UP on the family farm. His family moved to Tennessee in 1806, when he was eleven years old. His boyhood friends called him Black Pony because of his passion for horse racing. He had a small black horse that won a lot of races.

SCHOOL: As a boy, James was too sickly to go school. He learned to read and write at home. When he was 16, his doctor discovered that he was suffering from a gallstone. A gallstone is a stone-like object that can form in the gallbladder. It is a very painful condition. In Polk's day, it was also very dangerous. He had an operation to have the stone removed. In those days, surgery was very risky. Doctors didn't put the patient to sleep before they operated. James survived the surgery, and became a healthy and vigorous youth.

When he was 17, James went to an academy to prepare for college. He went on to the University of North Carolina, where he graduated at the head of his class in 1818.

In 1819 Polk went to Nashville, Tennessee, and studied law with a lawyer named Felix Grundy. He became a practicing lawyer in 1820.

MARRIAGE AND FAMILY: Polk married Sarah Childress on New Year's Day, 1824. She was the daughter of a wealthy plantation owner in Murfreesboro, Tennessee. She was one of the few women of her era to go to college. James and Sarah did not have any children. Sarah devoted her life to helping her husband's political career. Besides being a gracious hostess, she was also James's personal secretary.

EARLY POLITICAL CAREER: While studying law, Polk became interested in politics. He joined the **Democratic Party** and was elected to the state legislature in 1823. While he was there, he opposed the powerful land speculators and bankers and fought for the interests of the common people. He also became a supporter of his friend and mentor **Andrew Jackson**, who was then governor of Tennessee.

U.S. CONGRESS: Polk was elected to the U.S. **House of Representatives** in 1825. He served in the House for 14 years. While there, he worked hard for Jackson's election to the Presidency in 1828. He became a leader in **Congress** and made sure that Jackson's policies were carried out in the House.

Polk became Speaker of the House in 1835. The Speaker runs the House of Representatives, and is the third most powerful member of the U.S. government. He was the only President who also served as Speaker of the House.

In 1839, Polk left Congress and returned to his home in Tennessee. That same year he was elected Governor and served for two years. He ran again for Governor in 1841 and 1843, but was narrowly defeated both times.

PRESIDENT OF THE UNITED STATES: In 1844, Polk was a candidate for Vice President at the Democratic Convention. The two leading candidates for President that year were **Martin Van Buren** and Lewis Cass. Neither candidate could get a majority of votes to win the nomination. Finally, on the ninth ballot, the party delegates nominated Polk as their presidential candidate, because all the party factions trusted him.

Polk is known as America's first "dark horse" candidate. A "dark horse" is a candidate that isn't likely to win, but is successful

President James K. Polk.

anyway. Polk ran as "Young Hickory," because he was known as a supporter of his old mentor, Andrew Jackson, called "Old Hickory."

The great issue of the 1844 election campaign was whether or not to admit Texas into the Union. At that time, Texas was an independent country that had recently broken away from Mexico. Polk was for annexing Texas right away. His opponent, Henry Clay, was against it. Polk was elected President, winning 170 **electoral votes**, to Clay's 105.

LIFE AT THE WHITE HOUSE: The Polks were both strict Presbyterians who believed in the value of hard work. They also had very strict morals. Drinking, dancing and card games were banned from the White House. Even so, Sarah Polk was known as a gracious hostess. Dinners and parties at the White House were famous for their lively and stimulating conversation. Sarah hosted the first annual Thanksgiving dinner at the White House.

First Lady Sarah Polk.

Polk worked very hard as President. He was one of the strongest and most successful Presidents of the 19th century. Under his leadership, Congress passed laws that restored an independent treasury, and reduced tariffs — taxes on imports.

Polk's greatest achievement was the expansion of American control in the west. Disputes over the Texas bor-

*Many Americans moved West during Polk's Presidency,
as the boundaries of the nation expanded.*

der led to the **Mexican War** in 1846. When the war ended in 1848, the U.S. gained California and the Utah and New Mexico territories. Polk also settled the border between the Oregon territory and Canada.

RETIREMENT: When Polk was elected President, he promised to serve only one term. He wanted to work for the good of the country. He thought that reelection politics would distract him from his work.

In 1849, James and Sarah Polk returned to their home in Nashville, Tennessee. Polk had worked so hard as President that he left office in weak health. Only three months after leaving office, he became ill and died on June 15, 1849. He was 54 years old.

Sarah lived alone for another 42 years, and died on August 14, 1891, at the age of 87.

WHAT DID HE LOOK LIKE? Polk was 5 feet 8 inches tall. He had long, white hair, a high forehead, and sharp gray eyes.

FAMOUS QUOTE:

"I prefer to supervise the whole operation of government myself."

FOR MORE INFORMATION ON JAMES K. POLK:

Historic Sites:

Birth Site:
U.S. 521, Box 475
Pineville, NC 28134
Phone: 704-889-7145

Polk Home:
P.O. Box 741
Columbia, TN 38402
Phone: 931-388-2354

WORLD WIDE WEB ADDRESSES:

The White House offers young readers information on the U.S. government and the Presidents on a Web site called "**White House 101.**" The address is:
http://www.whitehouse.gov/about/white_house_101/

The **Internet Public Library** has a site on the Presidents. The address is:

http://www.ipl.org/div/potus

American Memory is a site maintained by the Library of Congress that contains biographical and historical information on the Presidents. It also provides links to Presidential portraits.
For James K. Polk:

http://memory.loc.gov/ammem/today/nov05.html

James K. Polk Ancestral Home
http://www.jamespolk.com

Zachary Taylor
1784-1850
12th President of the United States (1849-1850)
"Old Rough and Ready"

ZACHARY TAYLOR WAS BORN November 24, 1784, in Orange County, Virginia. His parents were Richard and Sarah Taylor. Richard had fought in the **Revolutionary War** with George Washington and was later a planter. Sarah was a homemaker.

Zachary was the third of nine children. He had three sisters and five brothers. His sisters were named Elizabeth, Sarah, and Emily. His brothers' names were Hancock, William, George, Joseph, and Strother. He was related to a number of notable Americans, including **President James Madison** and Civil War General Robert E. Lee.

ZACHARY TAYLOR GREW UP in Kentucky. His father had moved the family there from Virginia when Zachary was a baby. In Kentucky, the family started a farm near Louisville. The land had been given to Taylor's father for his Revolutionary War service.

ZACHARY TAYLOR WENT TO SCHOOL briefly at a school in Louisville. He was needed on the farm to help out, so there wasn't time for formal school. His parents taught him to read and write at home.

BECOMING A SOLDIER: Taylor worked on the farm while growing up. In 1808, when he was 24, he joined the army. Over the next 40 years, he served his country at posts throughout the growing American west.

MARRIAGE AND FAMILY: When he was 26, Taylor met Margaret Mackall Smith. She was a planter's daughter from Maryland. They were married June 21, 1810. They had five daughters and one son. Two of the girls died in infancy. The surviving daughters were named Anne, Sarah, and Mary Elizabeth. Their son was named Richard.

The Taylor family lived in many places on the western frontier. The children were used to the military way of life. When they grew up, the girls married men in the army. Sarah married Jefferson Davis, who became the first president of the **Confederacy** in the **Civil War**. Richard became a general in the Army of the Confederacy.

Taylor at the Battle of Buena Vista, February 23, 1847.

While he was in the army, Taylor bought property to farm. He had two large plantations, one in Louisiana and one in Mississippi. Over the years, the family spent time at their properties when they could.

MILITARY CAREER: Taylor's early military career took him to the area that is now the Midwest. During the **War of 1812**, he fought in what is now Indiana.

Throughout this period of American history, battles broke out between the U.S. and Native American tribes. In the 1830s Taylor led troops in the Black Hawk War in what is now Wisconsin and Illinois. From 1837 to 1840 he took troops to Florida to fight the Seminole Indians.

In the 1840s Taylor became a war hero for his leadership in the **Mexican War.** In that war, his troops defeated the Mexican army at three decisive battles in what is now Texas and Mexico. For his courage in battle, Taylor earned the nickname "Old Rough and Ready." He was honored in **Congress** and became a national hero.

GETTING INVOLVED IN POLITICS: Taylor thought of himself as a life-long soldier. He had never planned on running for President. In fact, when the **Whig Party** asked him to run in 1848, he refused. He later changed his mind and ran for President as the Whig candidate.

Taylor was a very popular and well-known hero to the American people. Even though he had no experience in politics, he won the election. He defeated his **Democratic** opponent, Lewis Cass, with 163 **electoral votes** to Cass's 127. He became the first career soldier to be elected President.

Taylor had never voted before the Presidential election of 1848. Because he was a soldier, he was never in one place long enough to register to vote. The first time he cast a ballot, he voted for himself.

PRESIDENT OF THE UNITED STATES: The most difficult issue facing the nation when Taylor took office was **slavery.** Taylor himself owned more than 100 slaves. But he didn't want slavery to be allowed in the new Western territories of the U.S. He stood by his beliefs and was willing to fight for them.

The Northern and Southern states had fought over the issue of slavery for years. During Taylor's presidency, the Southern states threatened to leave the U.S. over the issue.

Taylor's stance against the expansion of slavery was unpopular, especially with Southerners. Yet he believed that the Union should be preserved — that the Northern and Southern states should remain united as one nation. He was willing to lead an army to keep slavery out of the territories and save the Union. In his brief presidency, he was able to keep peace. But these tensions eventually led to the **Civil War.**

LIFE AT THE WHITE HOUSE: Margaret Taylor was ill when Zachary Taylor became President. She did not attend public functions as First Lady. Instead, the Taylor's daughter Mary Elizabeth took on the duties of White House hostess.

Taylor enjoyed taking walks around Washington, D.C. He also kept his horse, Old Whitey, at the White House. Old Whitey had been Taylor's horse through some of his fiercest battles. Taylor let him graze on the White House lawn.

DEATH IN THE WHITE HOUSE: On July 4, 1850, Taylor went to a special Fourth of July celebration in Washington, D.C. It was a very hot day, so after the festivities, Taylor went back to the White House and drank some cold water and milk. He also ate some fruit, probably cherries.

Taylor suddenly became quite ill. He died five days later, on July 9, 1850. No one is sure of the exact cause of his death. Taylor had served just 16 months of his term. Grieving deeply, Margaret Taylor moved back to their home in Mississippi, where she died in 1852.

Taylor's Vice President, **Millard Fillmore**, became the next President.

Taylor with his horse, Old Whitey, who grazed on the White House lawn.

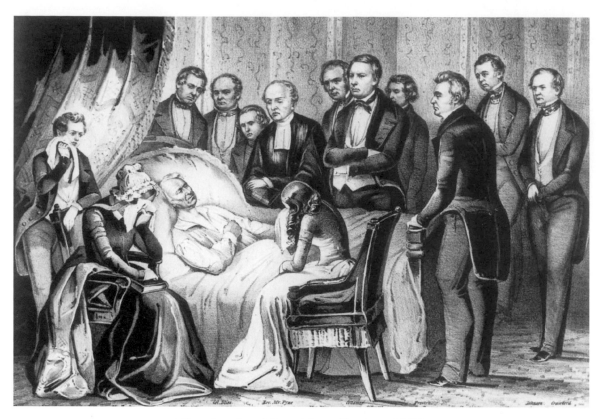

The death of President Taylor, 1850.

WHAT DID HE LOOK LIKE? Taylor was 5 feet, 8 inches tall and had a solid build. He had black hair and gray eyes.

FOR MORE INFORMATION ON ZACHARY TAYLOR:

Historic Sites:

Birth Site:
Montebello
Gordonsville, VA 22942

Springfield
5608 Apache Rd.
Louisville, KY 40207
Phone: 502-897-9990

WORLD WIDE WEB ADDRESSES:

The White House offers young readers information on the U.S. government and the Presidents on a Web site called **"White House 101."** The address is:
http://www.whitehouse.gov/about/white_house_101/

The **Internet Public Library** has a site on the Presidents. The address is:
http://www.ipl.org/div/potus

American Memory is a site maintained by the Library of Congress that contains biographical and historical information on the Presidents. It also provides links to Presidential portraits.
For Zachary Taylor:
http://memory.loc.gov/ammem/today/may08.html

Millard Fillmore

1800-1874
13th President of the United States (1850-1853)
"Wool-Carder President"

MILLARD FILLMORE WAS BORN January 7, 1800, in Locke township (now Summerhill), New York. His father, Nathaniel Fillmore, was a farmer. His mother, Phoebe Millard Fillmore, was a homemaker. Millard was the second of nine children. He had three sisters and five brothers. His sisters' names were Olive, Julia, and Phoebe. His brothers' names were Cyrus, Aimon, Calvin, Darius, and Charles.

MILLARD FILLMORE

MILLARD FILLMORE GREW UP on his family's frontier farm in Cayuga County, New York. They were very poor. Millard helped work the farm. He learned to plow, hoe corn, mow hay, and harvest wheat.

MILLARD FILLMORE WENT TO SCHOOL at a one-room schoolhouse. He only attended school now and then, because he had to work on the farm. Most of what he learned from books, he learned on his own.

His father thought Millard should learn a trade. When he was 15, his father sent him away to be an "apprentice." An apprentice is someone who learns a trade from another person. The apprentice learns the job, then works in exchange for a room and food.

Millard worked in a cloth-making factory. That's how he got his nickname, the "Wool-Carder President." A wool-carder was a worker who ran a machine that spun wool into yarn. Fillmore knew he wanted to be more than a wool-carder. He wanted an education. In his limited free time, he attended an academy in New Hope, New York.

By 1819, Fillmore he had completed his apprenticeship. He became a clerk for Judge Walter Wood in Montville, New York. While he was there, he began studying law. Besides working as a clerk, he also taught school to make extra money. Fillmore became a practicing lawyer in 1823 and opened his own law office in East Aurora, near Buffalo.

MARRIAGE AND FAMILY: Fillmore met Abigail Powers in 1819, while he was going to school in New Hope. Abigail was the daughter of Rev. Lemuel Powers of Moravia, New York. She was 21 when they met. He was 19. Millard and Abigail had a long courtship. He

117

First Lady Abigail Powers Fillmore, who was often ill during her husband's Presidency.

didn't think he should marry until he could prove himself and support his wife. They were married on February 5, 1826, after Millard had become a successful lawyer.

Millard and Abigail had two children. Their son was named Millard Powers, and their daughter was named Mary Abigail.

Abigail Fillmore died in 1853, at the end of Fillmore's term as President. In 1858, Fillmore married again. His second wife was Caroline Carmichael McIntosh. They had no children.

GETTING INVOLVED IN POLITICS: Fillmore ran for office for the first time in 1828. He was elected to the New York state legislature, where he served for three terms. While he was there, he helped end the practice of jailing people who were in debt.

In 1836, Fillmore was elected to the U.S. House of Representatives. As a member of the **Whig Party**, he supported high **tariffs**—taxes on imports—and opposed citizenship for new immigrants. Fillmore served for terms, from 1836 to 1844.

In 1844, Fillmore ran unsuccessfully for Governor of New York. In 1847, he was elected state comptroller—head of the state treasury. As comptroller, he worked to improve the state's banking system.

VICE PRESIDENT: In 1848, the Whig party nominated the war hero **Zachary Taylor** for President and Millard Fillmore for Vice President. They won the election by a narrow margin. Even though they ran as President and Vice President, Taylor and Fillmore didn't know each other. In fact, they didn't even meet until after the election was over.

PRESIDENT OF THE UNITED STATES: Fillmore became President when Zachary Taylor died on July 9, 1850. He was the second Vice President in U.S. history to take over the office after the death of the President.

Campaign Poster for Fillmore.

The most difficult issue facing America when Fillmore took over the Presidency was **slavery**. Fillmore opposed slavery, but he thought that it was up to the individual states to settle the matter, not the federal government. At the time, there were an equal number of states that did and did not allow slavery.

One of the major battles over slavery had to do with whether it should be allowed in the new states and territories of the U.S. The population of California grew dramatically after the discovery of gold in 1849. Zachary Taylor wanted California to be admitted to the Union as a state right away. Since most of the people in California were against slavery, they wanted their state to be a free state. All the Senators from the southern states fought California's statehood, because they wanted the California territory to allow slavery.

COMPROMISE OF 1850: Fillmore supported a compromise that was put together by Senator Henry Clay, known as the Compromise of 1850. The compromise provided for statehood for California, the end of slave trade in Washington D.C., and the division of the remaining Southwest into two territories, Utah and New Mexico. It also called for stronger fugitive slave laws that would force escaped slaves to be returned to their owners. Congress voted to adopt the Compromise of 1850. Although it kept the country together for ten more years, it didn't settle the issue of slavery. By 1861, the tensions around the issue would lead the nation to civil war.

In other issues, Fillmore sent Commodore Matthew Perry to Japan in 1852 to open trade with that country. He also supported the first federal land grants for railroad construction.

In 1852, the Whigs, divided over the Compromise of 1850, did not renominate Fillmore. They chose war hero General Winfield Scott instead. Democrat **Franklin Pierce** won the election.

President Millard Fillmore.

LIFE AT THE WHITE HOUSE:
When the Fillmores moved into
the White House in 1850, they
discovered that there were no
books in the mansion, not even
a dictionary or Bible. Abigail
Fillmore had her husband ask
Congress for $250 to start a
White House library.

*Mary Abigail Fillmore, who often
served as White House hostess.*

Abigail made other
improvements to the White
House. She had the first stove
installed. Before then, the food
for the First Family was cooked
over an open fire in the kitchen
fireplace. The Fillmores also
brought the first bath tub with
running water into the White House.

Abigail was a shy person who liked her privacy. She also had a
permanently injured ankle, which made the many White House parties a painful ordeal. Her daughter Mary often served as White
House hostess.

While attending Franklin Pierce's inauguration in March 1853,
Abigail caught a cold. Her cold turned into pneumonia, and she
died on March 30, 1853, less than one month after leaving the
White House.

LIFE AFTER THE PRESIDENCY: Fillmore still had political ambitions. He ran for President again in 1856. He had been nominated

by both the Whig Party, and the American, or **"Know-Nothing"** Party. The "Know-Nothings" were a conservative group who wanted to stop immigration to America. Fillmore finished a distant third in the Presidential election of 1856. He retired from politics.

Fillmore returned to Buffalo, New York. There, he continued with his law practice and got involved in charity work. He was the first chancellor of the University of Buffalo and helped build Buffalo General Hospital.

In 1858, Fillmore married Caroline Carmichael McIntosh, who was a wealthy widow from Buffalo. They moved into a mansion on Niagara Square, a fashionable neighborhood in Buffalo. Caroline filled the mansion with portraits and busts of her famous husband. Their home became a center of generous hospitality.

Fillmore suffered a stroke on February 13, 1874, which left him paralyzed. Less than a month later, he had a second stroke, and died on March 8, 1874. He was 74 years old.

WHAT DID HE LOOK LIKE? Fillmore was a handsome man with a dignified appearance. He was 5 feet 9 inches tall. He had blue eyes, thin grayish hair, and a big, powerful chest.

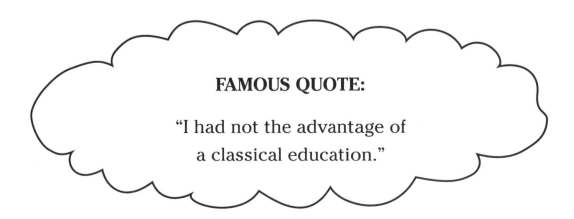

FAMOUS QUOTE:

"I had not the advantage of a classical education."

FOR MORE INFORMATION ON MILLARD FILLMORE:

Historic Sites:

Birth Site (marker):
Fillmore Road
Summerhill, NY

Birth Site (replica):
Fillmore Glen State Park
Rd.3, Box 26
Moravia, NY 13118
Phone: 315-497-0130

Childhood home (marker):
Carver Rd.
New Hope, NY

Millard Fillmore House Museum
24 Shearer Ave.
East Aurora, NY 14052
Phone: 716-652-8875

WORLD WIDE WEB ADDRESSES:

The White House offers young readers information on the U.S. government and the Presidents on a Web site called "**White House 101.**" The address is:
http://www.whitehouse.gov/about/white_house_101/

The Internet Public Library has a site on the Presidents. The address is:
http://www.ipl.org/div/potus

American Memory is a site maintained by the Library of Congress that contains biographical and historical information on the Presidents. It also provides links to Presidential portraits.
For Millard Fillmore:
http://memory.loc.gov/learn

The Millard Fillmore House
http://www.nps.gov/history/nr/travel/presidents/millard_fillmore_house.html

Franklin Pierce
1804-1869
14th President of the United States (1853-1857)
"Young Hickory of the Granite Hills"

FRANKLIN PIERCE WAS BORN November 23, 1804, in Hillsborough, New Hampshire. He was the first President who was born in the nineteenth century. His father was Benjamin Pierce, and his mother was Anna Kendrick Pierce. Benjamin was a former general from the **Revolutionary War** who also served as Governor of New Hampshire. Anna was a homemaker.

Franklin was the sixth of eight children. He had three sisters and four brothers. His sisters were named Nancy, Harriet, and

Charlotte. His brothers were named Benjamin, John, Charles, and Henry.

FRANKLIN PIERCE GREW UP in New Hampshire in a log cabin. While he was growing up, his father worked as a farmer. Benjamin told his son many stories of the Revolutionary War. Franklin's older brother fought in the **War of 1812.** Franklin thought he might be a soldier someday, too.

FRANKLIN PIERCE WENT TO SCHOOL at a school called Hancock Academy. He didn't like Hancock because it was very strict. One day he ran away. When he got home, his father said nothing at first. Then he made Franklin get in the carriage for the ride back to school. When they were halfway there, he told Franklin to get out and walk the rest of the way. Pierce said later he never forgot the experience. He said it taught him discipline.

After graduating from Hancock, Pierce attended Bowdoin College in Maine. There he studied Greek, Latin, science, and math. He graduated in 1824. After college, Pierce studied law and became a lawyer.

GETTING INTO POLITICS: Pierce's father Benjamin became Governor of New Hampshire in 1827. That sparked Franklin's interest in politics. He ran for the New Hampshire Congress in 1829 and served for four years. In 1833, he ran for the U.S. **House of Representatives**, where he also served for four years. Pierce's next political campaign was for the U.S. **Senate**. He won that election in 1837. He was just 33, the youngest person in the Senate at that time.

FRANKLIN PIERCE'S HOME AND FAMILY: Pierce met Jane Means Appleton while he was in college. They married on November 19, 1834.

The Pierces had three boys. Their first child, Franklin, was born in 1836. He died a few days after his birth. The next child, Frank, was born in 1839. Frank died of typhus when he was four. The Pierce's third son, Benjamin, was born in 1841.

U.S. SENATOR: In 1837, the Pierces moved to Washington, D.C., where Pierce began his Senate term. Although Franklin loved Washington and the political life, Jane did not. She hated Washington, and she let her husband know. In 1842, at Jane's urging, Pierce resigned from the Senate. They moved back to New Hampshire, where Pierce worked as a lawyer.

BRIEF CAREER AS A SOLDIER: When the **Mexican War** began in 1846, Pierce served in the army. He led troops in the battle for Mexico City in 1847, where he was wounded. By the end of the war, he had been made a general.

Returning to New Hampshire, Pierce again became a lawyer. In 1852, the **Democratic Party** wanted him to run for President. Over Jane's objections, Pierce accepted. The Democrats came up with the name "Young Hickory of the Granite Hills" to describe him. A previous Democratic President, **Andrew Jackson**, was called "Old Hickory," so the young Pierce would be "Young Hickory." He was from New Hampshire, called the "Granite State" for its mountains made of granite.

Most people didn't think Pierce had a chance to win the nomination. There were several powerful Democrats who wanted to be President in 1852. The candidates battled for the nomination, and the vote was split among them. None of the well-known politicians was able to get a majority of the votes needed for the nomination. The Democrats chose Pierce instead. According to reports, Jane Pierce fainted at the news.

PRESIDENT OF THE UNITED STATES: In the election of 1852, Pierce proved to be a popular candidate with the American people. He was elected, beating Winfield Scott, a war hero who had been his commanding officer in the Mexican War. Pierce received 254 **electoral votes**; Scott got 42.

LIFE AT THE WHITE HOUSE: Any happiness the Pierces might have known as President and First Lady disappeared after the death of their only

First Lady Jane Pierce.

surviving son. In January 1853, just two months after the election, 11-year old Benny was killed in a train accident.

Jane Pierce grieved deeply for her son. She didn't come to Washington until several months after her husband's inauguration. When she did move into the White House, she wanted to be alone in her grief. It was a terribly sad time for the Pierces. Franklin's aunt, Abby Kent Means, served as White House hostess.

SLAVERY AND PIERCE'S PRESIDENCY: During Pierce's presidency the country continued to argue over **slavery**. The nation had expanded its boundaries, and many Southerners wanted slavery extended into the new territories. Most of the Northerners opposed slavery. They wanted it abolished, and they certainly didn't want it in the new territories. These tensions would lead to the **Civil War** in 1861.

Pierce as a General in the Mexican War.

Pierce sided with most Southerners on the issue of slavery. He believed that the Constitution protected slavery. He also believed that slavery should be expanded into the new territories.

So fierce was the debate over slavery that it led to a split in the Democratic Party. Democrats opposed to slavery created a new party, the **Republican Party**. As Republicans, they fought for abolition—doing away with slavery. Pierce bitterly opposed the abolitionists.

One of the positive achievements of Pierce's administration was the Gadsden Purchase. In 1853, the U.S. bought 30,000 square miles of what is now Arizona and New Mexico from Mexico. It would later provide an important railroad route from east to west. He also arranged trade agreements with both Canada and Japan.

Pierce was a very unpopular President. In 1857, the Democratic Party refused to renominate him for President. He is the only elected President who wanted but did not receive his party's renomination. The Pierces left Washington in 1857.

RETIREMENT AND LIFE AFTER THE PRESIDENCY: After they left Washington, the Pierces decided to travel. They toured Europe and returned to New Hampshire to live. Franklin Pierce died in Concord, New Hampshire, on October 8, 1869. Jane Pierce had died earlier, in 1863.

WHAT DID HE LOOK LIKE? Franklin Pierce has often been called the most handsome President. He was 5 feet 10 inches tall and slender, with dark hair and gray eyes.

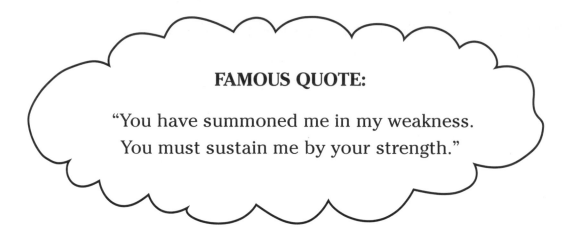

FAMOUS QUOTE:

"You have summoned me in my weakness.
You must sustain me by your strength."

FOR MORE INFORMATION ON FRANKLIN PIERCE:

Historic Sites:

Pierce Homestead
State Hwy. 31
Box 896
Hillsboro, NH 03244
Phone: 603-478-3165

Pierce Manse
P.O. Box 425
Concord, NH 03302
Phone: 603-224-5954

WORLD WIDE WEB ADDRESSES:

The White House offers young readers information on the U.S. government and the Presidents on a Web site called **"White House 101."** The address is:
http://www.whitehouse.gov/about/white_house_101/

The **Internet Public Library** has a site on the Presidents. The address is:
http://www.ipl.org/div/potus

American Memory is a site maintained by the Library of Congress that contains biographical and historical information on the Presidents. It also provides links to Presidential portraits.
For Franklin Pierce:
http://memory.loc.gov/ammem/today/nov23.html

Pierce Manse
http://www.piercemanse.org/

James Buchanan
1791-1868
15th President of the United States (1857-1861)
"The Bachelor President"

JAMES BUCHANAN WAS BORN April 23, 1791, in Cove Gap, Pennsylvania. His parents were James and Elizabeth Speer Buchanan. James Buchanan Sr. had come to America from Ireland in 1783. He ran a general store. Elizabeth was a homemaker. James was the second of 11 children. Three died in infancy. James had three brothers and four sisters who lived to be adults. His brothers were named William, George, and Edward. His sisters were named Jane, Maria, Sarah, and Harriet.

JAMES BUCHANAN GREW UP in the countryside of Pennsylvania. He often helped out at the family store. His father wanted him to learn about money and responsibility. James's mother was known to be quite a storyteller. She told her children stories of American heroes.

JAMES BUCHANAN WENT TO SCHOOL at the local public school. His parents encouraged him to do well in school, and he did. When he was 16, Buchanan went to college at Dickinson College in Carlisle, Pennsylvania.

During his first year of college, Buchanan got into what he called "mischief." He was expelled for bad behavior. After promising to improve, he was allowed to return. He was a very good student after that, doing well in math, history, and Latin. Buchanan graduated with honors in 1809.

After college, Buchanan studied law. He became a lawyer in 1812 and made a good deal of money. While still practicing law, Buchanan ran for office.

GETTING INTO POLITICS: In 1814, Buchanan began his political career. He was elected to the Pennsylvania legislature, where he served for four years.

MARRIAGE AND FAMILY: While he was serving in the legislature, Buchanan met Ann Coleman. She was the daughter of a wealthy Pennsylvania businessman. Ann and James fell in love. In 1819, they became engaged. Ann's parents opposed the marriage. They thought Buchanan only cared about her because she was rich. They forced Ann to break up the relationship.

Buchanan as Secretary of State, 1847.

Sadly, Ann became ill and died soon after the break up. Buchanan was so upset that he promised never to marry, and he never did.

MOVING TO WASHINGTON: In 1820, Buchanan ran for a seat in the U.S. **House of Representatives.** He won and was reelected five times. When Buchanan first was elected, he was a member of the **Federalist Party**. In 1828, he became a **Democrat,** the party of **President Andrew Jackson**.

In 1831, President Jackson chose Buchanan to be Minister to Russia. While serving as Minister, Buchanan developed the first trade agreement between Russia and the U.S. In 1833, Buchanan moved back to the U.S. In 1834, he ran for the U.S. Senate and won, serving for two terms.

SECRETARY OF STATE: In 1845, **President James Polk** chose Buchanan to be Secretary of State. As Secretary of State, he advised Polk on how to handle problems with other countries. One such problem was the **Mexican War**. Buchanan developed a treaty with Mexico that ended the war in 1848. As part of that agreement, the U.S. bought lands from Mexico. These lands spanned the territory from Texas to the Pacific Ocean. Buchanan also worked on a treaty with England that determined the border between Canada and the U.S.

BRIEF RETIREMENT FROM POLITICS: Buchanan retired briefly from politics in 1848. He moved back to Pennsylvania. There he bought an estate, called Wheatland. Buchanan had become the guardian for a number of nieces and nephews, who lived at Wheatland with him.

BACK TO POLITICS: In 1852, Buchanan decided to end his retirement and return to political life. He wanted to run for President. He tried to get the Democratic nomination, but in 1852 the Democrats chose **Franklin Pierce**. Pierce won the Presidency, and he named Buchanan Minster to England. Buchanan held that post for four years.

In 1856, Buchanan won the Democratic Party's nomination for President. He won the election, defeating his opponent, John C.

Wheatland, Buchanan's home in Pennsylvania.

Fremont, with 174 **electoral votes**. Fremont received 114. Buchanan began his term during one of the most difficult times in the nation's history.

PRESIDENT OF THE UNITED STATES: One main issue dominated American politics at this time—**slavery**. As the territory of the U.S. expanded, the people of the nation disagreed violently over whether slavery should be allowed in the new areas. Buchanan thought the states should decide for themselves. The Northern states, who were opposed to slavery, thought that Buchanan was pro-slavery. The Southern states, who wanted slavery in all the new areas, were ready to leave the **Union** over the issue.

Buchanan was opposed to slavery, but he wanted to reach a "compromise" between the North and the South and save the Union. During his first week as President, the **Supreme Court** made one of its most famous and controversial decisions, the Dred Scott Decision.

Dred Scott was a slave who had been taken to a nonslave territory. He wanted to be treated as a free man, because he lived in a free area. He sued to be allowed his freedom. At that time, the U.S. **Congress** had passed a law that said that slavery could not exist in a free territory. But the Supreme Court ruled that the Congress had no right to pass a law limiting slavery.

The nation was in an uproar over the decision. The Northern states were furious and threatened to disobey the ruling. The country moved closer to **Civil War**. Buchanan still fought for compromise between the two sides, but he failed.

Weary of the Presidency, Buchanan did not seek a second term. Even his party had split over the issue of slavery. The Democrats nominated two candidates for the Presidency in 1860, one from the

President James Buchanan.

Harriet Lane, Buchanan's niece, served as White House hostess.

North, one from the South. Buchanan supported the Southern Democratic candidate, John Breckinridge. Breckinridge lost to **Abraham Lincoln.**

BUCHANAN AND THE CIVIL WAR: In February 1861, just before Buchanan left office, seven states left the Union. The Civil War began that April. Some people blamed Buchanan for the war. Others thought that no one could have stopped the Southern states from leaving the Union and the war that followed.

Today many people think that Buchanan best served his nation as a statesman. His work as Minister to Russia and Britain and as Secretary of State was very important to the U.S. It is true that he could not keep the country from going to war, but many people believe that no one could have done that.

LIFE AT THE WHITE HOUSE: Buchanan had promised never to marry after the death of his first love, Ann Coleman. He kept that promise and became the only "Bachelor President."

Because he had no wife, Buchanan asked his niece, Harriet Lane, to be the White House hostess. Harriet was a popular social figure in Washington. During Buchanan's term, they entertained the first Japanese visitors to the White House. When the Prince of Wales visited from England, he brought so many people with him that they filled all the bedrooms. President Buchanan had to sleep in a hallway.

RETIREMENT AND LIFE AFTER THE PRESIDENCY: Buchanan retired to his estate at Wheatland in 1861. He worked on a book about his Presidency, which was published in 1865. Buchanan died at Wheatland on June 1, 1868, at the age of 77.

WHAT DID HE LOOK LIKE? Buchanan was 6 feet tall, with blond hair and blue eyes. He had problems with his eyes, and often had to cock his head to one side to see properly. That is why his head is tipped to one side in most of the pictures we have of him.

FAMOUS QUOTE: Buchanan was happy to leave the Presidency. He told Abraham Lincoln as he entered the White House:

"If you are as happy, my dear sir, on entering this house as I am in leaving it and returning home, you are the happiest man in the country."

FOR MORE INFORMATION ON JAMES BUCHANAN:

Historic Sites:

Birth Site (Marker):
Buchanan's Birthplace Historical State Park
Cowans Gap State Park
Fort Loudon, PA 17224
Phone: 717-485-3948

JAMES BUCHANAN

Birth Site (cabin):
Mercersburg Academy
Mercersburg, PA 17236
Phone: 717-328-2151

Wheatland
1120 Marietta Ave.
Lancaster, PA 17603
Phone: 717-392-8721

WORLD WIDE WEB ADDRESSES:

The White House offers young readers information on the U.S. government and the Presidents on a Web site called **"White House 101."** The address is:
http://www.whitehouse.gov/about/white_house_101/

The **Internet Public Library** has a site on the Presidents. The address is:
http://www.ipl.org/div/potus

American Memory is a site maintained by the Library of Congress that contains biographical and historical information on the Presidents. It also provides links to Presidential portraits.
For James Buchanan:
http://memory.loc.gov/learn/

Wheatland
http://www.wheatland.org/

Abraham Lincoln

1809-1865
16th President of the United States (1861-1865)
"Honest Abe"

ABRAHAM LINCOLN WAS BORN February 12, 1809, in Hardin County, Kentucky. His father was Thomas Lincoln, and his mother was Nancy Hanks Lincoln. Thomas was a farmer, and Nancy was a homemaker. Thomas built the log cabin that Abraham was born in. Abraham had one sister, Sarah, and one brother, Thomas. Thomas died when he was a baby.

ABRAHAM LINCOLN GREW UP in Kentucky. The children worked hard helping out on the farm. When Abraham was eight, the family moved to Indiana.

In Indiana, Abe helped his father clear the land and build a cabin on their new property. It was, he remembered, "a wild region, with many bears and other wild animals." He also became very good with an ax, splitting logs for the cabin and for fences. In later years, one of his nicknames was "The Rail-Splitter."

Abe didn't like hunting. When he was eight, he shot a wild turkey. Later he said he "never since pulled a trigger on any larger game."

When Abe was just 10 years old, his mother died. It was a very sad time for him. One year later his father married Mrs. Sarah Johnston. She was a widow with three children. Abe grew to love her very much. He said "she proved a good and kind mother" to him.

ABRAHAM LINCOLN WENT TO SCHOOL only occasionally. He said he "went to ABC schools by littles." He meant that he went to school when he could, and when he wasn't needed on the farm. He never graduated from elementary or high school and never went to college. He said he could "read, write, and cipher." To "cipher" means to do math. Altogether, his schooling "did not amount to one year," he recalled.

Even though he didn't have a lot of formal education, Lincoln loved to read from an early age. At home he read the family Bible. He walked long distances to borrow books from other people. He especially enjoyed *Robinson Crusoe, Aesop's Fables,* and an early biography of George Washington. Later in his life, he studied law. But his formal education ended at the elementary level.

FIRST JOBS: When Lincoln was 20, the family moved to Illinois. Lincoln began to work in a general store. Around this time he also worked as a lumberman, cutting down trees and taking them down the Mississippi River by boat.

First Lady Mary Todd Lincoln.

In 1832 he served briefly in the voluntary army fighting Indian wars. He was elected captain, which he said, gave him "much satisfaction." Next he decided to run for the Illinois legislature. He wasn't elected, so he found another business to get involved in.

He opened a general store that soon went broke. He also worked as the local postmaster and a surveyor. He made enough, he said, to buy "bread, and kept body and soul together."

In 1834 Lincoln ran again for the Illinois House of Representatives as a **Whig**, and this time he won. He served four terms from 1834 to 1842. He also began to study law, borrowing books from a friend. On his own, Lincoln also studied grammar. He wanted to study the English language and learn to use it well. He would go on to become one of the greatest speakers and writers in American history.

Lincoln with his son Tad, 1864.

WORKING AS A LAWYER: Lincoln began to practice law in 1836, while he served in the legislature. He became known as a fair and honest lawyer.

ABRAHAM LINCOLN'S HOME AND FAMILY: Lincoln met Mary Todd in Springfield, Illinois, where he practiced law. She was small and lively, just 5 feet 2 inches tall. Lincoln, who was 6 feet 4 inches and lanky, was quite a contrast. The two married on November 4, 1842.

Abraham and Mary Lincoln had four sons, Robert, Edward, William, and Thomas, called Tad. Three of the Lincoln children died before adulthood. Edward died at the age of four, Willie died at 11, and Tad died at 18. Robert went on to become a distinguished statesman. He served as Secretary of War for **President James Garfield.**

GETTING INTO NATIONAL POLITICS: In 1846 Lincoln ran for national office for the first time. He was elected to the U.S. **House of Representatives**, where he served for two years. After his term was over, he moved his family back to Illinois.

THE ISSUE OF SLAVERY: Throughout the nineteenth century, the issue of **slavery** dominated politics in the U.S. By the 1850s, the issue threatened to tear the country apart.

Since the founding of the nation in the 1770s, the country had argued over slavery. By the early 1800s the North didn't allow slavery. Some Northerners despised slavery so much that they wanted to "abolish" it, or do away with it. These were the "abolitionists" (ab-oh-LISH-in-ists).

In the South, slaves had worked on plantations since the time of the first settlers. The system of slavery was part of life for white Southerners. Despite its inhumane treatment of black people, the South wanted to keep slavery. And they wanted to extend it.

The nation was growing as new territories were added in the West. As settlers from the North and South moved into the new territories, the issue of whether there should be slavery in those areas became a major topic. In the 1850s the U.S. **Congress** tried to work out compromises that would satisfy the North and the South. The compromises didn't work.

In 1854, the **Republican Party** was formed by people who were opposed to slavery in the new territories. Abraham Lincoln shared the views of the Republicans. He joined the party in 1856.

THE LINCOLN-DOUGLAS DEBATES: In 1858, Lincoln ran as a Republican against Stephen Douglas for the U.S. **Senate**. The two had a series of debates with slavery as the main issue. These became some of the most famous debates in U.S. history. They also established Lincoln's reputation as a great speaker and an important Republican. Lincoln lost the senatorial election, but he had gained a national following.

PRESIDENT OF THE UNITED STATES: The Republicans chose Lincoln as their candidate for President in 1860. The country was on the brink of civil war, and the parties were in an uproar. Lincoln faced three opponents. Stephen Douglas and John C. Breckinridge ran for separate factions of a divided **Democratic Party**. John Bell represented the Constitutional Party. Lincoln won the election, even though he received very few votes from the South. He received 182 **electoral votes**. The remaining votes were split between Breckinridge, with 72; Bell, with 31; and Douglas, with 12.

The Southern states knew that a vote for Lincoln was a vote against slavery. Two months after the election, seven Southern states "seceded" from the Union. That means that they chose to break away from the United States. Instead, they formed their own new country, called the **Confederate States of America**, or the Confederacy.

*Lincoln with his Cabinet at the first reading of
the Emancipation Proclamation, 1862.*

On April 12, 1861, Confederate soldiers fired on Fort Sumter, a
fort held by Union (Northern) troops in South Carolina. It was an act
of rebellion. The Civil War began.

THE CIVIL WAR: The Civil War lasted from 1861 to 1865. The battles
of the war were fought in several states, including Virginia,
Mississippi, Pennsylvania, and Tennessee. Some of the fiercest and
most decisive battles took place at Bull Run, Antietam, Chancellorsville, Vicksburg, and Gettysburg. The loss of life was terrible. All
together, more than 300,000 people died in the Civil War.

THE EMANCIPATION PROCLAMATION: On January 1, 1863, Lincoln
issued "**The Emancipation Proclamation**." It said that all slaves living

*Lincoln with Sojourner Truth, presenting a Bible
from the African-Americans of Baltimore, Maryland, 1864.*

in Confederate states were free. Many former slaves fled to the North, where they joined the army and fought for the Union.

THE GETTYSBURG ADDRESS: The battle of Gettysburg in July 1863 was one of the major battles of the war and a major Union victory. It had also resulted in the loss of many lives. In November 1963, Lincoln gave a speech at the battlefield that became one of the most memorable in U.S. history. In his Gettysburg Address, Lincoln talked about the meaning of the lives sacrificed on that battlefield.

Lincoln said that the soldiers "gave their lives that this nation might live." He said that they fought to preserve the promise of what the nation stood for. He pledged that the nation "shall have a new birth of freedom. And that government of the people, by the people, for the people, shall not perish from this earth."

Throughout the war, Lincoln was a strong, compassionate leader. Preserving the Union — keeping the North and South together as one nation — remained his unwavering goal. He agonized over the loss of life on both sides, for all who died were Americans. Sometimes he was depressed and in despair. Yet he remained determined to bring the nation together.

LIFE AT THE WHITE HOUSE: The Lincolns' life at the White House was often unhappy. Mary Lincoln came under attack in the press because some thought that she spent too much money on White House furnishings. More seriously, as the war continued, Mary was accused of sympathizing with the South because she had family members fighting for the Confederacy. She was even accused of being a spy. Lincoln had to go before Congress and pledge that Mary was loyal to the Union.

In 1862, the Lincolns faced a terrible tragedy when their son Willie, just 11 years old, died of typhoid. Mary Lincoln almost lost her sanity over Willie's death. Abraham Lincoln, occupied with the burdens of the war, also grieved, and he saw how his wife suffered. He wrote to her sister, "I feel worried about Mary, her nerves have gone to pieces."

Lincoln mourned the death of his son, and for all those lost in the war. His son Tad brought some sunshine to his life, though. Tad used to visit his father's office, and would sometimes fall asleep there. Tad could also be a mischief maker. According to a modern White House source called "The First Family at Home," he would "bombard the door with his toy cannon during a Cabinet meeting," Tad was also known to "stop his father's callers to sell refreshments and wheedle money for war charities at stands he set up at the mansion." Such boisterous behavior brought laughter at a time when it was much needed at the White House.

REELECTION: In 1864, Lincoln ran for reelection and won. He defeated his opponent, George McClellan, with 212 electoral votes to McClellan's 21. By that time, the war was going in the North's favor. There were several decisive victories for the North under the leadership of General **Ulysses S. Grant.** With the end of the war in sight, Lincoln worked on a plan to bring the country back together.

THE END OF THE CIVIL WAR: The Northern forces won many decisive battles in 1864 and 1865. On April 9, 1865, the Confederacy surrendered. The ceremony ending the war took place at the court house in Appomattox, Virginia. There, General Robert E. Lee, head of the Confederate forces, surrendered to General Grant. The war was finally over.

Maj. Rathbone.   Miss Harris.   Mrs. Lincoln.   President.   Assassin.

THE ASSASSINATION OF PRESIDENT LINCOLN,
AT FORD'S THEATRE WASHINGTON. D.C. APRIL 14TH 1865.

Lincoln's assasination, April 14, 1865.

ASSASSINATION: Just five days after the war ended, Abraham Lincoln was shot and killed. He was attending a play called "Our American Cousin" at Ford's Theatre in Washington, D.C. One of the actors, John Wilkes Booth, shot Lincoln as he sat in his seat. Lincoln died the next morning, April 15, 1865.

The country was in shock and mourning over the death of their President. He had guided the Union through its most difficult times and brought the nation back together. Lincoln's body traveled in a funeral train across the nation to Springfield, Illinois, where he was buried. All along the route, people stood by the train tracks and paid their final respects. Mary Lincoln lived on in Springfield until her death in 1882.

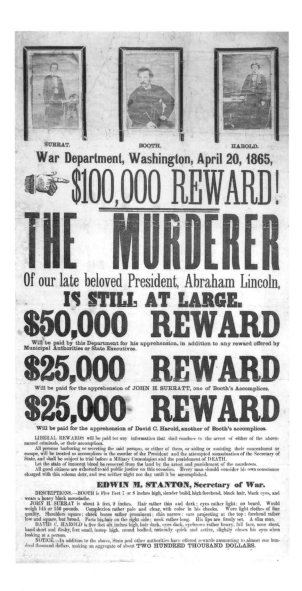

Lincoln's Vice President, **Andrew Johnson**, was sworn in as President on April 15, 1865.

John Wilkes Booth was found and shot by federal agents 12 days after he shot Lincoln. Six other people involved with the assassination were found, tried, and hung for their crimes.

Many Americans and historians consider Lincoln to be the greatest President. In simple, elegant language he expressed his high ideals for the nation. His courage and commitment to equality and the preservation of the Union have brought him the gratitude and admiration of generations of Americans.

WHAT DID HE LOOK LIKE? Once Lincoln was asked to describe himself. He said: "I am, in height, six feet four inches, nearly; lean in flesh, weighing on an average one hundred and eighty pounds; dark complexion, with coarse hair, and grey eyes—no other marks or brands recollected."

Lincoln was our tallest President and the first to wear a beard. Even though he was tall, he didn't eat much. It is said that he had one of the smallest appetites of any President. His favorite meal was fruit salad, cheese, and crackers.

ABOUT LINCOLN'S BEARD: While campaigning for the Presidency, Lincoln received the following letter:

Dear Sir:

I am a little girl 11 years old, but want you should be President of the United States very much so I hope you won't think me very bold to write to such a great man as you are.

Have you any little girls about as large as I am, if so give them my love and tell her to write me if you cannot answer this letter. I have got four brothers and part of them will vote for you any way and if you will let your whiskers grow I will try to get the rest of them to vote for you. You would look a great deal better for your face is so thin. All the ladies like whiskers and they would tease their husbands to vote for you and then you would be President.

Grace Bedell

Lincoln sent Grace the following letter:

My Dear Little Miss:

Your very agreeable letter of the 15th is received. I regret the necessity of saying I have no daughters. I have three sons, one seventeen, one nine, and one seven years of age. They, with their mother, constitute my whole family. As to the whiskers, having never worn any, do you not think people would call it a piece of silly affectation if I were to begin it now?

Your very sincere well-wisher,

A. Lincoln

(Lincoln did indeed grow a beard, after his election to the Presidency in 1860.)

FAMOUS QUOTE: Lincoln said and wrote many memorable things. One of his most famous quotes comes from his Second Inaugural Address. In that document, he spoke of what needed to be done to bring the nation back together after the Civil War. He said:

"With malice toward none, with charity for all, with firmness in the right, as God gives us to see the right, let us strive to finish the work we are in, to bind up the nation's wounds."

These words are engraved next to the statue of Lincoln at the Lincoln Memorial in Washington, D.C.

FOR MORE INFORMATION ON ABRAHAM LINCOLN:

Historic Sites:

Birth Site:
Lincoln Birthplace National Historic Park
2995 Lincoln Farm Rd.
Hodgenville, KY 42748,
Phone: 270-358-3137

Childhood Home:
Knob Creek Farm
7120 Bardstown Rd.
Hodgenville, KY 42748
Phone: 502-549-3741

Abraham Lincoln Presidential Library and Museum
112 North Sixth Street
Springfield, IL 62701
Phone: 217-558-8844

Ford's Theatre National Historic Site
511 10th Street NW
Washington, DC 20004
Phone: 202-233-0701

Lincoln Boyhood National Memorial
Box 1816
Lincoln City, IN 47552
Phone: 812-937-4541

Lincoln Home National Historic Site
413 S. Eighth St.
Springfield, IL 62701
Phone: 217-391-3226

Lincoln Memorial
900 Ohio Drive, S.W.
Washington, DC 20024
Phone: 202-426-6841

WORLD WIDE WEB ADDRESSES:

The White House offers young readers information on the U.S. government and the Presidents on a Web site called **"White House 101."** The address is:

http://www.whitehouse.gov/about/white_house_101/

The Internet Public Library has a site on the Presidents. The address is:
http://www.ipl.org/div/potus

American Memory is a site maintained by the Library of Congress that contains biographical and historical information on the Presidents. It also provides links to Presidential portraits.
For Abraham Lincoln:
http://memory.loc.gov/ammem/today/mar04.html

Abraham Lincoln Presidential Library and Museum
http://www.alplm.org/

Ford's Theatre National Historic Site
http://www.nps.gov/foth/index.html

Lincoln Birthplace National Historic Park
http://www.nps.gov/abli

Lincoln Boyhood National Memorial
http://www.nps.gov/libo/index.html

Lincoln Home National Historic Site
http://www.nps.gov/liho/index.html

Lincoln Memorial
http://www.nps.gov/linc/index.html

Andrew Johnson
1808-1875
17th President of the United States (1865-1869)
"Tennessee Tailor"

ANDREW JOHNSON WAS BORN December 29, 1808, in Raleigh, North Carolina. His parents were Jacob and Mary McDonough Johnson. Jacob made his living doing odd jobs. Mary did laundry and sewing to help support the family. Andrew had one brother, William, who was older. He also had a sister who died when she was a baby.

ANDREW JOHNSON GREW UP very poor and sometimes hungry. He came from the poorest background of any U.S. President. His father died when he was three. His mother remarried, but the family never had much money. Johnson remembered "the gaunt and haggard monster called hunger."

BECOMING A TAILOR'S APPRENTICE: When Andrew was just 13, his mother sent him away to be an "apprentice." An apprentice is someone who learns a trade from another person. The apprentice learns the job, then works in exchange for a room and food.

Andrew worked for a tailor named James Selby in Raleigh. Over the next several years, he learned to make men's clothing. There were several other boys working for Selby, and one day they got in trouble.

Andrew and a few of the boys threw stones at the window of the home of some local girls. The girls' mother became angry and threatened to tell the police. Andrew and his friends ran away to another town. There, they started their own tailor business.

SCHOOL: Andrew Johnson never went to school. His father and mother couldn't read or write, and Andrew didn't learn to read until he was an apprentice. A friend of the tailor he worked for read aloud to the boys, and that made Andrew want to learn, too. He taught himself to read, then later, after his marriage, his wife taught him how to write and do basic math.

MAKING A LIVING AS A TAILOR: In 1826, Johnson moved his mother and stepfather to Greeneville, Tennessee, where he had started his own tailor shop. He did well in his business, and the family finally had enough to eat.

MARRIAGE AND FAMILY: In Greeneville, Johnson met Eliza McCardle. They fell in love and married in 1827. They were very

First Lady Eliza Johnson.

young—Johnson was just 18 and Eliza was 16. In fact, he married at a younger age than any other President. Andrew and Eliza had five children, Martha, Charles, Mary, Robert, and Andrew.

GETTING INVOLVED IN POLITICS: Johnson's business prospered, and he bought property in Greeneville. His tailor shop became the center for political debates in town. Soon, Johnson became interested in public office. His first job in politics was as a member of the town council in Greeneville in 1829. He was elected mayor in 1831.

Johnson was a **Democrat**, and his hero was **Andrew Jackson**. Jackson had also come from a humble background and was a man of the people. Like Jackson, Johnson believed in states' rights. He thought that the federal government should stay out of the lives of the citizens.

After serving as mayor, Johnson ran for the Tennessee legislature. He was first elected to the state legislature in 1835, where he served for several years. He was elected as a State Senator in 1841. In 1843, he was elected to the U.S. **House of Representatives**, where he served for 10 years.

Johnson returned to Tennessee in 1853, where he was elected Governor. After four years in that job, he ran for and was elected to the U.S. **Senate** in 1857.

THE CIVIL WAR: While Johnson was rising in politics, the country was heading toward the **Civil War**. The Southern states wanted to defend **slavery** and extend it into the territories. They were willing to secede—break away—from the U.S. to get what they wanted. The Northern states wanted slavery abolished, and they wanted the country to stay together.

In 1860, the country elected **Abraham Lincoln** as President. Lincoln, who was against slavery, got little support from the South. Instead, southern states began to secede from the **Union** shortly after Lincoln's election. They created a new separate country called the **Confederate States of America**, or the Confederacy. The Civil War began.

Johnson was a Southerner and a slave owner. Yet he believed that the Union needed to be held together. When Tennessee seceded from the Union in 1861, Johnson remained loyal to the U.S. government. He was the only Senator from the South to continue to serve in the Senate during the Civil War.

Johnson risked his life for his beliefs. He was considered a traitor in the South, and more than once his life was threatened. Once, as he traveled in Tennessee, a mob stopped his train and threatened to hang him. He held them off with a pistol.

President Lincoln was grateful for Johnson's loyalty. He made him the military governor of Tennessee during the war.

VICE PRESIDENT OF THE UNITED STATES: In 1864, Lincoln ran for reelection. Even though Johnson was a Democrat, the **Republicans** chose him to run as Vice President. Lincoln and Johnson won in 1864.

Johnson's term as Vice President was very brief. Tragically, just as the Civil War came to an end, Lincoln was assassinated, in April 1865. Johnson had to take over a nation that had been at war for four years.

PRESIDENT OF THE UNITED STATES: President Johnson served during one of the most difficult times in the country's history. He wanted to follow his plan for **"Reconstruction"** — rebuilding the nation after the war. That plan would have allowed the Southern states to decide for themselves how they reestablished their governments and how they treated former slaves.

Problems with this plan came up right away. Several of the Southern states wanted to restrict the rights of blacks. They passed "black codes." These codes included rules that denied the newly freed blacks equal rights. Members of Congress from the Northern states were furious. They created laws that they believed would protect the rights of blacks.

Johnson, as President, was at the center of the argument. As a Southerner and a believer in states' rights, he wanted the South to determine its future. He argued with the U.S. **Congress**, but they couldn't agree. Johnson fought vigorously for what he believed. The Congress thought he was stubborn and unable to compromise. After several years of bitter disagreements, the Congress and Johnson had a final fight.

IMPEACHMENT: The U.S. **Constitution** states that if the U.S. House of Representatives thinks that a President has broken a law, they

The impeachment trial of Andrew Johnson, 1868.

can accuse him. That is called "**impeachment**." After a President is impeached, he is tried in the Senate for breaking the law. The Senate listens to the accusation, then votes to decide if the President should be removed from office.

In 1868, the House of Representatives accused Johnson of breaking a law. The law they accused him of breaking said that a President could not fire someone from a federal office unless the Senate approved. Johnson had fired his Secretary of War, Edwin Stanton, in 1868, without the approval of the Senate. The House accused him of breaking the law in firing Stanton. After he was accused, Johnson was tried in the Senate. The Senate found him innocent, but only by one vote. Johnson remained President, but his effectiveness as a political leader was over.

Johnson was the first President ever to be impeached. After the impeachment crisis, he wanted to run for President again. However, he did not win the nomination. In the election of 1868, **Ulysses S. Grant** became the next President.

Johnson's troubled Presidency is remembered most for his impeachment. Yet two important amendments—additions — to the Constitution were passed during his term. The 13th Amendment (1865) freed all remaining slaves in all states and territories. The 14th Amendment (1868) made all male former slaves U.S. citizens.

LIFE AT THE WHITE HOUSE: Johnson's wife Eliza was ill with tuberculosis when he became President. She was unable to serve as White House hostess, so those duties fell to their eldest daughter, Martha. Martha kept two cows on the White House lawn.

While he was President, Johnson became the first U.S. head of state to welcome a queen to the White House. In 1866, Queen Emma of Hawaii visited the U.S. and met with President Johnson.

When Johnson turned 60 in 1868, the White House put on a Children's Ball. More than 400 children attended the party.

ELECTION TO THE SENATE: Johnson returned to Tennessee in 1869. He wanted to stay in politics and ran for office several times. In 1874, five years after leaving Washington, he won election to the U.S. Senate. He became the only person to serve in the Senate after serving as President.

Johnson's term as Senator lasted only four months. In July 1875, he suffered a stroke. He died July 31, 1875, at the age of 66. Eliza Johnson lived just six months after her husband's death. She died on January 15, 1876.

WHAT DID HE LOOK LIKE? Johnson was 5 feet 10 inches tall and stocky. He had long brown hair.

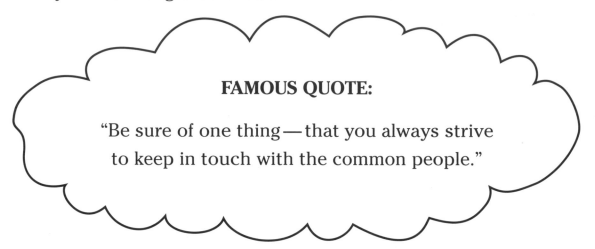

FAMOUS QUOTE:

"Be sure of one thing—that you always strive to keep in touch with the common people."

FOR MORE INFORMATION ON ANDREW JOHNSON:

Historic Sites:

Birth Site:
Mordecai Historic Park
1 Mimosa St.
Raleigh, NC 27604
Phone: 919-834-4844

Andrew Johnson National Historic Site
121 Monument Ave.
Greeneville, TN 37743
Phone: 423-638-3551

WORLD WIDE WEB ADDRESSES:

The White House offers young readers information on the U.S. government and the Presidents on a Web site called **"White House 101."** The address is:
http://www.whitehouse.gov/about/white_house_101/

The **Internet Public Library** has a site on the Presidents. The address is:
http://www.ipl.org/div/potus

American Memory is a site maintained by the Library of Congress that contains biographical and historical information on the Presidents. It also provides links to Presidential portraits.
For Andrew Johnson:
http://memory.loc.gov/ammem/today/dec29.html

Andrew Johnson National Historic Site
http://www.nps.gov/anjo/

Ulysses S. Grant
1822-1885
18th President of the United States (1869-1877)
"Unconditional Surrender"

ULYSSES S. GRANT WAS BORN April 27, 1822, in Point Pleasant, Ohio. His father was Jesse Root Grant and his mother was Hannah Simpson Grant. Jesse Grant was a farmer and a tanner. A tanner is someone who makes leather from animal hides. Hannah was a homemaker.

Ulysses was the oldest of six children. He had two brothers and three sisters. His brothers' names were Samuel and Orville. His sisters' names were Clara, Virginia, and Mary.

When Grant was born, his parents named him Hiram Ulysses Grant. When he got older, he didn't like the way his initials spelled HUG, so he switched the names to Ulysses Hiram. Later, when he went to West Point, he was mistakenly entered as Ulysses Simpson Grant. He decided to keep the name instead of changing it back.

ULYSSES S. GRANT GREW UP on the family farm in Georgetown, Ohio. He worked hard doing chores as a boy. When he was 8 years old, he would drive the wagon to haul firewood. He plowed the fields when he was 11. Ulysses liked horses and became an excellent rider.

ULYSSES S. GRANT WENT TO SCHOOL at the local elementary school in Georgetown. He was an average student and wasn't very interested in school.

In 1839, Grant was accepted to the Military Academy in West Point. (The military academies are like colleges. They offer courses and give degrees while training people for military careers.) Many of his fellow cadets — James Longstreet, Thomas "Stonewall" Jackson, and William T. Sherman — would also become great military leaders in the **Civil War**. Grant graduated in 1843. He became a second lieutenant in the U.S. Army.

MARRIAGE AND FAMILY: Grant was sent to Jefferson Barracks in Missouri after graduation. While he was there, he met 17-year-old Julia Dent. Julia was the sister of Grant's West Point roommate and friend. She was a lively and determined young lady. Ulysses was pleased to learn that she liked to ride horses. They fell in love and became engaged in 1844.

Shortly afterward, the Army sent Grant to Louisiana. His military duties and the **Mexican War** kept them apart until 1848. After the Mexican War ended, they were married, on August 22, 1848.

169

First Lady Julia Grant.

Ulysses and Julia had three sons and one daughter. Their sons' names were Frederick, Ulysses, and Jesse. Their daughter's name was Ellen. Her parents called her Nellie.

EARLY MILITARY CAREER: When the U.S. declared war on Mexico in 1846, Grant served under General **Zachary Taylor,** who later became President. Taylor was known as "Old Rough and Ready." His informal dress and simple manners later influenced Grant's own style. Grant fought in most of the major campaigns of the Mexican War. He was promoted to first lieutenant for his bravery in battle.

After the war, Grant spent the next four years in military posts in Sackets Harbor, New York, and Detroit, Michigan. In 1852, his regiment was sent to Fort Vancouver, in the Oregon Territory. Grant was unhappy because his family could not live with him in Oregon. In 1854, after two years of loneliness and boredom at the frontier fort, he resigned from the Army and returned home.

Grant settled in Missouri with his family and started a small farm. It was a poor farm, and he called it "Hard Scrabble." After four years of hard work, he abandoned farming and moved to St. Louis.

Grant as a Civil War General.

There, he started a real estate business. The business failed, and by 1860, he was working in his father's leather shop in Galena, Illinois.

CIVIL WAR HERO: While Grant was struggling to make a living, the country was getting ready for the **Civil War**. The Southern states wanted to defend **slavery** and extend it into the territories. They were willing to secede—break away—from the U.S. to get what they wanted. The Northern states wanted slavery abolished, and they wanted the country to stay together.

In 1860, the country elected **Abraham Lincoln** as President. Lincoln, who was against slavery, got little support from the South. Instead, Southern states began to secede from the **Union** shortly after Lincoln's election.

After the Civil War began, Grant returned to military service. He organized a regiment of volunteers from Illinois. In 1861, Lincoln appointed him brigadier general of volunteers. In February 1862, he captured Fort Henry and Fort Donelson. Those battles were the first major Union victories of the war. When the Confederate commander at Fort Donelson asked for terms of surrender, Grant replied "No terms except an unconditional and immediate surrender can be

General Grant in 1865, during the Civil War.

accepted. I propose to move immediately upon your works."
The commander gave up, and Grant took the fort and 14,000 rebel soldiers.

Shortly after, Lincoln promoted Grant to Major General. He was put in charge of all the Union troops fighting in Tennessee. His most famous victory was the capture of Vicksburg, Mississippi. During this campaign, he showed his ability as a great military commander. He defeated two Confederate armies and captured the fort at Vicksburg, along with its 30,000 rebel soldiers. Grant's victory gave the Union control of the Mississippi River and was one of the most important victories of the war.

In March of 1864, Lincoln put Grant in charge of all the Union armies. In May 1864, Grant began the long and bloody final campaign against the Confederate army. Finally, on April 9, 1865, Confederate commander Robert E. Lee surrendered his exhausted army. The Civil War was ended.

PRESIDENT OF THE UNITED STATES: Grant was a soldier, not a politician. However, his fame as a war hero made him the natural choice of the **Republicans** to run for President in 1868. Grant won easily, defeating **Democrat** Horatio Seymour by 214 to 80 **electoral votes**.

Grant picked his friends and political supporters to serve in his Cabinet. He was content to let the Congress and his Cabinet run the country. Although he was not very active as President, he was very popular with the people. Grant was reelected in 1872, easily defeating Democrat Horace Greeley, with 286 electoral votes to Greeley's 3.

Grant's second term was tarnished by scandal. Although Grant himself was an honest man, he trusted his friends too much. He didn't get involved in their work for the government. Many of them were guilty of stealing money from the government. Cabinet officers, Congressmen, and other officials took advantage of Grant's hands-off attitude toward leadership. They became rich, while he ignored the mounting complaints against them. By the end of his

President Ulysses S. Grant.

second term, his administration was better known for scandal and greed than for Grant's heroic military service.

In 1876, the Republican Party nominated **Rutherford B. Hayes** instead of Grant. He returned to private life.

LIFE IN THE WHITE HOUSE: Ulysses and Julia lived in the White House with their two youngest children, Jesse and Nellie. Fred was attending West Point, and Ulysses Jr. was at Harvard.

The White House became once again a center of elegant hospitality. This was due to Julia's ability as a lively hostess. Unlike his wife, Grant was a simple man and not an active socializer. He once said that he only knew two tunes, "one was Yankee Doodle, the other wasn't."

Nellie married an Englishman named Algernon Sartoris on May 21, 1874. It was the first White House wedding since Elizabeth Tyler's in 1842.

RETIREMENT: In 1876, after leaving the White House, Grant traveled around the world with Julia and their youngest son, Jesse. Their trip lasted two years. Everywhere he went, he was received with honors as the hero of the Civil War.

Grant's last years were not happy ones. His business investments failed, and he was short of money. He began to write his memoirs in 1884. He hoped to pay off his debts and provide for Julia with the proceeds from the book sales. While he was writing his book, he was dying of throat cancer. He had smoked 20 cigars a day since his Civil War days. He finished his book a few days before he died, on July 23, 1885.

Grant's *Personal Memoirs* was published by the famous American author Mark Twain. It became an immediate best seller. The profits from the book's sales provided for Julia until her death on December 14, 1902. Grant's book is still read today and is considered one of the best books ever written about war.

WHAT DID HE LOOK LIKE? Grant was 5 feet 8 inches tall. He had a beard and a firm-set mouth.

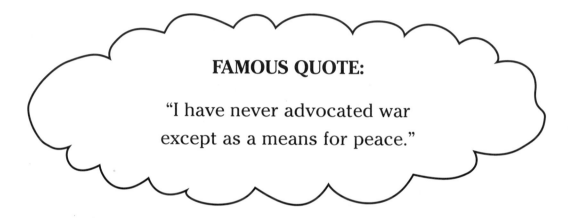

FAMOUS QUOTE:

"I have never advocated war except as a means for peace."

FOR MORE INFORMATION ON ULYSSES S. GRANT:

Historic Sites:

Birth site:
Grant Birthplace Historic Site
1551 State Rt., 232
Point Pleasant, OH 45157
Phone: 800-283-8932

City Point Unit Residence
Petersburg National Battlefield
Box 549
Petersburg, VA 23804
Phone: 804-732-3531

Grant Cottage State Historic Site
Mount McGregor
P.O. Box 2294
Wilton, NY 12831
Phone: 518-587-8277

Grant's "Hardscrabble" Farm
10501 Gravois Rd.
St. Louis, MO 63123
Phone: 314-743-1700

Ulysses S. Grant National Historic Site
7400 Grant Rd.
St. Louis, MO 63123
Phone: 314-842-3298

U.S. Grant Home
500 Bouthillier St., Box 333
Galena, IL 61036
Phone: 815-777-0248

Appomatox Court House
National Historical Park
P.O. Box 218
Appomatox, VA 24522
Phone: 434-352-8987

Burial site:
General Grant National Memorial
Riverside Dr. and W. 122nd St.
New York, NY 10027
Phone: 212-666-1640

WORLD WIDE WEB ADDRESSES:

The White House offers young readers information on the U.S. government and the Presidents on a Web site called **"White House 101."** The address is:
http://www.whitehouse.gov/about/white_house_101/

The **Internet Public Library** has a site on the Presidents. The address is:
http://www.ipl.org/div/potus

American Memory is a site maintained by the Library of Congress that contains biographical and historical information on the Presidents. It also provides links to Presidential portraits.
For Ulysses S. Grant:
http://memory.loc.gov/ammem/today/apr27.html

Appomattox Court House
http://www.nps.gov/apco/

Fort Donelson National Battlefield
http://www.nps.gov/fodo

General Grant National Memorial
http://www.nps.gov/gegr/

Ulysses S. Grant: History
http://www.nps.gov/history/logcabin/html/usg.html

Ulysses S. Grant National Historic Site
http://www.nps.gov/ulsg

Rutherford B. Hayes
1822-1893
19th President of the United States (1877-1881)
"Dark Horse President"

RUTHERFORD B. HAYES WAS BORN October 4, 1822, in Delaware, Ohio. His full name was Rutherford Birchard Hayes. His parents were Rutherford and Sophia Birchard Hayes. Rutherford Sr. died two months before young Rutherford was born. Before his death, Rutherford Sr. had been a storekeeper. Sophia was a homemaker.

Rutherford was the youngest of five children. A brother and sister had died before he was born. Another brother, Lorenzo, died when Rutherford was two. He and his sister Fanny were the only children in the family to live to adulthood.

RUTHERFORD B. HAYES GREW UP in Fremont, Ohio, raised by his mother and his uncle, Sardis Birchard. Sardis Birchard, a successful businessman, took care of his sister and her two children.

RUTHERFORD B. HAYES WENT TO SCHOOL at local private schools in Ohio. He went to high school at a private school in Connecticut. After high school, he returned to Ohio, where he attended Kenyon College. Hayes always did well in school. When he graduated from college in 1842, he was first in his class.

After college, Hayes went to law school at Harvard. He graduated in 1845. He was the first President to graduate from law school.

MAKING A LIVING AS A LAWYER: Hayes returned to Ohio and tried to make his living as a lawyer in Fremont. He wasn't able to find many clients, so he moved to Cincinnati. There, he soon had a successful law practice.

MARRIAGE AND FAMILY: In Cincinnati, he met Lucy Ware Webb. At a time when very few women attended college, Lucy was a college graduate. In fact, she was the first President's wife to graduate from college. She and Hayes married on December 20, 1852. They had eight children, but only five lived to be adults. They were Birchard, James, Rutherford, Fanny, and Scott.

THE CIVIL WAR: While becoming a successful lawyer, Hayes got involved in local politics. Because he was against slavery, he joined the **Republican Party**. The Republicans were opposed to slavery

Wedding portrait of Rutherford and Lucy Hayes, 1852.

and were the party of **Abraham Lincoln**. When the **Civil War** broke out in 1861, Hayes joined the army. He started out as a major in the Ohio Infantry.

During the war, Hayes fought in many fierce battles. He was wounded four times, once very seriously. In 1864, while he was away fighting, the people of Ohio elected him to the U.S. **Congress**. He didn't campaign for the position. He said that "any officer fit for duty who at this crisis would abandon his post to electioneer ought to be scalped." He won the election anyway, but didn't serve in the post until after the war.

In 1865, when the war was over, Hayes retired as a major general. He returned to Ohio, then moved to Washington, D.C., to serve in Congress.

GETTING INVOLVED IN POLITICS: In 1867, after serving his term in Congress, Hayes ran for Governor of Ohio. He won the race and served for one term. In 1872, he ran for U.S. Congress, but lost. Hayes was elected Governor again in 1875, but served for just one year.

In 1876, Hayes's political supporters wanted him to run for President as the Republican nominee. Hayes didn't really want the job. He ran because he thought his opponent, Samuel J. Tilden, would win easily.

THE ELECTION OF 1876: The Presidential election of 1876 was one of the most hotly debated election in U.S. history. Tilden beat Hayes in the popular vote by almost 300,000 votes. He received 184 **electoral votes**, but he needed 185 to win. Hayes had only 165 electoral votes. The 20 remaining electoral votes were "contested." That means that no one was sure who would receive those final 20 votes.

THE ELECTORAL COLLEGE AND THE ELECTION OF HAYES: The President is *not* elected by direct vote of the people. Instead, Presidential elections are decided by members of the **Electoral College**. When a voter casts a vote for a Presidential candidate, he or she is really voting for an "elector." That is someone who is pledged to vote for one of the Presidential candidates. After the election, the electors meet and cast their ballots for the candidates they are pledged to.

The number of electors is equal to the total number of members of the U.S. **House of Representatives** and **Senate**. In 1876, when Hayes ran, that number was 369. To win the election, the winner needed a majority of all the possible electoral votes, or 185.

In 1876, Hayes needed all 20 disputed electoral votes to win. Tilden needed just one. Congress created a special commission to decide who would get the electoral votes. The commission took months to make its decision. Finally, just three days before the new President was to take office, the commission decided to give all the votes to Hayes. He won the Presidency by just one electoral vote.

Hayes won by the slimmest margin in U.S. history. That is why he is called the "Dark Horse President." A "dark horse" is a candidate that isn't likely to win, but is successful anyway.

PRESIDENT OF THE UNITED STATES: Hayes began his term after the Presidency of **Ulysses S. Grant**. Grant's administration had been accused of political wrongdoing. Hayes wanted to bring back the American people's faith in government.

RECONSTRUCTION: Hayes is known as the President who ended **"Reconstruction."** Reconstruction was the program that rebuilt the South after the Civil War. As part of the program, the federal government was in control of the South. Federal troops were responsible for keeping order. The Southerners resented the troops. Still, many Northerners thought that the only way to guarantee rights to newly freed blacks was by using federal authority.

First Lady Lucy Hayes.

Hayes knew the South wanted the soldiers removed. He also wanted to restore "wise, honest, and peaceful local self-government." In 1877, he removed the federal soldiers. Before he removed the troops he tried to make sure that southern states would respect the rights of black Americans.

In 1877, Hayes had to deal with violent railroad strikes. Striking railroad workers fought against local police and destroyed property. Hayes used federal troops to stop the violence.

In 1880, Hayes became the first President to visit the West Coast of the U.S. He traveled by train across the nation, arriving in San Francisco in September, 1880. In another "first," Hayes signed a bill that allowed women lawyers to try cases before the U.S. Supreme Court.

Hayes had always promised that he would only serve one term. In 1880, he declined to run for reelection. In 1881, he and his wife, Lucy, returned to their home in Ohio.

LIFE AT THE WHITE HOUSE: Rutherford and Lucy Hayes didn't drink alcohol, and they didn't serve it in the White House. Because of that, the First Lady was called "Lemonade Lucy" for serving nonalcoholic drinks. Sometimes visitors to the White House brought rum to put in the nonalcoholic punches she served. But

Lucy was too smart for them. She flavored the punches to taste like rum, even though they didn't contain any alcohol.

The Hayes White House enjoyed many "firsts." The first phone in the White House was installed by the inventor, Alexander Graham Bell. Hayes also brought the first typewriter to the White House.

In 1878, Lucy Hayes gave the first Easter Egg Roll at the White House. This event takes place every year now, when the President invites children to roll Easter Eggs on the White House lawn.

RETIREMENT TO OHIO: Hayes was very happy to leave office. He said that "Nobody ever left the Presidency with less regret than I do." He and Lucy returned to Ohio, where over the years they had

Spiegel Grove, the Hayes home, in Fremont, Ohio.

built an estate called Spiegel Grove. Hayes spent the last years of his life there doing charity work. He devoted his time to improving education, libraries, and the conditions in prisons.

Lucy Hayes died in 1889. Rutherford B. Hayes lived on at Spiegel Grove. He died January 17, 1893, at the age of 70. He and Lucy are both buried at Spiegel Grove.

WHAT DID HE LOOK LIKE? Hayes was 5 feet 8 inches tall and weighed 170 pounds. He had dark hair, blue eyes, and a full beard.

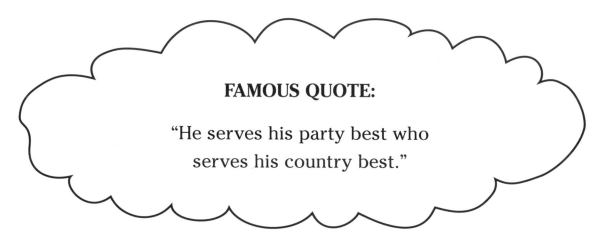

FAMOUS QUOTE:

"He serves his party best who serves his country best."

FOR MORE INFORMATION ON RUTHERFORD B. HAYES:

Historic Sites:

Birth Site:
East William and Winter St.
Delaware, OH 43420

Spiegel Grove National Historic Landmark
Rutherford B. Hayes Presidential Center
1337 Hayes Ave.
Fremont, OH 43420
Phone: 800-998-7737

WORLD WIDE WEB ADDRESSES:

The White House offers young readers information on the U.S. government and the Presidents on a Web site called **"White House 101."** The address is:
http://www.whitehouse.gov/about/white_house_101/

The Internet Public Library has a site on the Presidents. The address is:
http://www.ipl.org/div/potus

American Memory is a site maintained by the Library of Congress that contains biographical and historical information on the Presidents. It also provides links to Presidential portraits.
For Rutherford B. Hayes:
http://memory.loc.gov/ammem/today/oct04.html

Rutherford B. Hayes Presidential Center
http://www.rbhayes.org/

James A. Garfield
1831-1881
20th President of the United States (1881)
"Teacher President"

JAMES A. GARFIELD WAS BORN November 19, 1831, in Orange, Ohio. He was the last President who was born in a log cabin. His full name was James Abram Garfield. His parents were Abram and Eliza Ballou Garfield. Abram was a farmer, and Eliza was a home-maker. James was the youngest of five children. Only four of the children lived to be adults. His brothers and sisters were named Mehitabel, Thomas, and Mary.

JAMES A. GARFIELD GREW UP on the family farm. His father died when he was just 17 months old. The family was very poor. James's mother worked hard to raise her children, and all of them had to find work as soon as they were old enough.

JAMES A. GARFIELD WENT TO SCHOOL only three months a year, because he was needed to help out on the farm. Still, he did well in school and he loved to read. He could read parts of the Bible at the age of three. He was very religious, and later in life he became a lay preacher for his church.

James got jobs as a farm hand while still in elementary school. When he was 16, he got a job on a canal boat. At that time, canal boats pulled by teams of horses carried goods along the rivers of the U.S. Garfield remembered that he was pulled into the river 14 times before he was able to handle the horses. He caught malaria while working on the canals and had to go home to recover.

In his late teens, Garfield went to Geauga Academy to continue his schooling. He went on to study at Western Reserve Eclectic Institute in Ohio. He was an excellent student. He majored in Latin and Greek and also learned German.

BECOMING A TEACHER: Garfield wanted to be a teacher. He decided to finish his college degree at Williams College in Massachusetts. He graduated with honors in 1856. After graduation he took a job teaching at Western Reserve, his former school. Just one year later, he was named president of the college. While serving as college president, Garfield also studied law.

MARRIAGE AND FAMILY: Garfield met Lucretia Rudolph when he was in college in Ohio. They fell in love and married on

President James A. Garfield.

November 11, 1858. They had seven children, two girls and five boys. Two children died in infancy. The surviving children were named Harry, James, Mary, Irvin, and Abram.

GETTING INVOLVED IN POLITICS: Garfield joined the **Republican Party** in the 1850s. He won election to the Ohio Senate in 1859. He served there until the **Civil War** broke out in 1861.

THE CIVIL WAR: Garfield entered the war in 1861 as a lieutenant colonel. Always the teacher, he taught his soldiers how to fight with a book on military procedures in his hand.

Garfield fought at several of the major batttles in the Civil War, including the Battle of Shiloh. He led his men to one of the few early **Union** victories at the Battle of Middle Creek. During the war, the citizens of Ohio elected Garfield to the U.S. **House of Representatives**. In 1862, he left the army at the rank of major general.

BACK IN POLITICS: Garfield served in the U.S. House for 17 years, from 1863 to 1880. He was one of the most powerful Republicans in **Congress**. During his years in the House, Garfield worked on the policies of **"Reconstruction."** Reconstruction was the name of the program created to rebuild the South after the Civil War. Garfield was particularly concerned about the fate of the newly freed slaves. He worked to guarantee their freedom.

In 1880, Garfield was elected to the U.S. **Senate** from Ohio. That same year, in a surprise vote, he won the Presidential nomination for the Republican Party. There were several powerful Republicans running for the nomination that year, including former **President Ulysses S. Grant**. The Republicans were divided into two groups, the Stalwarts and the Half-Breeds. These two groups couldn't find

First Lady Lucretia Garfield.

enough supporters to get a majority for either of their candidates. Surprisingly, Garfield won the nomination, even though he was not the favorite.

Garfield was popular on the campaign trail. He could speak German well, and he used that ability to talk to German-American voters in his native Ohio. In the Presidential election of 1880, Garfield ran against Winfield Scott Hancock. The election was very close, and Garfield won by less than 10,000 votes. In the electoral vote, Garfield won 214 **electoral votes**; Hancock received 155.

PRESIDENT OF THE UNITED STATES: Throughout history, people have tried to get jobs in a new President's administration. Some feel they are "owed" a job because of their support for the new President. This system is called "political patronage."

When Garfield became President, many people went to Washington to look for jobs in his administration. Garfield was offended by them. "These people would take my very brain, flesh, and blood if they could," he said. One of the people looking for a job was a lawyer named Charles J. Guiteau. He was a Stalwart and wanted a government job, but didn't get it.

ASSASSINATION: On July 2, 1881, Garfield was in a Washington railroad station when Guiteau shot him twice. One bullet just missed his arm, but the other hit him in the back. Garfield was taken to the White House, where doctors tried to remove the bullet. At the time, doctors didn't use sterile instruments. Garfield developed an infection and grew weaker.

Alexander Graham Bell, the inventor of the telephone, brought a new invention to the White House that he hoped could find the bullet. But he wasn't able to save the President. Garfield was moved to the New Jersey shore to recover, but he never did. He died in Elberon, New Jersey, on September 19, 1881. Garfield was 49 years old and just six months into his term at the time of his

The assassination of President Garfield, July 2, 1881.

death. He was the second President to be assassinated, after **Abraham Lincoln**.

Garfield's Vice President, **Chester A. Arthur**, became the next President. The man who had shot Garfield, Charles Guiteau, was arrested. Although some people thought he was insane, he was tried, found guilty, and hung for his crime.

LIFE AT THE WHITE HOUSE: The Garfield family had very little time to live in the White House. After Garfield's death, supporters and friends collected money to help Lucretia Garfield and her children.

WHAT DID HE LOOK LIKE? Garfield was six feet tall, with blue eyes and a full beard. He was the first President who was left-handed.

FAMOUS QUOTE:

"I do not care what others say and think about me. But there is one man's opinion which I very much value, and that is the opinion of James Garfield. Others I need not think about. I can get away from them, but I have to be with him all the time."

FOR MORE INFORMATION ON JAMES A. GARFIELD:

Historic Sites:

Birth Site:
Abram Garfield Farm Site Park
Center and Jackson Rd.
Moreland Hills, OH 44022

President Garfield National Historic Site
8095 Mentor Ave.
Mentor, OH 44060
Phone: 440-255-8722

WORLD WIDE WEB ADDRESSES:

The White House offers young readers information on the U.S. government and the Presidents on a Web site called **"White House 101."** The address is:
http://www.whitehouse.gov/about/white_house_101/

The Internet Public Library has a site on the Presidents. The address is:
http://www.ipl.org/div/potus

American Memory is a site maintained by the Library of Congress that contains biographical and historical information on the Presidents. It also provides links to Presidential portraits.
For James A. Garfield:
http://memory.loc.gov/ammem/today/jul02.html

President Garfield National Historic Site
http://www.nps.gov/jaga/

Chester A. Arthur

1829-1886
21st President of the United States (1881-1885)
"The Gentleman Boss"

CHESTER A. ARTHUR WAS BORN October 5, 1829, in Fairfield, Vermont. His full name was Chester Alan Arthur. His parents were William and Malvina Stone Arthur. William had come to the U.S. from Ireland in the 1800s. He was a teacher and later a Baptist minister. Malvina was from an old New England family. She was a homemaker. Chester was the fifth of nine children. His sisters and brothers were named Regina, Jane, Almeda, Ann, Malvina, William, George, and Mary.

CHESTER A. ARTHUR GREW UP in several different towns in New York and New England. His father was a preacher, and the family moved often.

CHESTER A. ARTHUR WENT TO SCHOOL at local schools wherever the family lived. He always did well in school. When he was just 15, he went to college at Union College in New York. During his college vacations, he taught elementary school to make extra money. He graduated from college in 1848, at the age of 19.

After college, Arthur studied law. He began to practice law in New York City in 1854.

WORKING AS A LAWYER: When Arthur began his career as a lawyer, the country was deeply divided over the issue of **slavery**. Arthur joined the **Republican Party**, which was opposed to slavery. Early in his career he took the case of eight black men accused of being runaway slaves. Arthur successfully defended them and won their freedom.

In another important early case, Arthur represented a black woman named Lizzie Jennings. She had been denied a seat on a New York City streetcar because she was black. Arthur convinced the court that she had been treated unfairly. The court ruled that black people had the same right as whites to ride on streetcars.

MARRIAGE AND FAMILY: Arthur met Ellen Lewis Herndon while he was living in New York. They married on October 25, 1859. They had three children, but one died in infancy. Their two surviving children were a son, Chester, and a daughter, Ellen.

GETTING INVOLVED IN POLITICS: In the late 1850s Arthur got involved in New York politics. He helped run the campaign of

Edwin Morgan, who was elected Governor of New York in 1860. Morgan then made Arthur quartermaster general during the **Civil War**. In that job, Arthur was responsible for buying and distributing the food and supplies to the Union soldiers from New York.

MACHINE POLITICS, POLITICAL BOSSES, AND THE PATRONAGE SYSTEM: After the war, Arthur worked as a lawyer again. At that time, the Republican Party in New York was run by a powerful man named Roscoe Conkling. He was known as a political "boss." His party was so powerful that it was called a "machine." Conkling used his power to get jobs for people who were loyal to the party. This system is called the "spoils system," or "political patronage."

Arthur went to work for Conkling and the Republican Party. After **Ulysses S. Grant** was elected President in 1869, he named Arthur, a loyal fellow Republican, the Collector for the Port of New York. In that job, Arthur was responsible for collecting taxes on most of the goods that came into the U.S. He was also responsible for giving away more than 1,000 jobs.

Although Arthur himself was an honest man, many people thought the "political patronage" system was corrupt. Getting a job in that system wasn't based on whether someone was a good worker, but whether they were a loyal party member.

In 1880, the Republicans chose Arthur to run as Vice President with **James Garfield.** The Republicans were divided into two groups at the time. The "Stalwarts" were the group of Grant and Arthur. They liked the patronage system and wanted to leave things as they were. Garfield was part of the "Half-Breeds." They wanted the patronage system done away with.

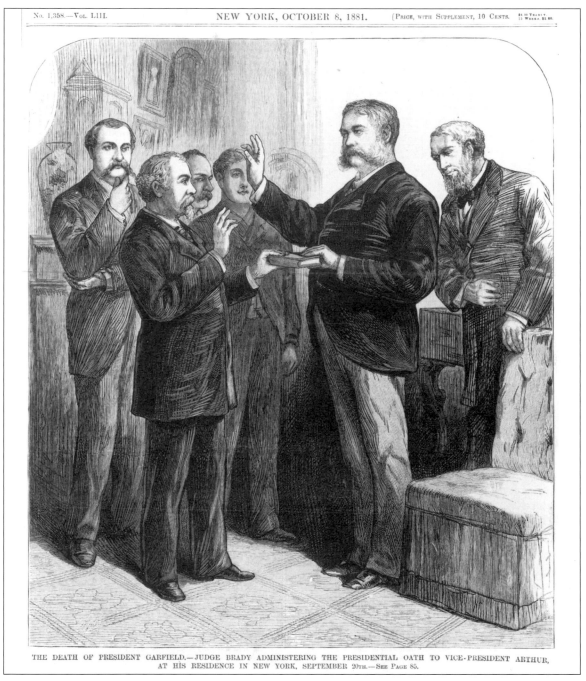

No. 1,358.—Vol. LIII.   NEW YORK, OCTOBER 8, 1881.   [Price, with Supplement, 10 Cents.

THE DEATH OF PRESIDENT GARFIELD.—JUDGE BRADY ADMINISTERING THE PRESIDENTIAL OATH TO VICE-PRESIDENT ARTHUR, AT HIS RESIDENCE IN NEW YORK, SEPTEMBER 20TH.—SEE PAGE 85.

Arthur sworn in as President following the death of James Garfield.

Roscoe Conkling, the political boss, didn't want Arthur to run with Garfield. But Arthur wanted the job. "The office of Vice President is a greater honor than I ever dreamed of attaining," he said.

President Chester A. Arthur.

VICE PRESIDENT OF THE UNITED STATES: Garfield and Arthur won the election of 1880. Sadly, Garfield's term was cut short. An assassin shot Garfield on July 2, 1881. The assassin was a Stalwart who was disappointed he hadn't gotten a job in the Garfield administration.

In September 1881, Garfield died of his wounds. Arthur became President of the United States.

PRESIDENT OF THE UNITED STATES: Arthur had never expected to become President. Many people thought he would be a bad President because he was so closely tied to the patronage system. But Arthur was determined to continue the reforms that Garfield had begun. He wanted to be his own man, not someone who answered to a political "boss."

Arthur's Presidency was not an easy one. The **Congress** was controlled by politicians who did not share his beliefs. Many favored high taxes as a way to raise money. Arthur disagreed. He thought the government had more than enough money. Some Congressmen wanted to pass laws that would benefit only their states. Arthur didn't like this type of favoritism for individual states.

Despite his frustrations, Arthur did make important reforms as President. His greatest achievement was the passage of the Pendleton Civil Service Act. It said that people wanting a government job had to be qualified and had to pass tests. The Pendleton Act helped do away with the patronage system.

In 1882, the second year of his term, Arthur found out he had Bright's disease. Bright's disease affects the kidneys, and in Arthur's time it was fatal. In 1884, he wanted to run for reelection, but he didn't win the nomination.

Ellen Arthur, who died before her husband became President.

By the time Arthur left Washington in 1885, he was considered an honest and hardworking President. A publisher named Alexander McClure said, "No man ever entered the Presidency so profoundly and widely distrusted, and no one retired more generally respected."

LIFE AT THE WHITE HOUSE: Arthur's wife, Ellen, had died in 1880, before he became President. In her memory, Arthur placed fresh flowers in front of her picture every day. Arthur's sister, Mary, took over the duties of White House hostess.

Arthur liked nice furnishings. He had the White House redecorated before he moved in. To make room for his own things, he had 24 wagon loads of old furniture and other items hauled away. Some of these things—old mattresses, stoves, and the like—were auctioned off to people who wanted a little piece of White House history.

Arthur was also known as a man who loved good food and drink. People eagerly awaited invitations to his fancy White House dinners. The President was fond of going for walks late at night, and he loved fishing. Once, he caught a bass that weighed 80 pounds.

RETIREMENT: Arthur was ill with Bright's disease when he left the Presidency. He moved back to New York City, where he practiced law again. He died on November 18, 1886, at the age of 56.

WHAT DID HE LOOK LIKE? Arthur was 6 feet tall with long sideburns, a mustache, and side whiskers. Sometimes called the "most handsome President,"Arthur was an elegant dresser. He had 80 suits hanging in his closet at the White House.

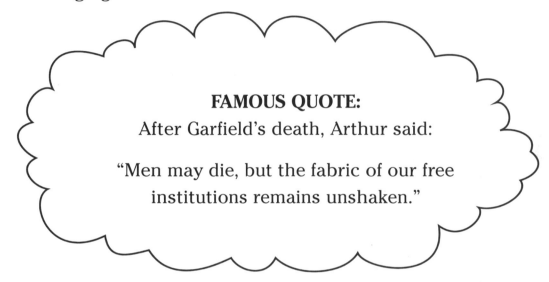

FAMOUS QUOTE:
After Garfield's death, Arthur said:

"Men may die, but the fabric of our free institutions remains unshaken."

FOR MORE INFORMATION ABOUT CHESTER A. ARTHUR:

Historic Sites:

Childhood Home (replica):
North Fairfield, VT 05450
Phone: 802-828-3051

WORLD WIDE WEB ADDRESSES:

The White House offers young readers information on the U.S. government and the Presidents on a Web site called **"White House 101."** The address is:
http://www.whitehouse.gov/about/white_house_101/

The Internet Public Library has a site on the Presidents. The address is:

http://www.ipl.org/div/potus

American Memory is a site maintained by the Library of Congress that contains biographical and historical information on the Presidents. It also provides links to Presidential portraits.
For Chester A. Arthur:

http://memory.loc.gov/learn/

Grover Cleveland

1837-1908
22nd President of the United States (1885-1889)
24th President of the United States (1893-1897)
"Grover the Good"

GROVER CLEVELAND WAS BORN March 18, 1837, in Caldwell, New Jersey. His parents were Richard and Anne Neal Cleveland. His father was a minister in the Presbyterian Church, and his mother was a homemaker.

Grover was the fifth of nine children. His given name was Stephen Grover, but he changed it to Grover when he was a boy. He had five sisters and three brothers. His sisters' names were

Anna, Mary, Margaret, Susan, and Rose. His brothers' names were William, Richard, and Lewis.

GROVER CLEVELAND GREW UP in Fayetteville, New York. His family moved there when Grover was four years old. Young Grover spent much of his time hunting and fishing. Discipline was strict in the Cleveland household, with much time devoted to prayer.

As a boy, Grover was known for his honesty. One day, a neighbor's chicken wandered into the Cleveland's yard and laid an egg. Grover returned the egg to the chicken's owner.

GROVER CLEVELAND WENT TO SCHOOL at the local public school in Fayetteville. He was not a brilliant student, but was remembered for his common sense and hard work.

Cleveland's family moved to Clinton, New York, in 1850, where Grover finished high school. In 1853, his father died. Grover was 16 years old. He went to live with his uncle in Buffalo, who helped him find a job as a clerk in a law office. Cleveland never went to college. Instead, he worked as a legal clerk and later studied law. He became a lawyer in 1859.

EARLY POLITICAL CAREER: Soon after Cleveland became a lawyer he joined the **Democratic Party**. For the next several years he practiced law and held minor offices within the party. In 1871, he served as sheriff of Erie County. Throughout this period, he gained a reputation for being hard-working and trustworthy.

In 1881, citizens concerned with honesty in Buffalo government persuaded Cleveland to run for mayor. He won the election and restored honesty and efficiency to the city's government. His

The wedding of Grover and Frances Cleveland, 1886.

success as mayor made him popular throughout the state of New York. He was elected Governor of New York in 1883. In 1884 he won the Democratic nomination for President.

PRESIDENT OF THE UNITED STATES: Cleveland won the 1884 presidential election by a narrow margin. He defeated his **Republican** opponent, James G. Blaine, 219 **electoral votes** to 182. He became the first Democratic President since **James Buchanan** won the office in 1857.

As President, Cleveland worked hard to restore honesty to the federal government, which many believed had become corrupt. He was politically conservative and believed that the federal government should have a limited role in American society. He vetoed

Frances Cleveland with her daughter Ruth, called "Baby Ruth."

laws that he thought gave special favors to businesses, groups, or individuals.

MARRIAGE AND FAMILY: Cleveland was still a bachelor when he became President. That changed in 1886, when he married Frances Folsom, the daughter of his former law partner. Cleveland had looked after Frances and helped her get an education after her father died. When Frances graduated from college in 1885, they fell in love and became engaged.

The Cleveland's marriage was the first time a President was married in the White House. Frances was 27 years younger than Cleveland, and, at 21, the youngest First Lady in history.

Grover and Frances Cleveland had three daughters and two sons. Their daughters' names were Ruth, Esther, and Marion. Their sons' names were Richard and Francis. Their oldest daughter was called "Baby Ruth." The popular candy bar was named after her.

LIFE AT THE WHITE HOUSE: Frances became one of the most popular First Ladies. She was very attractive, and women all over the country copied her fashions. One of Cleveland's political foes once said, "I detest him so much that I don't even think his wife is beautiful." She hosted two receptions each week. One of them was held on Saturday afternoons, so women who worked could attend.

ELECTION OF 1888: Cleveland ran for reelection in 1888. The principal issue of the 1888 campaign involved **tariffs**—taxes on imports. Cleveland and the Democrats wanted to lower tariffs. His Republican opponent, **Benjamin Harrison**, favored high tariffs. Although Cleveland received 90,000 more popular votes than his opponent, Harrison won the election with 233 electoral votes to Cleveland's 168.

The Cleveland family.

THE ELECTORAL COLLEGE AND THE ELECTION OF 1888:
Americans vote for President in a different way than they do for
any other elected official. The rules for the election of a President
and Vice President are outlined in the **Constitution**.

The President is *not* elected by direct vote of the people.
Instead, he is elected by members of the **Electoral College**. When a
voter casts a vote for a Presidential candidate, he or she is really
voting for an "elector." That is someone who is pledged to vote for
one of the presidential candidates. After the election, the electors
meet and cast their ballots for the candidates they are pledged to.

The number of electors is equal to the total number of members of the U.S. **House of Representatives** and **Senate**. To win the
election, the Presidential candidate must get a majority of all the
possible electoral votes. In 1888, Grover Cleveland got the majority
of popular votes in the election. But when the electors got together
to vote, more of them were pledged to Harrison, so Harrison won
the election, 233 electoral votes to 168 for Cleveland.

It is said that when the Cleveland's left the White House in
1889, Mrs. Cleveland told one of the servants "to take good care of
all the furniture and ornaments in the house, for I want to find
everything just as it is now when we come back again."

RETURN TO THE WHITE HOUSE: Cleveland spent the years 1889
to 1892 working as a lawyer in New York City. The Democratic
Party nominated him again to run for President in 1892. This time,
he defeated Benjamin Harrison, with 277 to 145 electoral votes. He
is the only President to serve two non-consecutive terms.

During Cleveland's second term the U.S. suffered through difficult economic times. Millions of people were out of work. Some

First Lady Frances Cleveland.

lost their homes and savings. Cleveland continued to govern based on what he thought was right, even though it often made him unpopular. In 1894, he sent the army to end a railroad strike. Many people disagreed with him, yet he stood by his ideas.

Frances remained a very popular First Lady. In 1893, their second child, Esther, was born. This was the first time a President's child was born in the White House.

Their third daughter, Marion, was also born in the White House in 1895.

RETIREMENT AND LIFE AFTER THE PRESIDENCY: After the end of his term in 1897, Cleveland retired from politics and moved to Princeton, New Jersey. He taught at Princeton University and later became a trustee. Cleveland died on June 24, 1908, at the age of 71.

Frances outlived her husband by many years. In 1913, she married Thomas J. Preston, Jr., an archeology professor at Princeton, and was a leading member of the community. She died at the age of 84, on October 29, 1947.

WHAT DID HE LOOK LIKE? Cleveland was a heavy man. He was 5 feet, 11 inches tall and weighed 260 pounds. He had thin gray hair, and a large, drooping mustache.

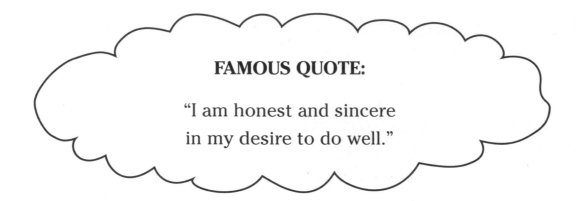

FAMOUS QUOTE:

"I am honest and sincere
in my desire to do well."

FOR MORE INFORMATION ON GROVER CLEVELAND:

Historic Sites:

Birth Site:
207 Bloomfield Ave.
Caldwell, NJ 07006
Phone: 973-226-1810

Oak View
3536 Newark St., N.W.
Washington, DC 20016

Burial Site:
Princeton Cemetery
29 Greenview Ave.
Princeton, NJ 08542
Phone: 609-924-1369

WORLD WIDE WEB ADDRESSES:

The White House offers young readers information on the U.S. government and the Presidents on a Web site called **"White House 101."** The address is:
http://www.whitehouse.gov/about/white_house_101/

The Internet Public Library has a site on the Presidents. The address is:

http://www.ipl.org/div/potus

American Memory is a site maintained by the Library of Congress that contains biographical and historical information on the Presidents. It also provides links to Presidential portraits. For Grover Cleveland:

http://memory.loc.gov/ammem/today/jun02.html

Benjamin Harrison
1833-1901
23rd President of the United States (1889-1893)
"Little Ben"

BENJAMIN HARRISON WAS BORN August 20, 1833, in North Bend, Ohio. His father was John Scott Harrison, and his mother was Elizabeth Irwin Harrison. John Harrison ran the large family farm and also served in the U.S. Congress. Elizabeth Harrison was a homemaker. Benjamin was the second of ten children. Three children died in infancy. His surviving sisters and brothers were named Archibald, Mary Jane, Anna, John, Carter, and James.

Benjamin Harrison came from a long line of distinguished Americans. He was named for his great-grandfather, who was a signer of the Declaration of Independence. His grandfather was **William Henry Harrison**, the ninth President of the United States.

BENJAMIN HARRISON GREW UP on the family farm, which covered 2,000 acres. As a boy, young Ben Harrison loved to fish, hunt, and roam the farm.

BENJAMIN HARRISON WENT TO SCHOOL at the local public schools and always did well. When he was 14, he went to Cary's Academy in nearby Cincinnati. There, he studied Greek, Latin, and science. He also met his future wife, Caroline Scott, called Carrie. She was the daughter of one of his teachers.

After two years at Cary's Academy, Harrison entered Miami University in Ohio. He was a good student, and he also began to develop his skills as a speaker and debater. Harrison graduated from Miami with honors in 1852.

After college, Harrison studied law. He became an attorney in 1853 and started a small practice.

MARRIAGE AND FAMILY: On October 20, 1853, Benjamin and Carrie Harrison were married. Her father, who was a Presbyterian minister, performed the service. The Harrisons had a son, Russell, and a daughter, Mary. Another child died as a baby.

GETTING INVOLVED IN POLITICS: In 1854, Harrison moved his family to Indianapolis, Indiana, where he worked as a lawyer. He joined the newly formed **Republican Party,** and he campaigned for the Republican candidates. In 1857 he ran for city attorney for

Indianapolis and won. Moving up the political ranks, he won a job with the state **Supreme Court**. He served in that job until the **Civil War**.

THE CIVIL WAR: In 1861, the Civil War broke out. The governor of Indiana chose Harrison to lead a regiment. He was made a colonel. His troops called him "Little Ben" because he was just 5 feet 6 inches tall. He was a strict but a brave leader.

Harrison led his men in several battles of the war and became a hero. When the war was over, **President Abraham Lincoln** made him a brigadier general.

RETURNING TO POLITICS: After the war, Harrison returned to Indianapolis. He practiced law again and entered politics. He ran for governor in 1876, but lost. In 1877, he became the leader of the state party. He won national office in 1880, when he was elected to the U.S. Senate.

Harrison served six years in the Senate. He supported the political ideas of the Republicans. He voted for rights for blacks and also favored high "**tariffs**," or taxes on goods coming into the U.S.

In 1888, the Republicans chose Harrison to be their nominee for President. Although he was sometimes called an "iceberg" because he was cool and formal with people, Harrison was a good campaigner.

Harrison used a new approach in his campaign, giving "front-porch" speeches. Having shown his skill in speaking since college, Harrison brought groups to his house and talked with them about issues. Almost 30,000 people heard Harrison speak in his "front-porch" campaign.

President Benjamin Harrison.

Harrison also made use of his famous family name. One campaign slogan of the time was "Grandfather's Hat Fits Ben," That meant that Ben was as able as his famous grandfather, President William Henry Harrison.

In the election of 1888, Harrison ran against **President Grover Cleveland**. Cleveland won the popular vote by almost 90,000 votes, but Harrison won the electoral vote, and the Presidency.

THE ELECTORAL COLLEGE AND THE ELECTION OF HARRISON: Americans vote for President in a different way than they do for any other elected official. The rules for the election of a President and Vice President are outlined in the **Constitution**.

The President is *not* elected by direct vote of the people. Instead, he is elected by members of the **Electoral College**. When a voter casts a vote for a Presidential candidate, he or she is really voting for an "elector." That is someone who is pledged to vote for one of the Presidential candidates. After the election, the electors meet and cast their ballots for the candidates they are pledged to.

The number of electors is equal to the total number of U.S. Representatives and Senators. To win the election, the Presidential candidate must get a majority of all the possible electoral votes. In 1888, Grover Cleveland got the majority of popular votes in the election. But when the electors got together to vote, more of them were pledged to Harrison, so Harrison won the election, 233 electoral votes to 168 for Cleveland.

PRESIDENT OF THE UNITED STATES: Harrison became President when the nation was 100 years old. That is why he is sometimes called the "Centennial President." As President, he was a

Republican with a Republican Congress. That made it easier for him to get the laws he wanted passed in his term.

While Harrison was President, Congress passed several important laws. One guaranteed a pension for all Civil War veterans. Another important law, the Sherman Antitrust Act, protected small businesses from "monopolies." A monopoly is a business that controls the entire market for a product. A monopoly is so powerful that other businesses can't make products and compete for customers.

Harrison also supported high tariffs. These taxes on imported products were supposed to protect U.S. businesses. They became the major issue when Harrison ran for reelection in 1892.

Harrison ran for another term, but by the time the election campaign took place in 1892, his wife was ill with tuberculosis. Harrison didn't campaign at all. Out of respect for Mrs. Harrison, Grover Cleveland, running against Harrison, didn't campaign, either. Cleveland won the election of 1892.

LIFE AT THE WHITE HOUSE: Harrison brought several generations of his family to live with him in the White House. His children, grandchildren, and Mrs. Harrison's father lived with him during his term.

One of the most famous relatives was Harrison's grandson, Benjamin Harrison McKee. Known as "Baby McKee," little Ben was the son of Harrison's daughter Mary. "Baby McKee" often rode in a cart pulled by one of Harrison's pet goats, whose name was His Whiskers. Once, the goat took off with the cart and Baby McKee. The President, huffing and puffing, ran into Pennsylvania Avenue to rescue his grandson.

The Harrisons were the first family to have electricity in the White House. But the new invention scared them. They made the White House electrician turn the lights off and on, because they were afraid of getting a shock.

First Lady Carrie Harrison.

Carrie Harrison was known as a gracious White House hostess. She set up the very first Christmas tree in the White House. She raised money for Johns Hopkins University, a famous medical school in Baltimore, but only when they agreed to admit women. She loved flowers and grew orchids in the White House. She also painted china.

Sadly, Carrie Harrison became ill with tuberculosis in 1892. She died of the disease on October 25, 1892, just two weeks before the Presidential election. The First Family that had been so happy and bustling when she was alive was in mourning when Harrison departed in March 1893.

RETURN TO INDIANAPOLIS AND REMARRIAGE: After his term, Harrison returned to Indianapolis. He practiced law again and was very successful. He wrote a book on the workings of government that was used in colleges throughout the U.S.

Harrison also married again. In 1896, he married Mary Scott Lord Dimmick. She was a widow and a niece of Harrison's first wife. They had one daughter, Elizabeth, in 1897.

Harrison died of pneumonia on March 13, 1901, in Indianapolis. He was 67 years old. His wife Mary lived on in Indianapolis until her death in 1948.

WHAT DID HE LOOK LIKE? "Little Ben" was one of our shortest Presidents, just 5 feet 6 inches tall. He had gray hair and blue eyes.

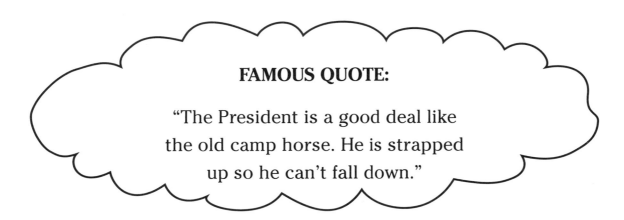

FAMOUS QUOTE:

"The President is a good deal like the old camp horse. He is strapped up so he can't fall down."

FOR MORE INFORMATION ON BENJAMIN HARRISON:

Historic Sites:

Benjamin Harrison Home
1230 N. Delaware St.
Indianapolis, IN 46202
Phone: 317-631-1888

WORLD WIDE WEB ADDRESSES:

The White House offers young readers information on the U.S. government and the Presidents on a Web site called **"White House 101."** The address is:
http://www.whitehouse.gov/about/white_house_101/

The Internet Public Library has a site on the Presidents. The address is:
http://www.ipl.org/div/potus

American Memory is a site maintained by the Library of Congress that contains biographical and historical information on the Presidents. It also provides links to Presidential portraits.
For Benjamin Harrison:
http://memory.loc.gov/learn/

Benjamin Harrison Home
http://www.presidentbenjaminharrison.org/

William McKinley
1843-1901
25th President of the United States (1897-1901)
"Idol of Ohio"

WILLIAM McKINLEY WAS BORN January 29, 1843, in Niles, Ohio. His parents were William and Nancy Campbell McKinley. His father worked in an iron foundry and his mother was a homemaker. The seventh of nine children, William had three brothers and five sisters. His siblings' names were David, Anna, James, Mary, Helen, Sarah, Abbie, and Abner.

WILLIAM McKINLEY GREW UP in the countryside around Niles, Ohio. It was the edge of the frontier in those days, and he enjoyed playing outside. His mother remembered that "the thing he loved best of all was a kite."

WILLIAM McKINLEY WENT TO SCHOOL at the local public schools. He was a bright and serious student. He attended Poland Academy in Poland, Ohio, then went on to college at Allegheny College in Pennsylvania.

McKinley attended college for less than a year. He left college to teach at a school in a rural area. In 1861, when **Civil War** broke out, he enlisted in the army.

THE CIVIL WAR: McKinley joined the Ohio Volunteer Infantry as a private. He served under **Rutherford B. Hayes**. Hayes later became President and guided McKinley's early political career. McKinley was a brave soldier, and when the war was over in 1865, he left the army with the rank of major.

GETTING INVOLVED IN POLITICS: McKinley returned to Ohio and began to study law. He settled in Canton, Ohio, and started his law practice in 1867. His former officer, Rutherford B. Hayes, encouraged him to get involved in politics.

In 1869, McKinley ran for office for the first time. He was elected prosecuting attorney. It was the first office he held in a political career that lasted until his death.

MARRIAGE AND FAMILY: In the late 1860s, McKinley met Ida Saxton, the daughter of a local banker. They fell in love and married on January 25, 1871. They had two daughters, Katherine, born in 1871, and Ida, born in 1873. Baby Ida died when she was just a few months old. Katherine died of typhoid when she was four.

The deaths of her two daughters shattered Ida McKinley. She became an invalid and suffered from seizures for years. William McKinley was devoted to his wife. He treated her with the greatest gentleness throughout their marriage. Even though she was ill, Ida did not stand in the way of her husband's political career.

First Lady Ida McKinley.

U.S. HOUSE OF REPRESENTATIVES: In 1877, McKinley was elected to the U.S. **House of Representatives**, where he served until 1890. He was a member of the **Republican Party** and served on the powerful Ways and Means Committee. That is a group that determines how money is spent by the government.

From his earliest jobs in government, McKinley was known as an honest man. He got along with members of both parties, even those who disagreed with him. He enjoyed a reputation for fairness and the ability to compromise.

TARIFFS: Like most Republicans, McKinley believed in high "**tariffs.**" A tariff is a tax on imported goods. He thought that high tariffs protected American business. High tariffs meant that foreign goods would be more expensive, and therefore less desirable, than American-made products. In 1890, a major bill, called the McKinley Tariff Act, passed in Congress. It made high tariffs the law of the land.

McKinley's second inauguration, 1901.

Some people disagreed with McKinley on tariffs. In 1890, when he ran for reelection to Congress, he was defeated. He ran for Governor of Ohio, and he was elected to two terms, serving from 1891 to 1896.

In 1896, the Republicans chose McKinley as their nominee for President. McKinley's campaign was managed by a powerful businessman named Marcus Hanna. Some people thought that Hanna would control McKinley's thinking. But McKinley proved to be his own man. Hanna helped him get elected, but McKinley followed his own values.

In the election of 1896, McKinley ran against William Jennings Bryan, a popular Democratic Congressman. Bryan set off on a train tour of the country, making speeches and stumping for votes.

McKinley approached the voters differently. He used a "front porch campaign" to share his views with Americans. Speaking from the front porch of his home in Ohio, McKinley talked to more than 750,000 people. When the voters went to the polls in November 1896, McKinley was the winner. In the **Electoral College**, McKinley received 271 votes; Bryan got 176.

PRESIDENT OF THE UNITED STATES: McKinley expected his term as President to be focused on issues like the tariff. Instead, he spent most of his term working on U.S. interests outside the country.

THE SPANISH-AMERICAN WAR: In the late 1890s, Spain controlled Cuba and Puerto Rico as colonies. Many Americans were disturbed by reports that Spain was treating Cubans cruelly. In 1898, the U.S. battleship *Maine* was destroyed in the harbor of Havana, Cuba. Although no one was sure who sank the *Maine*, most Americans blamed Spain.

Congress declared war on Spain in April 1898. The **Spanish-American War** lasted only four months. The fighting took place on Cuba and in the Philippine Islands in the Pacific Ocean, also a colony of Spain. The U.S. forces defeated Spain in both places.

After the war, the U.S. gained control of Cuba, Puerto Rico, and the Philippine Islands. The U.S. was becoming a world power. At this time, many countries were interested in developing trade with China. McKinley's Secretary of State, John Hay, negotiated an agreement, called the "Open Door" policy on China. It stated that all nations should have equal trading opportunities in China.

REELECTION: In 1900, McKinley ran for reelection. He had a new Vice Presidential candidate, **Theodore Roosevelt**, because his former Vice President, Garrett Hobart, had died. McKinley ran against William Jennings Bryan again, and he defeated him again. His reelection victory was decisive: he received more popular votes than any other candidate up to that time. In the electoral vote, he received 292 votes; Bryan got 155.

LIFE AT THE WHITE HOUSE: McKinley's life at the White House was devoted to his wife's well-being. Ida McKinley was an invalid by the time her husband became President. She still took part in White House social activities, however, greeting her guests from a chair. She always sat next to husband at White House dinners, in case she had a seizure.

ASSASSINATION: Just six months into his second term, McKinley was assassinated. It happened on September 6, 1801, in Buffalo, New York, where he was visiting the Pan-American Exposition. While McKinley was shaking hands with a group of people, a man

McKinley's assassination, September 6, 1901.

named Leon Czolgosz (CHOL-goz) shot him twice. When McKinley was shot, his first thoughts were for his wife. "My wife," he said to an aide, "be careful how you tell her." Eight days after being shot, on September 14, 1901, McKinley died. He was 58 years old. **Theodore Roosevelt** became the next President.

Czolgosz was an anarchist — someone who does not believe in governmental authority. He was tried and convicted of McKinley's murder and was executed October 29, 1901.

First Lady Ida McKinley arranged for the President's body to travel by train from Washington to their home in Ohio. Grieving Americans lined the tracks to pay their final respects to him.

McKinley was buried in Canton, Ohio. Ida McKinley lived on in Canton until her death in 1907.

WHAT DID HE LOOK LIKE? McKinley was 5 feet 7 inches tall and balding.

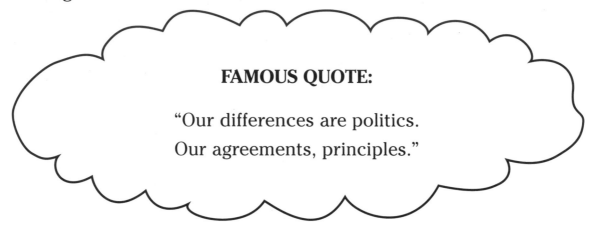

FAMOUS QUOTE:

"Our differences are politics.
Our agreements, principles."

FOR MORE INFORMATION ON WILLIAM McKINLEY:

Historic Sites:

Birth Site:
40 S. Main St.
Niles, OH 44446
Phone: 330-652-1774

The McKinley National Memorial
800 McKinley Monument Dr., N.W.
Canton, OH 44708
Phone: 330-455-7043

National McKinley Birthplace Memorial and Library
40 N. Main St.
Niles, OH 44446
Phone: 330-652-1704

WORLD WIDE WEB ADDRESSES:

The White House offers young readers information on the U.S. government and the Presidents on a Web site called **"White House 101."** The address is:
http://www.whitehouse.gov/about/white_house_101/

The Internet Public Library has a site on the Presidents. The address is:
http://www.ipl.org/div/potus

American Memory is a site maintained by the Library of Congress that contains biographical and historical information on the Presidents. It also provides links to Presidential portraits.
For William McKinley:
http://memory.loc.gov/ammem/today/sep06.html

National McKinley Birthplace Memorial and Library
http:www.mckinley.lib.oh.us/

Theodore Roosevelt
1858-1919
26th President of the United States (1901-1909)
"The Rough Rider"

THEODORE ROOSEVELT WAS BORN October 27, 1858, in New York City. His parents were Theodore and Martha Bulloch Roosevelt. His father was a successful merchant, and his mother was a homemaker. Theodore was the second of four children. His sister Anna was older, and his brother Elliott and sister Corinne were younger.

THEODORE ROOSEVELT GREW UP in the family's large, comfortable home in New York City. He was a weak, sickly child. His eyesight was so bad that he had to wear glasses from a young age. Theodore also had very bad asthma. Sometimes he could barely breathe. At night, when his breathing was difficult, his father would walk with him, holding him upright to help him breathe.

Theodore's father and mother were devoted to their son. His father encouraged him to build up his body by getting vigorous exercise. Over the years, Theodore grew stronger and eventually became an energetic, robust, and healthy man. His father was also concerned with his moral upbringing. He taught Theodore right from wrong and the importance of being a thoughtful, responsible man.

THEODORE ROOSEVELT WENT TO SCHOOL at home until he was college age. His parents hired tutors who taught him all his subjects until he was 18. Roosevelt was an active, curious boy. He loved to collect specimens from nature, like mice and birds. He sometimes stored them in his dresser drawers.

Roosevelt went to college at Harvard University, where he did very well. While he was still in college, Roosevelt began to write books. His first book was about the War of 1812. He finished it after he graduated from Harvard in 1880.

Roosevelt went on to law school at Columbia University in New York City. After one year of studying law, he decided that he wanted to run for office.

GETTING INVOLVED IN POLITICS: Roosevelt's first elected office was as a state assemblyman from New York. He served three one-year terms, from 1881 to 1884.

FIRST MARRIAGE: Roosevelt met Alice Hathaway Lee in 1878. The two fell in love and married on October 27, 1880. In 1884, Alice

Roosevelt from his days in the Dakota Territory.

gave birth to their only child, a daughter also named Alice. Two days after giving birth, Alice Roosevelt died. That same day, Roosevelt's beloved mother, Martha, also died. Roosevelt was overwhelmed with grief. Leaving his infant daughter with relatives, he set out for the Dakota territory.

LIVING IN THE DAKOTA TERRITORY: Roosevelt spent the next few years living on a ranch he had built on land in what is now North Dakota. Roosevelt loved the land. He later said that "I never would have been President if it had not been for my experiences in North Dakota."

He raised cattle and learned to be a cowboy. He even captured an outlaw. Roosevelt also developed an interest in conservation during these years in the Dakotas. He saw what had happened after the buffalo and other wild game were nearly wiped out by greedy hunters. He saw the damage done to the land from over-grazing. Later, when he became President, he would set up national parks and wildlife refuges to protect the land and animals.

SECOND MARRIAGE AND FAMILY: In 1886, Roosevelt returned to New York. He became reacquainted with Edith Kermit Carow, who had been a friend since childhood. They fell in love and were married on December 2, 1886, in London, England. They had five children, Theodore, Kermit, Ethel, Archibald, and Quentin. Ethel also raised Alice, who was just two when they married. She was a loving and gentle mother who was lot of fun. One of her sons once said, "When Mother was a little girl, she must have been a boy!"

RETURNING TO POLITICS: Roosevelt decided to devote his life to politics again. He ran for mayor of New York City and lost, but he was not discouraged. In 1889, he took a job as head of the United States Civil Service Commission. That is the part of the government that sets policy for government workers. In that job, he worked for a more honest and responsible civil service.

Next, Roosevelt became head of the New York City police board. He brought his energy and enthusiasm to that job, too. He was known to check on the police by walking the streets of the city after midnight, making sure that everyone did their jobs.

Roosevelt then began to work for the administration of **President William McKinley** as assistant secretary of the Navy. While he was in that job, the United States went to war against Spain and Teddy Roosevelt became a war hero.

THE SPANISH-AMERICAN WAR AND THE ROUGH RIDERS: In the late 1890s, Spain controlled Cuba and Puerto Rico as colonies. Many Americans were disturbed by reports that Spain was treating Cubans cruelly. In 1898, the U.S. battleship *Maine* was destroyed in the harbor of Havana, Cuba. Although no one was sure who sank the *Maine*, most Americans blamed Spain.

Congress declared war on Spain in April 1898. The **Spanish-American War** lasted only four months. The fighting took place on Cuba and in the Philippine Islands in the Pacific Ocean, which were also a colony of Spain. Roosevelt and his troops fought in Cuba.

Roosevelt in his Rough Rider uniform.

Roosevelt was head of the First United States Volunteer Cavalry Regiment, known as the "Rough Riders." They were a group of soldiers made up of former cowboys and college sports stars. Roosevelt led them in a famous battle, called the Battle of San Juan Hill. They won that battle and the war.

GOVERNOR OF NEW YORK: Now a war hero, Roosevelt was asked by the **Republican Party** to run for Governor of New York. He won and served for two years. He was not what the Republican political "bosses" thought he was. They were used to telling their candidate what to do, but Roosevelt set his own priorities. He fought for reforms he thought needed to be made in government. He taxed wealthy corporations and tried to end "sweatshops," factories where people worked in miserable conditions.

VICE PRESIDENT OF THE UNITED STATES: Many of the Republican bosses and their supporters were angry with Roosevelt for his reforms. They wanted him out of New York. So, in 1900, they nominated him for Vice President to run with **William McKinley** in his second term. The ticket of McKinley and Roosevelt won the election.

MCKINLEY'S ASSASSINATION: Roosevelt's term as Vice President lasted only six months. On September 6, 1901, McKinley was shot by an assassin. He died September 14, and Theodore Roosevelt became the 26th President.

PRESIDENT OF THE UNITED STATES: Roosevelt was just 42 when he became President. He is the youngest person ever to hold the office. He took the reins of the country with his characteristic energy, bursting with new ideas for the country.

Roosevelt thought the President should be a powerful political leader. He thought of himself as the President of all the people, not just the wealthy and powerful. He was known as the "trust buster." Trusts were large groups of companies that controlled money and jobs across the country. Roosevelt wanted their power broken up.

Roosevelt also supported the labor movement to create unions to represent workers. He expanded the influence of the U.S. in foreign countries, too. He is known for the phrase, "Speak softly and carry a big stick." He meant that the U.S. should be thought of as a world power that could use force if necessary.

Roosevelt was the first President to travel outside of the U.S. In 1903 he worked on the treaty to build the Panama Canal. He visited the site of the canal, a deep trench being dug across the country of Panama in Central America. When completed, the Panama Canal created a shipping lane that linked the Atlantic and Pacific Oceans. It allows ships to travel between the two Oceans without having to travel far south to go around South America or far North to go around North America.

THE TEDDY BEAR: While on a hunting trip in 1902, Roosevelt came upon a mother bear and her cub. He refused to allow the bears to be shot. The story made its way into the newspapers, where it appeared in a cartoon. A candy store owner in New York heard the story and decided to make a stuffed bear, using Roosevelt's nickname, "Teddy." Roosevelt agreed to have his name used on the toy, and the "Teddy Bear" was born.

President Theodore Roosevelt.

*Roosevelt with the famous conservationist John Muir
at Yosemite National Park in California.*

SECOND TERM: In 1904, Roosevelt ran for reelection and won by a huge majority, beating his opponent, Alton Parker. He won 336 **electoral votes**, to 140 for Parker. During his second term, he turned again to issues guarding the welfare of the common people. He helped to pass the Pure Food and Drug Act. That law made manufacturers responsible for producing safe food and medicine.

Roosevelt had always favored conservation policies. In his second term, he set up over 125 million acres of the nation as national forests. He also created 51 wildlife refuges. Through these policies, he helped to protect the land and wildlife he loved for all the people.

The lively and curious Theodore Roosevelt was the first President to ride in a car, an airplane, and a submarine. He lived the "life of strenuous endeavor" he loved. Sometimes, still full of energy at the end of a long work day, he would take a brisk walk around the capital.

THE NOBEL PRIZE: Roosevelt became the first President to receive the Nobel Peace Prize. He won the award in 1906 for his help in ending the war between Russia and Japan. By this time, he was a well-known and much-loved figure around the world.

Roosevelt had said he would not run again in 1908. He didn't really want to leave office, but after seeing his friend **William Howard Taft** elected President, he retired.

LIFE IN THE WHITE HOUSE: The White House of Teddy Roosevelt was a lively place. The Roosevelt children were as energetic as their father. They kept a wide assortment of pets, including many dogs and cats, a bear, a lion, a rooster, a garter snake, a parrot, a guinea pig, and a pony. The pony, named Algonquin, belonged to Roosevelt's youngest son, Quentin. One day, when his brother Archie was sick, Quentin took the pony up the stairs at the White House to cheer him up.

First Lady Edith Roosevelt.

The rough and tumble Roosevelt children also liked to take large platters and use them to slide down the staircases at the White House. Roosevelt encouraged his young children's activities, and he loved to play with them.

By this time, Alice, Roosevelt's oldest daughter, was growing up. She liked to shock people by smoking in public and going to horse races. When told of this, Roosevelt said, "I can run the country or control Alice, but not both." Alice married Nicholas Longworth in the White House on February 17, 1906.

RETIREMENT FROM POLITICS: After leaving office, Roosevelt went on safari in Africa and toured Europe. He missed politics, however, and after a year, he returned to the U.S.

RETURN TO POLITICS: In 1912, Roosevelt tried to get the Republican nomination to run again as President. But the Republicans chose Taft again. Not discouraged, Roosevelt formed a new party. It was called the National Progressive Party, known as the "**Bull Moose Party**." It got the nickname because Roosevelt told reporters that he felt "as fit as a Bull Moose" running for President again.

Roosevelt ran against both Taft, the Republican candidate, and **Woodrow Wilson,** the Democrat. He beat Taft in the voting, but lost to Wilson. Back at his family home, called Sagamore Hill, he continued to write. His autobiography, which came out in 1913, was a success.

In 1914, Roosevelt went on a trip to explore a river in Brazil. He came down with a jungle fever that almost killed him. He returned home sick and exhausted to his house in Oyster Bay, New York. During **World War I** (1914-1918), Roosevelt lost his youngest son, Quentin, who was killed in France in 1918.

Roosevelt became ill and died on January 6, 1919, at the age of 60. Edith Roosevelt lived on in Oyster Bay for almost 30 more years. She died September 30, 1948, at the age of 87.

WHAT DID HE LOOK LIKE? Roosevelt was 5 feet 8 inches tall and had a powerful, muscular body. He had thick glasses and a full mustache.

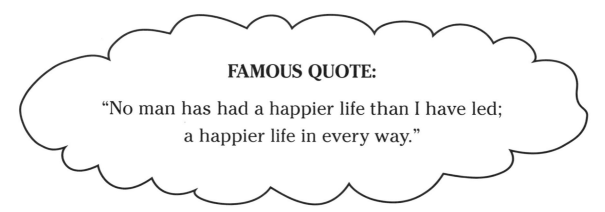

FAMOUS QUOTE:

"No man has had a happier life than I have led; a happier life in every way."

FOR MORE INFORMATION ON THEODORE ROOSEVELT:

Historic Sites:

Birth site:
28 E. 20th St.
New York, NY 10003
Phone: 212-260-1616

Sagamore Hill National Historic Site
20 Sagamore Hill Rd.
Oyster Bay, NY 11771
Phone: 516-922-4447 or 516-922-4788

Theodore Roosevelt Inaugural National Historic Site
641 Delaware Ave.
Buffalo, NY 14202
Phone: 716-884-0095

Theodore Roosevelt Island Park
George Washington Memorial Parkway
McLean, VA 22101
Phone: 703-289-2500

Theodore Roosevelt National Park
Maltese Cross Cabin
Box 7
Medora, ND 58645
Phone: 701-623-4466

WORLD WIDE WEB ADDRESSES:

The White House offers young readers information on the U.S. government and the Presidents on a Web site called **"White House 101."** The address is:
http://www.whitehouse.gov/about/white_house_101/

The Internet Public Library has a site on the Presidents. The address is:
http://www.ipl.org/div/potus

American Memory is a site maintained by the Library of Congress that contains biographical and historical information on the Presidents. It also provides links to Presidential portraits.
For Theodore Roosevelt:
http://memory.loc.gov/ammem/today/feb03.html

Theodore Roosevelt Birthplace National Historic Site
http://www.nps.gov/thrb/

Theodore Roosevelt National Park
http://www.nps.gov/thro/

Theodore Roosevelt Island National Memorial
http://www.nps.gov/this/

William Howard Taft
1857-1930
27th President of the United States (1909-1913)

WILLIAM HOWARD TAFT WAS BORN September 15, 1857, in Cincinnati, Ohio. His parents were Alphonso Taft and Louise Torrey Taft. Alphonso was a judge and had served as Secretary of War and Attorney General for **President Ulysses S. Grant**. Louise was a homemaker.

William was the second of five children. He had three brothers, Samuel, Henry, and Horace, and one sister, Frances. He also had two half-brothers named Charles and Peter. They were the children of his father's first marriage. Alphonso Taft's first wife died in 1852.

WILLIAM HOWARD TAFT GREW UP in Cincinnati. He had lots of friends and enjoyed swimming, ice skating, and playing baseball. He was always large for his age and grew very heavy as an adult.

WILLIAM HOWARD TAFT WENT TO SCHOOL at the local schools in Cincinnati where he was a good student. His parents thought he could do better in school, though, and cautioned him not to be lazy. He graduated from high school second in his class and went on to college at Yale University.

Taft did well at Yale, graduating with honors in 1878. He had always been interested in law and returned to Cincinnati to study it. After graduating from Cincinnati Law School in 1880, he began working as a lawyer.

GETTING INVOLVED IN POLITICS: Taft's career in politics began with his legal career. He was from a family with long-standing ties to the **Republican Party** and was given his early legal positions by Republican leaders.

In 1881, Taft was named assistant attorney for a county in Ohio. In 1887, he became a judge on the Ohio state court. In 1890, **President Benjamin Harrison** named him solicitor general of the United States. That is the second most important position in the Justice Department. After two years in that job, Taft became a federal court judge.

MARRIAGE AND FAMILY: In 1879, Taft met Helen Herron, whose nickname was Nellie, at a sledding party. They courted for several years and were married on June 19, 1886. The Tafts had three children, Robert, Helen, and Charles.

First Lady Helen Taft.

Helen Herron Taft had a great influence on her husband. She encouraged his political career and advised him. She wanted him to be President, even though he really didn't want the office. Instead, he wanted to be a **Supreme Court** Justice. Helen Taft enjoyed the political life of Washington, D.C., and liked to travel. In 1901, she accompanied her husband to the Philippines.

GOVERNOR OF THE PHILIPPINES: In 1901, **President William McKinley** named Taft Governor of the Philippine Islands. As a result of the **Spanish-American War** in 1898, the U.S. had come into control of the Philippines, a group of islands in the Pacific Ocean. The people of the islands wanted their independence. Taft helped manage their government and prepare them for independence.

Taft was an excellent Governor. He helped the Filipinos build roads and schools. He took the job very seriously. In fact, when **President Theodore Roosevelt** offered to name him to the Supreme Court while he was in the Philippines, Taft refused. He wanted to stay and help the Filipinos until the job he started was done.

SECRETARY OF WAR: Taft returned to the U.S. in 1904. He was now a national political figure. He was also a close political friend of Roosevelt. Roosevelt named Taft Secretary of War, a position he held until 1908.

In 1908, Taft ran, reluctantly, for President. Roosevelt had just completed two terms as President. He wanted Taft to run so that he could carry on the reforms Roosevelt had begun. Mrs. Taft was also enthusiastic about her husband running for President. The Republicans nominated Taft overwhelmingly in 1908. Taft won the election over his Democratic rival, William Jennings Bryan. He received 321 **electoral votes** to Bryan's 162.

PRESIDENT OF THE UNITED STATES: Taft was an unhappy President. He didn't have the skills for compromise needed in the job. His own party, the Republicans, were divided. Some wanted the party to be focused on reforms, as Roosevelt had been. Some wanted the party to be more conservative.

Taft followed Roosevelt's reforms in some areas. Roosevelt had been known as the "Trust Buster." Trusts were large groups of companies that controlled money and jobs across the country. Roosevelt wanted their power broken up. Taft oversaw the breakup of some of the biggest trusts in the country during his Presidency.

Taft did not follow Roosevelt's policies in the area of conservation. Roosevelt had been devoted to preserving lands and wildlife. Taft fired Roosevelt's chief forester over a disagreement about mining in Alaska. This made him unpopular with reform-minded Republicans.

When it came time to run for reelection in 1912, Taft did so, again reluctantly. In a surprise to Taft, Roosevelt decided to run

President William Howard Taft.

President Taft playing golf, 1908.

against his old friend for the nomination. Roosevelt was disappointed in what Taft had done in the office, and he wanted to be President again. The Republicans renominated Taft, but Roosevelt ran anyway. He was the Presidential candidate of the **Bull Moose Party.**

The election of 1912 was a three-way race. Taft, Roosevelt, and the **Democratic** candidate, **Woodrow Wilson**, all ran for President.

The Republican voters in the country split their vote between Taft and Roosevelt, and Wilson won the election. Taft received only eight electoral votes.

LIFE AT THE WHITE HOUSE: Soon after Taft's inauguration, Helen Taft suffered a stroke. She struggled to learn to speak and walk again, and she succeeded. She loved living in the White House. One of her favorite memories was of the Taft's 25th wedding anniversary. They invited several thousand people to a party on the White House lawn.

Helen Taft was also responsible for planting the beautiful cherry trees in Washington. They were a gift from the Japanese government.

The Tafts kept a cow, named Pauline, on the White House lawn. She provided fresh milk for the children. Taft was also the first President to have a car. He had the old horse stables at the White House converted into garages for his automobiles.

Taft loved baseball and golf. He began the tradition of the President throwing out the first ball at the opening day of the baseball season. On April 14, 1910, he threw the first ball at a game between the Washington Senators and the Philadelphia Athletics. Taft also loved to play golf. One of the things he disliked most about being President was that it left him little time for his favorite game.

CAREER AFTER THE PRESIDENCY: Taft was happy to leave the White House. He was soon chosen to teach at Yale Law School. When World War I started in 1914, he served on the National War Labor Board. After several years in that job, he finally received the job he had always wanted. He became a Supreme Court Justice.

President Taft speaking at Manassas Court House, November 1910.

CHIEF JUSTICE OF THE SUPREME COURT: In 1921, William Taft finally achieved his highest goal. **President Warren G. Harding** named him Chief Justice of the Supreme Court. The Chief Justice is the head of the Court and writes some of its major decisions. Taft served on the Court for nine years. He is remembered for his efforts to streamline the court system.

Taft is the only person to serve as both President and Chief Justice. He considered the Chief Justice position his greatest achievement. After having served in the job for several years, he said, "I don't remember that I ever was President."

RETIREMENT: Ill from heart disease, Taft retired from the Supreme Court in February 1930. He lived only one month more, dying in Washington, D.C., on March 8, 1930. He was 72 years old. Mrs Taft lived on in Washington until her death on May 22, 1943.

WHAT DID HE LOOK LIKE? William Howard Taft was our largest President. He was six feet tall and weighed over 300 pounds. He was so large that he got stuck in the bathtub at the White House. A new tub was made for him that was large enough to fit four men.

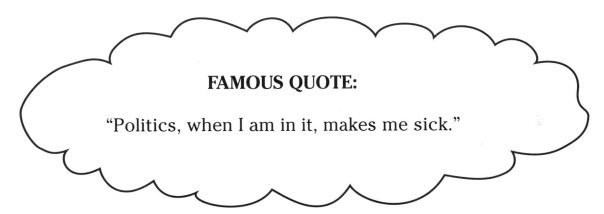

FAMOUS QUOTE:

"Politics, when I am in it, makes me sick."

FOR MORE INFORMATION ON WILLIAM HOWARD TAFT:

Historic Site:

William Howard Taft National Historic Site
2038 Auburn Ave.
Cincinnati, OH 45219
Phone: 513-684-3262

WORLD WIDE WEB ADDRESSES:

The White House offers young readers information on the U.S. government and the Presidents on a Web site called **"White House 101."** The address is:

http://www.whitehouse.gov/about/white_house_101/

The Internet Public Library has a site on the Presidents. The address is:
http://www.ipl.org/div/potus

American Memory is a site maintained by the Library of Congress that contains biographical and historical information on the Presidents. It also provides links to Presidential portraits.
For William Howard Taft:
http://memory.loc.gov/ammem/today/sep15.html

William Howard Taft National Historic Site
http://www.nps.gov/wiho/

Woodrow Wilson

1856-1924
28th President of the United States (1913-1921)
"Schoolmaster in Politics"

WOODROW WILSON WAS BORN December 29, 1856, in Staunton, Virginia. His father was Joseph Ruggles Wilson, and his mother was Jessie Janet Woodrow Wilson. His father was a Presbyterian minister. His mother was a homemaker.

Woodrow was the third of four children. He had two sisters and one brother. His sisters' names were Marion and Annie. His brother's name was Joseph. Woodrow's given name was Thomas Woodrow Wilson. His family and friends called him "Tommy" when he was a

First Lady Ellen Wilson, who died in 1914, during Wilson's first term.

child. After he graduated from college, he preferred to be called Woodrow.

WOODROW WILSON GREW UP in Augusta, Georgia. His father became the minister at the local church in 1857. When **Abraham Lincoln** was elected President in 1860, the **Civil War** began. Wilson's father served as a chaplain in the Army for the **Confederacy**. Woodrow's earliest memories were of the Civil War and the hardships that it brought to the people.

The Wilson family was very close. Woodrow later called his father "the best instructor, the most inspiring companion that a youngster ever had."

WOODROW WILSON WENT TO SCHOOL at home and at private schools. When he was five, the local schools were closed because of the Civil War. His father taught him at home until he was nine years old. After that, he went to private schools.

Wilson entered Davidson College in North Carolina when he was 17. He left Davidson after his first year. In 1875 he enrolled at the College of New Jersey, which later became Princeton University. Although Wilson was not an outstanding student, he loved history and literature. After graduating from college in 1879, he went to the University of Virginia to study law. He had to leave after one year because of poor health. He finished his law studies at home.

Wilson opened a law office in Atlanta, Georgia in 1882. His law practice was unsuccessful, so he decided to go back to school. He entered Johns Hopkins University and earned a Ph.D. — doctor of philosophy — in political science in 1886.

MARRIAGE AND FAMILY: When Wilson was practicing law in Atlanta, he met Ellen Axson, the daughter of a Presbyterian minister. Ellen was an artistic and intelligent young woman. Wilson fell in love with her at first sight. They became engaged in 1883 and were married in 1885.

Woodrow and Ellen had three daughters. Their names were Margaret, Jessie, and Eleanor. Wilson was devoted to his family and always found time to play with his girls.

Ellen Wilson died in 1914. Wilson remarried in 1915. His second wife's name was Edith Bolling Galt. They had no children.

CAREER AS A PROFESSOR: In 1885, Wilson became a professor of history at Bryn Mawr College, in Pennsylvania. He taught there for three years. In 1888, he moved his family to Wesleyan University in Connecticut. He taught history and coached the school's football team for the

President Wilson's second wife, First Lady Edith Wilson.

next 12 years. In 1889, he published a textbook on modern governments. He was becoming known as a leading scholar.

In 1890, he began teaching at Princeton University and was soon one of the most popular teachers on campus. He was elected president of Princeton in 1902. As president, he introduced new teaching methods that are still used in colleges across the U.S. today.

POLITICAL CAREER: In 1910, Wilson was nominated to run for Governor of New Jersey by the **Democratic Party**. He won the election by a large majority. He set about reforming the state's government. He worked on election reform and improving education.

PRESIDENT OF THE UNITED STATES: Wilson's success as Governor made him a leading candidate for President in 1912. He won the Democratic nomination that year, and defeated **William Howard Taft** and **Theodore Roosevelt** in the Presidential election. Although Wilson only won 42 percent of the popular vote, he won 435 of the 531 **electoral votes**. He had gone from college president to President of the United States in just two years.

As President, Wilson worked on a program of major reforms. He called his program the "New Freedom." He formed new laws and got them approved by **Congress**. In 1913, he reformed the nation's banking system by creating the Federal Reserve. The Federal Reserve System consists of 12 regional banks, and a board of Presidential appointees. This board is called The Federal Reserve Board, and it performs central banking functions and controls the money supply. It also created a new currency which is still used today. If you look at a dollar bill today, you will see the words "Federal Reserve Note" printed on it.

President Woodrow Wilson.

President and Mrs. Edith Wilson at his second inauguration, 1917.

In 1914, Wilson created the Federal Trade Commission. This department fought unfair trade practices and helped protect Americans from business monopolies. He also lowered **tariffs**—taxes on imports—and enacted the nation's first income tax.

WORLD WAR I: In August 1914, Great Britain and France went to war with Germany and Austria, and plunged Europe into **World War I.** Most Americans wanted to stay out of the war. Wilson worked hard to keep America out of the war and to defend America's neutrality.

REELECTION: Wilson was reelected in 1916, defeating **Republican** Charles Evans Hughes. He received 277 electoral votes to 254 for Hughes. His campaign slogan was "He Kept Us Out of War." Wilson offered to help work out a peace settlement with the warring nations, but he was turned down.

Then, in January 1917, Germany began a policy of unconditional submarine warfare. This meant that German submarines attacked any ship they saw, even if it was from a neutral country. By 1917, they threatened U.S. ships. On April 2, 1917, Wilson asked Congress to declare war on Germany. "The world must be made safe for democracy," he said.

THE U.S. ENTERS WORLD WAR I: Wilson got the nation ready for war. Men were recruited for the armed forces, and industry was shifted into war production. Wilson even had a flock of sheep that grazed on the White House lawn. The sheep's wool was sold to raise money for the Red Cross.

America's entry into the war gave the Allies (Britain and France) the advantage. Germany wanted to stop fighting, and a cease-fire was signed on November 11, 1918. Wilson went to the Peace Conference in Paris in 1919, to work out a final peace treaty. He had a plan he believed would lead to lasting peace. His plan was known as the Fourteen Points. Many of these points were part of the final peace treaty.

THE LEAGUE OF NATIONS: The most important of Wilson's Fourteen Points was the founding of the League of Nations. The League of Nations was an assembly of countries from around the world. It was much like today's United Nations. Its goal was to settle disputes between nations and avoid war.

After the peace treaty was signed on June 28, 1919, Wilson returned to the America to get the U.S. **Senate** to approve the treaty. The U.S. **Constitution** gives the power to negotiate treaties with other countries to the President. But the treaties are not valid until they are approved by two-thirds of the Senate. This is an example of the "separation of powers" that is a major feature of the U.S. Constitution.

The Republicans controlled the Senate. They were against the treaty. They didn't want the U.S. to join the League of Nations. These Senators were known as "isolationists." When the Senate refused to ratify the treaty, Wilson decided to take the issue directly to the people. He made a tour of the country. He covered 8,000 miles and gave 40 speeches to gain support for his treaty. The strain of this trip was too much for his health. Wilson collapsed after giving a speech in Pueblo, Colorado, on September 25, 1919. He returned to Washington, where he suffered a stroke on October 2. He was paralyzed and gravely ill.

While he was recovering from his illness, Edith Wilson took care of her husband. She acted as his nurse and executive secretary. During this time, she played a more active part in the government than any President's wife in U.S. history.

Despite Wilson's efforts, the U.S. never joined the League of Nations. The election of Republican **Warren G. Harding** in 1920 ended any chance of the U.S. of joining the League of Nations.

LIFE IN THE WHITE HOUSE: The White House was a busy place when Wilson was President. Two of his daughters were married in the White House. Jessie married Francis Sayre in 1913 and Eleanor married William McAddo in 1914. Although Ellen was a retiring person by nature, she was an active hostess at the White House. She also had a studio with a skylight installed in the White House attic, so she could paint.

Ellen also worked hard to improve the living conditions of poor black people who lived in Washington, D.C. She became ill with Bright's disease. Sadly, Ellen Wilson died on August 6, 1914. After Ellen's death, her daughter Margaret served as White House hostess.

While Wilson was grieving the loss of his beloved Ellen, he met Edith Bolling Galt. Edith was the widow of a successful Washington jeweler and was a descendant of the Indian princess Pocahontas. They became friends and soon fell in love. They were married on December 18, 1915.

The Wilson family, in 1913.

NOBEL PRIZE: Late in 1920, Wilson won the Noble Peace Prize for his efforts to build the League of Nations. He was the second President to be awarded this prize.

RETIREMENT: The Wilsons retired to their home in Washington, D.C. in 1921.

Wilson's health never recovered after leaving the White House. He died on February 3, 1924, at the age of 67. He was buried in the

National Cathedral in Washington. He is the only President buried in our nation's capital.

Edith Wilson outlived her husband by many years. She was a highly respected figure in Washington society and lived to ride in **President John Kennedy**'s inaugural parade. She died on her husband's birthday, December 28, in 1961.

WHAT DID HE LOOK LIKE? Wilson was 5 feet, 11 inches tall and slender. He wore eyeglasses, and had a sharp, angular face.

FAMOUS QUOTE:

"Sometimes people call me an idealist.
Well, that is the way I know I am an American."

FOR MORE INFORMATION ON WOODROW WILSON:

Historic Sites:

Birth Site:
Woodrow Wilson Presidential Library and Museum
20 N. Coalter St., Box 24
Staunton, VA 24402
Phone: 540-885-0897

Early Childhood Home:
419 Seventh St.
Augusta, GA 30901
Phone: 706-722-9828

Childhood Home:
1705 Hampton St.
Columbia, SC 29201
Phone: 803-252-1770

Woodrow Wilson House Museum
2340 S St., N.W.
Washington, DC 20008
Phone: 202-387-4062

WORLD WIDE WEB ADDRESSES:

The White House offers young readers information on the U.S. government and the Presidents on a Web site called **"White House 101."** The address is:
http://www.whitehouse.gov/about/white_house_101/

The Internet Public Library has a site on the Presidents. The address is:
http://www.ipl.org/div/potus

American Memory is a site maintained by the Library of Congress that contains biographical and historical information on the Presidents. It also provides links to Presidential portraits.
For Woodrow Wilson:
http://memory.loc.gov/ammem/today/dec28.html

Woodrow Wilson Presidential Library and Museum
http://www.woodrowwilson.org

Woodrow Wilson Boyhood Home
http://www.wilsonboyhoodhome.org

Woodrow Wilson House
http://www.woodrowwilsonhouse.org/

Warren G. Harding
1865-1923
29th President of the United States (1921-1923)

WARREN G. HARDING WAS BORN November 2, 1865, in Corsica, Ohio. His full name was Warren Gamaliel Harding. He was the first President to be born after the **Civil War**. His parents were George Tyron Harding and Phoebe Dickerson Harding. George was a doctor and farmer, and Phoebe was a homemaker.

Warren was the oldest of eight children. His sisters and brothers were named Charity, Mary, Eleanor, Charles, Abigail, George, and Phoebe.

WARREN G. HARDING GREW UP on the family farm. He often helped out with farm chores. His father said, "Warren was always willing to work hard if there was any money in it." Warren also worked in a mill that made brooms, and he learned to work the printing press at the local newspaper.

Young Warren Harding loved music, and he played several instruments. His first instrument was the cornet — a small trumpet. Later, he said he learned to play almost all the band instruments.

WARREN G. HARDING WENT TO SCHOOL at a one-room schoolhouse near his home. His mother taught him to read when he was quite young, and he always did well in school. In high school, he joined the debate team and edited the school newspaper. Harding graduated from high school at 14. He attended Ohio Central College for three years and graduated from college in 1882, at 17.

FIRST JOBS: Harding tried many things before he found a successful career. He worked for a short time as a schoolteacher. He gave it up, saying it was the "hardest job" he had ever had. He studied law briefly, but he didn't like that, either. After selling insurance for a few months, he finally found what he wanted to do.

BECOMING A NEWSPAPER EDITOR: In 1884, Harding bought a newspaper in Marion, Ohio, with two friends. It was called the Marion *Star*. Over the years, Harding became a successful newspaper editor and publisher.

MARRIAGE AND FAMILY: While living in Marion, Harding met a widow named Florence Kling De Wolfe. They fell in love and mar-

First Lady Florence Harding.

ried on July 8, 1891. Warren and Florence Harding had no children of their own, but they raised her son, Marshall, from her previous marriage.

Florence Harding was a strong, intelligent woman. She worked on the newspaper, too, and helped to make it a success. She also encouraged her husband's political ambitions. One of the newspaper reporters said: "she had faith in his future. She believed he had the makings of a great man." Harding called her "the Duchess." She said, "I have only one hobby — my husband."

GETTING INVOLVED IN POLITICS: Running as a **Republican**, Harding was elected to the Ohio State **Senate** in 1898. In 1902, he ran for and won the office of Lieutenant Governor. (A Lieutenant Governor is second in rank to a Governor.) In 1906, Harding returned to his newspaper business. After four years, he ran for Governor of Ohio, but lost. Then, in 1914, Harding ran for the U.S. Senate and won.

Warren and Florence Harding were very happy living in Washington, D.C. Harding called the Senate "a very pleasant place." In 1920, a reluctant Harding allowed his supporters to nominate him for President.

Harding ran a "front porch" campaign, making speeches from his home in Ohio. **World War I** had just ended, and the people of the U.S. wanted to return to quieter, simpler times. That is what Harding offered in his speeches. His slogan was "Back to normalcy with Harding." He was a tall, attractive man, who "looks like a President," his supporters said. He and his running mate, **Calvin Coolidge**, won the election of 1920. Harding beat the **Democratic** candidate, James A. Cox, with more than 60 percent of the vote. He won 404 **electoral votes**; Cox got 127.

PRESIDENT OF THE UNITED STATES: Unlike previous Presidents **Theodore Roosevelt** and **Woodrow Wilson**, Harding wasn't interested in strong Presidential powers. Instead, he let the Republican members of **Congress** make decisions about policy.

During Harding's term, the Congress passed bills limiting immigration. They also brought back high "**tariffs**," or taxes on import-

President Harding in the White House garden with his pet dog, Laddie.

ed goods. Unlike Wilson, Harding did not support the League of Nations, which was like the modern-day United Nations.

Harding wanted to be remembered as the "best-loved" President. But today he is remembered for the many scandals that took place during his term. The most famous of these was known as the **"Teapot Dome"** scandal.

TEAPOT DOME: Although he tried to hire intelligent, responsible men as his advisors, Harding trusted men he shouldn't have. Several members of his **Cabinet**, or advisers, were corrupt men. One of them, Secretary of the Interior Albert Hall, was found guilty of taking a bribe. Hall took money from oil developers to allow them to drill on federal lands in Wyoming, in an area known as "Teapot Dome."

The scandal began to surface in 1923. That summer, Harding and his wife took a trip he called a "Voyage of Understanding." During this trip, he became the first President to visit Alaska and Canada. But Harding was ill and concerned about the scandals brewing back in Washington. He had a heart attack and died in San Francisco, California, on August 2, 1923. He was 57 years old.

Calvin Coolidge became the next President.

Florence Harding escorted Harding's body back to Washington, then to Ohio for burial. She died about one year later, on November 21, 1924, at the age of 64.

LIFE AT THE WHITE HOUSE: The Hardings were gracious hosts in the White House. The previous President, **Woodrow Wilson** had been ill in the last part of his term. With the Hardings, the White House was once again open to guests. They liked to give dinner parties, where Harding's favorite food was pork and sauerkraut.

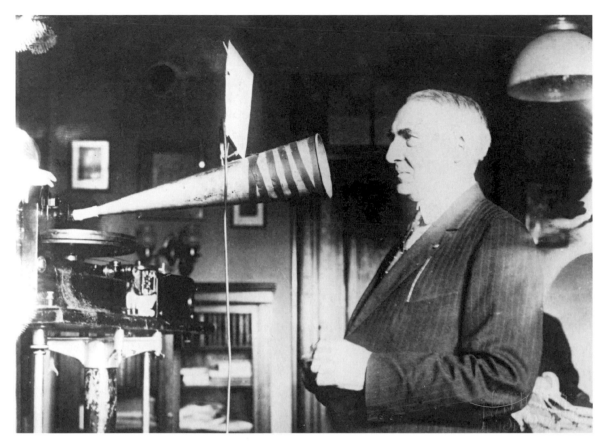

President Harding with an early recording device.

Harding also liked to have poker parties. Even though it was against the law to make, sell, or transport alcohol at the time, it was a law that was often ignored. Harding offered liquor to his guests.

Harding was the first President to have a radio in the White House and the first to ride to his inauguration in a car. He had an Airedale named Laddie.

FAMOUS QUOTE:

"My friends . . . they're the ones that keep me walking the floors nights!"

WHAT DID HE LOOK LIKE? Warren Harding was tall and handsome, with grey hair and heavy eyebrows.

FOR INFORMATION ABOUT WARREN G. HARDING:

Historic Sites:

Birth Site:
State Hwy. 97
East of County Rd. 20
Corsica, OH

Harding Home and Museum
380 Mt. Vernon Ave.
Marion, OH 43302
Phone: 614-387-9630

WORLD WIDE WEB ADDRESSES:

The White House offers young readers information on the U.S. government and the Presidents on a Web site called **"White House 101."** The address is:
http://www.whitehouse.gov/about/white_house_101/

The Internet Public Library has a site on the Presidents. The address is:
http://www.ipl.org/div/potus

American Memory is a site maintained by the Library of Congress that contains biographical and historical information on the Presidents. It also provides links to Presidential portraits.
For Warren G. Harding:
http://memory.loc.gov/learn/

Calvin Coolidge
1872-1933
30th President of the United States (1923-1929)
"Silent Cal"

CALVIN COOLIDGE WAS BORN July 4, 1872, in Plymouth Notch, Vermont. His name at birth was John Calvin Coolidge. When he was an adult, he dropped his first name and was known as "Cal." His parents were John Calvin Coolidge and Victoria Moor Coolidge. John was a farmer, storekeeper, and the local justice of the peace. Victoria was a homemaker. Calvin Coolidge had one sister named Abigail.

First Lady Grace Coolidge.

CALVIN COOLIDGE GREW UP in the countryside in Vermont. He often helped out on the farm. His family taught him the values he was known for throughout his life. They were hardworking, honest, plain speaking, and thrifty. They didn't waste money or words, and neither did their son.

CALVIN COOLIDGE WENT TO SCHOOL at the local public school, a one-room schoolhouse. He went to high school at Black River Academy in nearby Ludlow, Vermont. After high school, he attended Amherst College in Massachusetts.

Coolidge liked college and did well. Even though he wasn't much of a talker, he was on the debate team. Coolidge graduated from Amherst with honors in 1895.

After college, Coolidge moved to Northampton, Massachusetts, where he studied law. He began to practice law in 1898.

MARRIAGE AND FAMILY: While living in Northampton, Coolidge met the vivacious Grace Anna Goodhue. She was a graduate of the University of Vermont and taught at the Clarke School for the Deaf. Even though they were not alike, they fell in love. Referring to his own quiet nature, Coolidge said that "having taught the deaf to hear, Miss Goodhue might perhaps cause the mute to speak."

They were married on October 4, 1905, and had two sons, John and Calvin. Grace Coolidge always supported her husband's political career. She was warm and funny, and her personality seemed to ease her husband's shyness.

GETTING INVOLVED IN POLITICS: Coolidge had grown up in a family involved in politics. His father served for several terms in the Vermont state legislature. The family believed it was important to serve the community. Becoming involved in politics was a way to do that. Coolidge got involved in **Republican** politics in the 1890s while living in Massachusetts. In 1898, he was appointed to the city council in Northampton, his first political job.

In 1906, Coolidge won election to the Massachusetts **House of Representatives**. He served there for several years. In 1909, he was elected mayor of Northampton. He served in the state legislature again in 1911. In 1913, he became head of the **Senate**. He told his fellow Congressman to "Do the day's work," and "Be brief." Those were words he followed all of his career.

Coolidge was elected Lieutenant Governor of Massachusetts in 1915. (A Lieutenant Governor is second in rank to a Governor.) Then, in 1918, he was elected Governor.

Coolidge made a national name for himself as Governor of Massachusetts. In 1919, the Boston police went on strike. The city was in chaos, and there was violence and theft. Coolidge stood up to the police. He called in the state militia to restore order. He said, "There is no right to strike against the public safety by anybody, any-where, any time." His stand made him famous across the country.

VICE PRESIDENT OF THE UNITED STATES: In 1920, the Republicans chose Coolidge to run as Vice President on the ticket with **Warren G. Harding.**

They won the election easily.

DEATH OF HARDING: On August 2, 1923, Harding died while traveling in California. Coolidge was visiting his parents in Vermont when he received the news. His father, a justice of the peace, swore his son in as President at 2:30 in the morning on August 3, 1924.

PRESIDENT OF THE UNITED STATES: As Coolidge took office, several major scandals in Harding's administration came to light. Some members of Harding's **Cabinet**, or advisers, were corrupt men. One of them, Secretary of the Interior Albert Hall, was found guilty of taking a bribe. Hall took money from oil developers to allow them to drill on federal lands in Wyoming, in an area known as "**Teapot Dome**." That led to one of the biggest political scandals in American history, called Teapot Dome.

Coolidge made sure that anyone involved in wrongdoing was charged and tried for their crimes. He was thorough and effective in bringing them to justice. Because he was a man of such honesty, he helped people regain their trust in the President.

As President, Coolidge stuck by his conservative ideas. The economy was strong during his term. Most people had jobs and were making money. Coolidge didn't believe that the federal government should try to control the economy or business. "The business of America is business," he said. By that, he meant that American companies should be free to run their businesses without government interference.

REELECTION: Most of the people of the country agreed with Coolidge's policies. He ran for reelection in 1924 and easily defeated **Democrat** John W. Davis. He won 382 **electoral votes** to Davis's

President Coolidge shaking hands with baseball star Walter Johnson.

136. Coolidge was the first President to deliver his inaugural address by radio, which he did in March 1925.

During his first full term, Coolidge continued his program of not interfering with the American economy. He worked for lower taxes. He also supported a peace plan called the Kellogg-Briande Pact. It was developed by people from around the world to try to keep nations from going to war.

Always a man of few words, Coolidge made a brief announcement in 1928: "I do not choose to run for President in 1928." To the end of his career, he lived up to his nickname, "Silent Cal."

President Coolidge dressed in a cowboy outfit.

LIFE AT THE WHITE HOUSE: Even though her husband was known for his shy and quiet ways, Grace Coolidge was a lively and charming White House hostess. They entertained some of the most famous people of the day. One guest was Charles Lindbergh. The famous aviator had just completed the first flight from the U.S. to Europe when he visited in 1927.

Coolidge never got used to all the attention paid to the President. He used to like to sit on the porch at the White House after dinner. He had to stop doing that when so many people showed up to stare at him. Once, he took a stroll around the grounds with a Senator. As they came back to the White House, the Senator joked: "I wonder who lives there?" "Nobody," said Coolidge. "They just come and go."

One of Coolidge's favorite foods was pancakes smothered in Vermont maple syrup. He also spent a good deal of time in the White House kitchen, but not to study the cooking. Instead, he gave the staff hints on how to save money. The Coolidges had one of the first White House cats, a black cat named Tige.

One great tragedy occurred to the family during their White House years. The Coolidge's son, Calvin, died suddenly of blood poisoning in 1924, at the age of 16. It was a devastating loss for the family, but they remained very private about their grief.

RETIREMENT: After leaving Washington, the Coolidges moved back to Vermont. They were unable to find the privacy they wanted because so many people drove by their house. They moved to a new home, called The Beeches, in Northampton, Massachusetts. Coolidge was so thrifty that it was the first home he had ever bought. He spent the remaining years of his life writing. He wrote a newspaper column and published his autobiography. On January 5, 1933, he died of a heart attack, at the age of 60.

Grace Coolidge lived on at The Beeches until her death on July 8, 1957.

FAMOUS QUOTE:
One of the most famous quotes from this man of few words was often repeated by Mrs. Coolidge. Once, at a White House dinner, Coolidge was seated next to a woman who told him she had bet someone that she could get three words out of him. Coolidge replied:

"You lose."

WHAT DID HE LOOK LIKE? Coolidge was 5 feet 10 inches tall and slender, with red hair.

FOR MORE INFORMATION ON CALVIN COOLIDGE:

Historic Sites:

Birth Site:
P.O. Box 247
Plymouth Notch, VT 05056
Phone: 802-672-3773

Calvin Coolidge Presidential Library and Museum
Forbes Library
20 West St.
Northampton, MA 01060
Phone: 413-587-1014

Coolidge Homestead
P.O. Box 247
Plymouth Notch, VT 05056
802-672-3773

WORLD WIDE WEB ADDRESSES:

The White House offers young readers information on the U.S. government and the Presidents on a Web site called **"White House 101."** The address is:
http://www.whitehouse.gov/about/white_house_101/

The Internet Public Library has a site on the Presidents. The address is:
http://www.ipl.org/div/potus

American Memory is a site maintained by the Library of Congress that contains biographical and historical information on the Presidents. It also provides links to Presidential portraits.
For Calvin Coolidge:
http://memory.loc.gov/ammem/today/aug03.html

Calvin Coolidge Presidential Library and Museum
http://www.forbeslibrary.org/coolidge/coolidge.shtml

Herbert Hoover

1874-1964
31st President of the United States (1929-1933)
"The Great Humanitarian"

HERBERT HOOVER WAS BORN August 10, 1874, in West Branch, Iowa. He was the first U.S. President born west of the Mississippi River. His father was Jesse Clark Hoover, and his mother was Hulda Randall Minthorn Hoover. His father was a blacksmith and sold farm machinery. His mother was a homemaker.

Herbert was the second of three children. His older brother's name was Theodore, and his younger sister's name was Mary.

HERBERT HOOVER GREW UP in West Branch, Iowa. He learned to hunt and fish in the fields around West Branch. He especially loved to fish and enjoyed it all his life. The Hoovers were Quakers. The Quakers are a religious group that believes in a simple, peaceful way of of life. His parents taught him to value hard work and to help others in need.

Hoover's father died of typhoid fever in 1880, when Herbert was only six years old. Three years later, his mother died of pneumonia. Herbert was an orphan at the age of nine. He went to live with his uncle, Dr. Henry Minthorn, in Newberg, Oregon.

HERBERT HOOVER WENT TO SCHOOL at local public schools went he lived in Iowa. After he moved to Oregon, he attended a Quaker academy that his uncle helped run. Herbert was an average student, but was very good at mathematics.

In 1891, he enrolled in Stanford University, in California. He was just 17 years old. He wanted to be a mining engineer, so he studied geology and mathematics. In 1895, he was the youngest member of Stanford's first graduating class. He had earned a degree in geology.

MARRIAGE AND FAMILY: While at Stanford, Hoover met Lou Henry, who was also a geology student. She became the first American woman to earn a degree in geology. Herbert and Lou fell in love. They were married on February 10, 1899.

Lou was Hoover's partner in everything he did. She traveled around the world with her husband during his successful engineering career. She could speak several languages and published many books on geology and archeology. Lou was also very involved with the Girl Scouts. She was president of the Girl Scouts throughout much of the 1920s. She is credited with starting the first Girl Scout cookie sale.

First Lady Lou Hoover.

Lou and Herbert had two sons. Herbert Jr. was born in 1903 and Allan was born in 1907. Both boys were born in London and spent most of their childhood there.

ENGINEERING CAREER: After college, Hoover worked in gold mines in California and Nevada as an engineer. Then, in 1897, he joined a London mining firm. During the next ten years he built and supervised mines around the world. He and his family lived in Australia, China, and other foreign countries. He retired from mining a millionaire before he was 40 years old.

PUBLIC SERVANT: After retiring from the mining business, Hoover devoted himself to public service. In 1909 he gave lectures at Columbia and Stanford Universities. He also published a book, *Principles of Mining*. He became a trustee of Stanford in 1912.

Hoover was living in London when **World War I** began in 1914. The American ambassador asked him to start a group to help feed starving refugees in the war zones. He organized the Commission for Relief in Belgium, which fed 10 million Belgians and French during the war.

After the U.S. entered the war in 1917, **President Woodrow Wilson** called Hoover back to America. He was appointed food commissioner. In that job, he improved food production and distribution to help the war effort. After the war ended on November 11, 1918, he was put in charge of relief for the homeless and starving people in Europe. His organization fed and clothed over 200 million people while they recovered from the hardships of the war.

POLITICAL CAREER: Hoover was named Secretary of Commerce in 1920. In that post, he served under Presidents **Warren Harding** and **Calvin Coolidge.** He worked hard to reorganize and expand the Department of Commerce and helped improve foreign trade.

In 1922, Hoover wrote another book, *American Individualism*, which explained his personal and political beliefs. Many political leaders thought Hoover was one of the most qualified men in America to be President.

PRESIDENT OF THE UNITED STATES: After Calvin Coolidge decided not to run for President in 1928, Hoover became the **Republican** candidate. He defeated his **Democratic** opponent, Alfred Smith, 444 to 87 **electoral votes**. It was the largest margin of victory any President had yet received.

Hoover took office during a time of great prosperity in the U.S. That quickly changed when the stock market crashed in October 1929. This began the **Great Depression**, the worst economic crisis in American history. It was a time from 1929 to 1939 when up to one-quarter of Americans were out of work. People who had jobs lost them. Those who wanted jobs couldn't find them. Banks closed all over the country. People who had their life savings in banks lost all their money. It was a terrible, frightening time for the entire nation.

Hoover believed that the federal government should have a limited role in the economic recovery. He established the Reconstruction Finance Corporation. This agency gave federal loans to banks and businesses. It also sent funds to state governments for local relief. As the hardships of the Depression continued, people began to blame Hoover for their misery. Shantytowns full of homeless people were called "Hoovervilles."

Hoover ran for President again in 1932. His Democratic opponent was **Franklin D. Roosevelt** who promised more federal government involvement to help the people. Roosevelt defeated Hoover in a landslide victory.

LIFE IN THE WHITE HOUSE: Lou Hoover was known as an elegant first lady. She redecorated many of the rooms in the White House. She was a gracious hostess and was admired for the many lavish parties that she gave. Because times were hard, the Hoovers paid for their White House expenses with their own money.

As a man of great private wealth, Hoover never accepted his Presidential salary. He was the first President to donate his salary to charity.

Hoover exercised every day on the White House lawn. He worked out with a group of his aides before breakfast, regardless of the weather. They were known as the "medicine ball Cabinet," because they threw a heavy "medicine ball" as part of their exercises.

RETIREMENT: Hoover remained very active in public service for the rest of his long life. In 1936, he joined the board of the Boys Club of America and was immediately made its chairman.

At the end of **World War II** in 1945, **President Harry Truman** called on Hoover to run the Famine Emergency Commission. Once

President Hoover making a radio broadcast.

President Hoover addressing Congress on the 200th anniversary of George Washington's birth, 1932.

again, he saved millions of war refugees from starvation. He also helped to start the relief organizations UNICEF and CARE, which are still active today. These groups provide aid to needy people, especially children, in foreign countries.

When Hoover reached the age of 84, he had survived beyond his term of office longer than any other President. (John Adams had held the record until then.) By this time Hoover had written over 40 books. He had also received more than 80 honorary degrees from colleges and universities around the world.

By the end of his life, most Americans felt differently about Hoover than they did when he left office. When he left the

Presidency in 1932, many people still blamed him for the Depression. But most people now believe that Hoover was not responsible for that economic crisis. He is now recognized for his devotion to public service and for saving millions from starvation.

Hoover died in New York City on October 20, 1964. He was 90 years old. He was buried next to his wife, Lou, who had died in 1944. Their graves are on a hill overlooking the cottage where Hoover was born.

WHAT DID HE LOOK LIKE? Herbert Hoover was 5 feet 11 inches tall. He had a square face and a ruddy complexion.

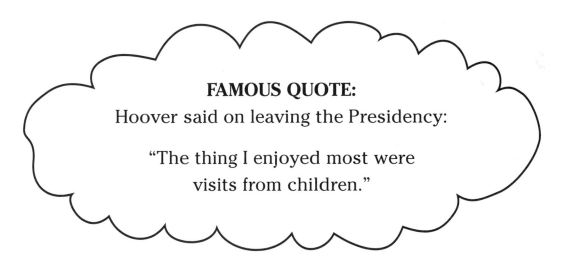

FAMOUS QUOTE:
Hoover said on leaving the Presidency:

"The thing I enjoyed most were
visits from children."

FOR MORE INFORMATION ON HERBERT HOOVER:

Historic Sites:

Birth Site:
Herbert Hoover National Historic Site
110 Parkside Drive
P.O. 607
West Branch, IA 52358
Phone: 319-643-2541

Herbert Hoover Presidential Library and Museum
210 Parkside Dr., Box 488
West Branch, IA 52358
Phone: 319-643-5301

Hoover Institution on War, Revolution and Peace
Stanford University
Palo Alto, CA 94305
Phone: 650-723-1754

Hoover-Minthorn House Museum
115 South River St.
Newberg, OR 97132
Phone: 503-538-6629

Shenandoah Camp Hoover
Shenandoah National Park
Rapidan River, VA
Park Address:
3655 U.S. Highway 211 East
Luray, VA 22835
Phone: 540-999-3500

WORLD WIDE WEB SITES:

The White House offers young readers information on the U.S. government and the Presidents on a Web site called **"White House 101."** The address is:
http://www.whitehouse.gov/about/white_house_101/

The Internet Public Library has a site on the Presidents. The address is:
http://www.ipl.org/div/potus

American Memory is a site maintained by the Library of Congress that contains biographical and historical information on the Presidents. It also provides links to Presidential portraits.
For Herbert Hoover:
http://memory.loc.gov/learn/

Herbert Hoover National Historic Site
http://www.nps.gov/heho/

Herbert Hoover Presidential Library and Museum
http://www.hoover.archives.gov/

Franklin D. Roosevelt
1882-1945
32nd President of the United States (1933-1945)
"F.D.R."

FRANKLIN D. ROOSEVELT WAS BORN January 30, 1882, in Hyde Park, New York. His full name was Franklin Delano Roosevelt. His parents were James Roosevelt and Sara Delano Roosevelt. James was a successful businessman and lawyer. Sara was a homemaker. Franklin had a half-brother, James, who was 28 years old when Franklin was born. He was the son of their father's first marriage. Rebecca Roosevelt, James Roosevelt's first wife, had died in 1876.

Franklin Roosevelt was part of a very distinguished family. He was related to 11 former Presidents, including **Theodore Roosevelt**, who was a distant cousin.

FRANKLIN D. ROOSEVELT GREW UP in a wealthy, privileged home. He was the only child of parents who spent a good deal of time with him. They traveled often and took Franklin with them. He began going to Europe when he was only three. The family also had a home on Campobello Island, off the coast of Canada. There, Franklin learned to love the water. He always loved to sail and swim.

FRANKLIN D. ROOSEVELT WENT TO SCHOOL at home until he was 14. In his early years, he was taught by a governess and a tutor. At 14, he went to Groton School, a famous private school in Massachusetts. At Groton, he spent time with boys his own age for the first time. Some of the boys made fun of him, calling him a "feather-duster," because they thought he was snobbish and a bit of a sissy.

Roosevelt was not a great student, but he enjoyed school. He wasn't very big—just 5 foot 3 inches and 100 pounds at 14—but he went out for football and baseball and had fun. He learned to make fun of himself, too. He wrote to his parents about playing on the school's worst baseball team. He was trying to catch a fly ball that "landed biff! on my stomach, to the great delight of all present."

Roosevelt learned things at Groton that influenced him throughout his life. Like him, most of the students at Groton were from wealthy backgrounds. The school principal taught them that those who are privileged owe something to society. Roosevelt began to think he might devote his life to public service.

First Lady Eleanor Roosevelt.

After graduating from Groton in 1900, Roosevelt went to college at Harvard University. He studied history and edited the school paper. After graduating in 1904, Roosevelt went to law school at Columbia University in New York.

MARRIAGE AND FAMILY: Franklin Roosevelt had met his future wife, Eleanor Roosevelt, when they were children. She was the niece of **Theodore Roosevelt** and was distantly related to Franklin. While Franklin was in college, he and Eleanor fell in love. They were married on March 17, 1905. Eleanor's father had died, so her uncle, Theodore Roosevelt, gave her away at the wedding ceremony.

Franklin and Eleanor had six children. One died as a baby. Their surviving children were Anna, James, Elliott, Franklin, and John.

Throughout their 40 years of marriage, Eleanor was a great help to Franklin's political career. She helped him campaign, and later, when he was stricken with polio, she acted as his "eyes and ears."

GETTING INVOLVED IN POLITICS: Roosevelt spent several years practicing law, but he didn't really like it. In 1910, he decided to run for the New York State Senate. He was an enthusiastic and optimistic man, and voters liked his confident manner. Even though he was a **Democra**t in a district that had usually voted **Republican,** Roosevelt won that first race.

Roosevelt served in the New York State Senate for two terms, until 1913. That year, he was chosen to be the Assistant Secretary of the Navy. He moved to Washington, D.C., and served in that job for 7 years.

In 1920, Roosevelt ran as the Democrat's Vice Presidential candidate. He and his running mate, James Cox, lost that race to **Warren Harding** and **Calvin Coolidge.**

Roosevelt wasn't ready to give up on politics. But just one year after losing the Vice Presidential race, he faced the greatest crisis of his life.

POLIO: In 1921, when he was 39 years old, Roosevelt came down with polio. Polio is a disease that can cause crippling, paralysis, and death. The disease became an epidemic in the first half of the 20th century. A vaccine was developed for polio in the mid-1950s. Since then the disease has become quite rare.

After getting polio, Roosevelt's legs became paralyzed. He could not move his legs and was never able to walk again without leg braces and canes. Roosevelt fought the disease with courage and determination. He swam and did exercises to regain his strength. His wife Eleanor nursed him through his illness and helped him regain his confidence. She remembered his bravery. "I think probably the thing that took the most courage in his life was his mastery of polio. I never heard him complain. He just accepted it as one of those things that was given you as discipline in life."

According to those close to him, having polio changed Roosevelt's outlook. Living with his own disability, he began to feel

Roosevelt as a young man.

a greater compassion for those who were poor and in need.

Roosevelt was a man of wealth and didn't need to work. But he wanted to stay in politics. In 1924 he gave a rousing speech at the Democratic convention for Presidential candidate Alfred Smith. Smith didn't win that year, but he remembered Roosevelt and his abilities.

GOVERNOR OF NEW YORK: In 1928 Alfred Smith encouraged Roosevelt to run for Governor of New York. Roosevelt won the election and served as Governor for two terms.

THE GREAT DEPRESSION: During Roosevelt's years as Governor, the era known as the "**Great Depression**" began. It was a time from 1929 to 1939 when up to one-quarter of Americans were out of work. People who had jobs lost them. Those who wanted jobs couldn't find them. Banks closed all over the country. People who had their life savings in banks lost all their money. It was a terrible, frightening time for the entire nation.

Herbert Hoover was President when the Depression began. He did not believe that the federal government should provide large relief programs. Many people in the country disagreed with him. Roosevelt believed that the federal government should provide aid in extremely difficult economic times. He decided to run for President to promote his ideas.

Roosevelt won the Democratic nomination for President in 1932. He promised to bring relief to "the forgotten man." In his speech accepting the nomination, he said, "I pledge you, I pledge myself, to a new deal for the American people."

PRESIDENT OF THE UNITED STATES: Roosevelt beat Hoover in a landslide victory in 1932. He received 472 **electoral votes** to Hoover's 59. As he took office, Roosevelt knew the country was in despair. In his inaugural address, he reassured the American people. "The only thing we have to fear is fear itself," he said.

Throughout his Presidency, Roosevelt inspired Americans with his confidence. Eleanor Roosevelt said, "I have never known a man who gave one a greater sense of security. I never heard him say there was a problem that he thought it was impossible for human beings to solve." Roosevelt communicated with Americans regularly over the radio in a program known as "fireside chats." In this way, he continued to explain his programs and encourage the American people.

Some of the programs that Roosevelt suggested worked. Some did not. But over the 12 years of his Presidency, he was optimistic and willing to try new ways to solve the economic problems of the country. "I have no expectation of making a hit every time I come to bat," he said. "What I seek is the highest possible batting average." Americans felt hope for the future with their new leader. After his first few days in office, "the spirit of the country seemed markedly changed," wrote a historian. "A feeling of hope had been reborn."

"THE NEW DEAL": Roosevelt's program to get American back on its feet was called the **New Deal**. The New Deal was a group of programs that Roosevelt presented to the **Congress**. The Congress passed the programs as laws. That is the way the New Deal policies began.

One of the first things Roosevelt did was close all the banks. He then lent money from the government to the banks to help them recover. The banks reopened, and Americans once again deposited their money. Roosevelt created the Federal Deposit Insurance Corporation, the FDIC. It insured the money in savings accounts. That way people with bank accounts wouldn't lose their money if the bank failed.

Other programs in the New Deal included direct cash relief to poor people. The federal government gave money to individuals to help them feed their families. The Agricultural Adjustment Administration, the AAA, controlled production and prices of food.

The New Deal program known as the National Recovery Administration, the NRA, helped businesses recover. It set up rules for fair competition. It also set up guidelines for minimum pay and maximum hours for workers.

Roosevelt also created works programs. One of these was the Works Progress Administration, the WPA. The WPA employed over 3 million Americans. They worked on buildings of all kinds, from schools to swimming pools. Other WPA workers created art, writing, and theater projects paid for by the WPA.

The Tennessee Valley Authority, the TVA, was another New Deal program. The TVA built dams that prevented flooding in the area around the Tennessee River. The dams provided inexpensive electric power to the people of the area.

Roosevelt created Social Security during his first term. That program still exists today. During the Depression, it provided money for the elderly, unemployed, disabled, and children.

Roosevelt's programs made him a popular and a controversial President. Poor and unemployed people looked to him as a champion. Businessmen thought he was taking too much power from them with some policies. Conservatives thought he was giving too much power to the federal government with his New Deal programs. The programs cost a lot of money, and the federal government went into debt to provide them. These were the major issues when Roosevelt ran for a second term in 1936.

REELECTION — 1936: Even though some Americans disagreed with Roosevelt's policies, he easily won reelection in 1936. That year, he faced Republican Alfred Landon. Roosevelt won with 523 electoral votes. Landon received 8.

When Roosevelt began his second term, more Americans were back to work and the economy was improving. Yet he believed that more needed to be done. "I see one third of a nation ill-housed, ill-clad, ill-nourished," he said in his second inaugural speech. He proposed increased government programs to help.

Two of Roosevelt's programs, the AAA and the NRA, had been canceled because the **Supreme Court** found them unconstitutional. Roosevelt decided to fight the Court. He wanted to add to the total number of judges and appoint people who supported his programs. This action became known as "packing the court," and was very controversial. The plan was blocked by the Congress.

During his second term, Roosevelt was unable to get Congress to back most of his new programs. They did, however, approve aid for public housing and continue other assistance programs.

Joseph Stalin, President Roosevelt, and Winston Churchill
meeting during World War II, December 1943.

WORLD WAR II: In the late 1930s, Europe was on the brink of war. In 1939, Adolf Hitler and the German army invaded Poland. World War II began. Germany, Italy, and Japan made up the "Axis" powers. They fought against the "Allies"—England, France, and the Soviet Union.

Most Americans wanted to stay out of the war. Roosevelt wanted to send arms and supplies to England and France. As he faced reelection in 1940, the war in Europe was a major issue.

REELECTION—1940: Roosevelt's popularity was decreasing when he ran for reelection in 1940. Also, he was running for a third term, which no one had done before. Still, he defeated his Republican opponent, Wendell Wilkie, with 449 electoral votes to Wilkie's 82.

At the beginning of his third term, Roosevelt increased production of arms and supplies for England and France. This production helped end the Great Depression, as more people went to work to support the war effort.

PEARL HARBOR: On December 7, 1941, Japanese planes bombed the U.S. naval base at Pearl Harbor, in Honolulu, Hawaii. Roosevelt immediately asked Congress to declare war. He called it a "day that will live in infamy." Congress approved Roosevelt's request, and the U.S. joined the Allies to fight the Axis powers.

Over the next four years, from 1941 to 1945, the U.S. and the Allies fought the Germans and Italians in Europe and Africa. In the Pacific, they fought the Japanese. Millions of American troops and millions of dollars in American-made weapons and supplies went to fight the war.

As President, Roosevelt met often with the leader of England, Winston Churchill, and the leader of the Soviet Union, Joseph Stalin. Together they determined how the war would be fought.

REELECTION — 1944: Roosevelt was ill with heart disease and high blood pressure at the time of the 1944 election. He was ready to retire, but he felt that the country needed him. He ran again, for a fourth term, something no one had ever done. Roosevelt was the last President to run for a third or fourth term. In 1951, the **Constitution** was amended, or changed, to limit a President to two terms.

Roosevelt won that race, with a new Vice President, **Harry Truman**. He defeated the Republican candidate, Thomas Dewey, with 432 electoral votes. Dewey got 99.

The Allies were winning the war in Europe against the Germans by 1945. But Franklin Roosevelt did not live to see the war end.

DEATH: Worn out by the demands of the war, Roosevelt had a stroke and died on April 12, 1945, in Warm Springs, Georgia. He was 63 years old. Harry Truman became the next President.

Roosevelt had served as President for 12 years, longer than any other man. He had been elected four times, also a record for a President. His loss was felt greatly throughout the world. Although some of his policies were controversial, he was also one of the most popular Presidents of all time. He had led the country during two of its greatest crises, the Great Depression and World War II. His influence on the role of the federal government in modern times is enormous.

ELEANOR ROOSEVELT: Like her husband, Eleanor Roosevelt was popular and controversial. She traveled extensively on behalf of the President, who couldn't travel easily because of his disability. She held press conferences and gave radio broadcasts and lectures. She wrote a newspaper column, called "My Day," about issues the country was facing. After Roosevelt's death, she continued in public life. She served as the U.S. delegate to the United Nations for several years. By the time of her death in 1962, she was known as the "first lady of the world."

LIFE AT THE WHITE HOUSE: Franklin and Eleanor Roosevelt were gracious White House hosts. Eleanor could stand and shake hands

Roosevelt's funeral procession, Washington, D.C., April 24, 1945.

for hours. Although Franklin had several favorite foods, including pancakes and sweet potatoes with marshmallows, Eleanor didn't really care about food. Once, when the King and Queen of England visited the U.S., she served them hot dogs at a picnic. She was criticized in the press for serving such simple food to such famous guests. Yet, she considered it appropriate and didn't feel bad about it.

As a pet, the President had a rather famous dog, a Scottie named Fala.

303

WHAT DID HE LOOK LIKE? By the time he became President, Roosevelt was confined to a wheelchair. But he rarely allowed his picture to be taken in his wheelchair. So he was most often photographed standing behind a podium or sitting down. He was 6 feet 2 inches tall and slender. He had gray hair, blue eyes, and wore glasses.

FAMOUS QUOTE:
As he took office in 1932,
Roosevelt tried to calm a frightened nation:

"We have nothing to fear but fear itself."

FOR MORE INFORMATION ON FRANKLIN D. ROOSEVELT:

Historic Sites:

Birth Site:
Franklin D. Roosevelt National Historic Site
4097 Albany Post Rd.
Hyde Park, NY 12538
Phone: 845-486-1966

Franklin D. Roosevelt Library and Museum
4097 Albany Post Rd.
Hyde Park, NY 12538
Phone: 845-229-8114

Little White House State Historic Site
401 Little White House Rd.
Warm Springs, GA 31830
Phone: 706-655-5870

Roosevelt Campobello International Park
P.O. Box 129
Lubec, Maine 04652
Phone: 506-752-2922

WORLD WIDE WEB ADDRESSES:

The White House offers young readers information on the U.S. government and the Presidents on a Web site called **"White House 101."** The address is:
http://www.whitehouse.gov/about/white_house_101/

The Internet Public Library has a site on the Presidents. The address is:
http://www.ipl.org/div/potus

American Memory is a site maintained by the Library of Congress that contains biographical and historical information on the Presidents. It also provides links to Presidential portraits.
For Franklin D. Roosevelt:
http://memory.loc.gov/ammem/today/jun16.html

Franklin D. Roosevelt Library and Museum
http://www.fdrlibrary.marist.edu/

Franklin D. Roosevelt National Historic Site
http://www.nps.gov/hofr/

Harry S. Truman
1884-1972
33rd President of the United States (1945-1953)
"The Man from Independence"

HARRY S. TRUMAN WAS BORN May 8, 1884, in Lamar, Missouri. His parents were John and Martha Young Truman. John was a farmer and livestock trader, and Martha was a homemaker. The "S." in Harry's middle name didn't stand for anything. His parents each had a relative with a name that started with an "S," but they couldn't decide who to name Harry after. So they left just it as an "S."

Harry was the oldest of three children. He had a brother named John Vivian, called Vivian, and a sister named Mary Jane. Harry's family had a tremendous influence on him. His parents and grand-parents were hardworking, plain-speaking people. They taught Harry the values of honesty, family love, and hard work.

HARRY S. TRUMAN GREW UP on a farm in Harrisonville, Missouri, and later in Independence, Missouri. He loved life on the farm. He and his brother would explore the fields and the creek. They had a dog named Tandy and a cat named Bob. Harry remembered those times as "wonderful days and great adventures."

When Harry was six, he got glasses. His eyes were so bad, he said he was "blind as a mole" without them. His mother, who had taught him to read before he was five, made sure Harry had plenty of books. He read the family Bible through twice before he was 12. He also loved to read history and biography. He remembered read-ing "everything I could get my hands on—histories and encyclope-dias and everything else." He also played the piano from a young age. He enjoyed playing all his life.

In 1890, the family moved to Independence, Missouri, not far from Kansas City. There, Harry went to school.

HARRY S. TRUMAN WENT TO SCHOOL at the local public schools in Independence. He loved school, and he always did well. He didn't have a lot of friends in elementary school, though, and he remem-bered feeling lonely.

Because he was afraid of breaking his glasses, Harry didn't get involved in sports. He often was teased because of his glasses. "To tell the truth, I was kind of a sissy," he said later. He didn't get in fights, and he preferred to be at home when he was young.

By the time he was in high school, Truman was feeling more at ease with people his age. He did well in school, and he still loved to read. He claimed to have read all the books in the Independence Library.

Even though he did very well in school, Truman didn't go to college after graduation. College was expensive, and his parents couldn't afford it. Instead, Truman started working.

Harry Truman at about age 10.

FIRST JOBS: Truman worked for the railroad and as a bank clerk after high school. When he was 22, he moved back to the country and worked on the family farm. For the next 11 years, he made his living as a farmer.

WORLD WAR I: In 1918, Harry Truman joined the army and went to France to fight in **World War I**. It was a major turning point in his life. Truman was an officer, and he and his troops were involved in fierce fighting. Once, a horse was shot out from under him and nearly crushed him. His men ran away from the battle. But Truman inspired them, through his own bravery, to return and fight. The experience taught him a lot about himself. He had courage, and he was a good leader.

MARRIAGE AND FAMILY: Returning from the war, Truman married his childhood sweetheart, Elizabeth Wallace, called Bess. Truman had first met her when he was a child, and he thought she was the loveliest girl he'd ever seen. He was too shy to talk to her when they were young. As he grew older and more confident, he let her know how he felt.

Harry and Bess Truman were married on June 28, 1919, in Independence. They had one daughter, Mary Margaret, who was called Margaret. They were a close, loving family. When he was President, Truman called Bess "the Boss," and Margaret the "Boss's Boss."

GETTING INVOLVED IN POLITICS: After Truman returned from World War I, he tried to make a living as the co-owner of a men's clothing store. The store failed, and Truman got into politics.

At that time, politics in most big cities were controlled by what is called a "political machine." In Kansas City in those days, the **Democratic Party** was run by a powerful man named Thomas Pendergast. He was known as a political "boss." His party was so powerful that it was called a "machine." Pendergast used his power to run the party his way. He was also corrupt and broke the law.

Truman got his first job in politics through the Democratic machine in Kansas City. Although he was never accused of any wrongdoing, he was always linked to Pendergast, and it affected his reputation.

Truman's first political post came in 1922, when he was made a county court judge. It was mainly an administrative job and didn't involve judging court cases. He served as a judge for the next 12 years. Next, he wanted to try for a national office. He ran for and won a seat in the U.S. **Senate** in 1934.

U.S. SENATOR: As a Democratic Senator, Truman was a great supporter of the **New Deal** policies of **President Franklin D. Roosevelt.** The country was suffering through the **Great Depression**, a time in the 1930s when up to one- quarter of Americans couldn't find work. Roosevelt's policies put many people back to work, and he was one of the most popular Presidents ever.

Truman loved his work in the Senate. He ran for reelection in 1940 and won by a narrow margin. By 1941, the U.S. had entered **World War II**. Truman became the head of an important committee that cut waste in war spending.

VICE PRESIDENT OF THE UNITED STATES: In 1944, many Democrats wanted Truman to run for Vice President. He wasn't interested. "I don't want to be Vice President," he told a friend. "I bet I can go down the street and stop the first 10 men I see and that they can't tell me the names of two of the last ten Vice Presidents." But President Roosevelt wanted Truman for his Vice President. By that time, Roosevelt had been President since 1933. He and Truman were elected in 1944 by a large majority.

By the time Truman became Vice President, Roosevelt was very ill with heart disease and high blood pressure. Truman had no idea how sick the President was. He was stunned when Mrs. Roosevelt called him on April 12, 1945, and told him that President Roosevelt was dead. Truman was now the President of the United States.

PRESIDENT OF THE UNITED STATES: After he took the oath of office on April 13, 1945, Truman met with reporters. "Boys, if you ever pray, pray for me now. When they told me yesterday what had happened, I felt like the moon, the stars, and all the planets had fallen on me."

President Harry S. Truman.

Truman became President when the country was fighting in World War II. He took over for a man who had been one of the nation's most beloved Presidents. Truman didn't feel he was worthy of the office, but he brought all his courage and ability to the job.

WORLD WAR II: In World War II, Americans and their allies — England, France, and the Soviet Union — were fighting in two places. In Europe they fought the Germans, and in Southeast Asia they fought the Japanese. Just one month after Truman took office, in May 1945, the Americans and their allies defeated the Germans. The war in Europe was over. But the war against Japan raged on.

The Americans had a new weapon, the atomic bomb. They knew it was the most powerful weapon that had ever been created.

Truman was clear with the Japanese. He said that unless they surrendered, the U.S. would use the most destructive weapon ever known. The Japanese refused to surrender. Truman told the U.S. forces to drop the bomb. After two atomic bombs were dropped on Japan, they finally surrendered, in August 1945. World War II was over at last.

Europe had been devastated by the war. Buildings were in ruins and people were starving. With the help of Secretary of State John Marshall, Truman developed the Marshall Plan. It helped the European nations rebuild their lands and economy.

Eastern Europe was fighting a new enemy — the Soviet Union. After World War II, the Soviet Union had invaded many of the countries of Eastern Europe. They controlled the people and the governments of these nations. This was the beginning of what is called the "**Cold War**."

THE COLD WAR: After World War II, the Soviet Union and the U.S. became the two strongest nations in the world. They represented two very different political systems. The U.S. was a democracy; the Soviet Union was a Communist state. For more than 40 years, the hostilities between these two powers determined world politics. This was known as the Cold War.

The countries of Europe were afraid for their freedom. Truman created the "Truman Doctrine." It stated that the U.S. would protect the other nations against threats to their freedom. He also helped create NATO — the North Atlantic Treaty Organization. Its purpose is to provide military protection to nations in Europe.

Clement Attlee, Harry S. Truman, and Joseph Stalin
at Berlin Conference, August 1945.

Truman believed in the social policies Roosevelt had created in his "New Deal." Truman called his plan for the U.S. the "Fair Deal." He wanted to create programs that offered good medical care, public housing, and jobs. He also fought for racial equality.

REELECTION: Despite his efforts for world peace and protection, Truman was not a very popular President. When he ran for reelection in 1948, no one thought he had a chance of winning. But Harry Truman had no doubts. He made a train tour throughout the country, with his wife and daughter at his side. He fought a long, tough campaign. He was known for his plain-speaking ways, and he went to the people with his message.

Truman holding up newspaper with headline "Dewey Defeats Truman," November 1948.

In 1948, Truman beat Thomas Dewey in one of the biggest upsets ever. Truman won 303 **electoral votes**, to Dewey's 189. His victory surprised everybody. One of the most famous photographs in American political history shows Truman holding up a newspaper announcing: "Dewey Defeats Truman." The newspaper was so sure that Truman would lose that they printed the headline before the election results were in.

Truman faced major problems at home and around the world in his second term. In 1950, the U.S. got involved in the **Korean War**. This was a civil war between North and South Korea. North Korea was backed by the Communist nations of China and the Soviet Union. The U.S. was part of a mission that included troops from other countries in the United Nations. They fought against the

Communist forces to protect the government of South Korea. The conflict lasted until 1953.

At home, Truman dealt with problems between labor unions and business owners. By 1952, Truman had decided not to run again. He retired to his home in Missouri.

LIFE AT THE WHITE HOUSE: Bess Truman was rather shy. She didn't like Washington, D.C., and wasn't much for White House entertaining. Also, the White House was in bad shape when the Trumans moved in. Walls and floors were literally falling apart. So the family lived for most of Truman's term at Blair House, across the street from the White House. As a pet, the First Family had an Irish setter named Mike.

The scrappy Truman was known for speaking his mind. He had a sign on his desk that said, "The buck stops here." One of his favorite sayings was "If you can't stand the heat, get out of the kitchen." While he was President, his daughter, Margaret, was studying to be a singer. She gave a concert in Washington, D.C., that was harshly criticized by a music reporter. Truman was furious. He fired off a letter to the critic threatening to break his nose.

First Lady Bess Truman.

When it was time to leave the White House, Truman said to Margaret, "Your dad will never be reckoned among the great. But you can be sure he did his level best and gave all he had to his country."

RETIREMENT TO MISSOURI: Truman returned to Independence with his family. Over the years, he wrote his memoirs and oversaw the building of a library that holds his Presidential papers. Truman died in Independence on December 26, 1972, at the age of 88. He wasn't very popular while in office. But by the time he died, many considered him one of our best Presidents. Bess Truman lived on in Independence until her death on October 18, 1982.

WHAT DID HE LOOK LIKE? Truman was 5 feet 9 inches tall, with thick glasses and grey hair.

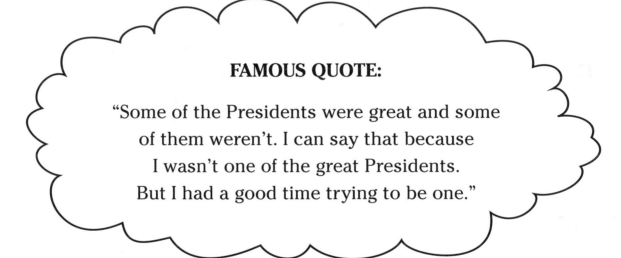

FAMOUS QUOTE:

"Some of the Presidents were great and some of them weren't. I can say that because I wasn't one of the great Presidents. But I had a good time trying to be one."

FOR MORE INFORMATION ABOUT HARRY S. TRUMAN:

Historic Sites:

Birth Site:
Harry S. Truman Birthplace State Historic Site
1009 Truman Ave.
Lamar, MO 64759
Phone: 800-334-6946

Harry S. Truman Presidential Library and Museum
U.S. Highway 24 and Delaware St.
Independence, MO 64050
Phone: 800-333-1225

Harry S. Truman National Historic Site
223 N. Main St.
Independence, MO 64050
Phone: 816-254-9929

WORLD WIDE WEB ADDRESSES:

The White House offers young readers information on the U.S. government and the Presidents on a Web site called **"White House 101."** The address is:
http://www.whitehouse.gov/about/white_house_101/

The Internet Public Library has a site on the Presidents. The address is:
http://www.ipl.org/div/potus

American Memory is a site maintained by the Library of Congress that contains biographical and historical information on the Presidents. It also provides links to Presidential portraits.
For Harry S. Truman:
http://memory.loc.gov/ammem/today/jan05.html

Harry S. Truman National Historic Site
http://www.nps.gov/hstr

Harry S. Truman Presidential Library and Museum
http://www.trumanlibrary.org

Dwight D. Eisenhower
1890-1969
34th President of the United States (1953-1961)
"Ike"

DWIGHT D. EISENHOWER WAS BORN October 14, 1890, in Denison, Texas. He was the first President born in Texas. His father was David Eisenhower, and his mother was Ida Stover Eisenhower. His father was a mechanic, and later, a businessman. His mother was a homemaker.

Dwight was the third of seven sons. His brothers' names were Arthur, Edgar, Roy, Paul, Earl, and Milton. One brother, Paul, died as a baby. His given name was David Dwight Eisenhower. Since his father's name was David also, his family called him Dwight. He had his name officially changed to Dwight David later in life.

DWIGHT D. EISENHOWER GREW UP in Abilene, Kansas. His family moved there in 1891. Dwight's family was poor. They had to make do without much money. His father worked at the local creamery, which made dairy products. The boys grew all the family's food on their small farm.

DWIGHT D. EISENHOWER WENT TO SCHOOL at the public schools in Abilene. He was an average student, but excelled in athletics. His schoolmates called him "Ike." This nickname stayed with him the rest of his life.

Eisenhower graduated from Abilene High School in 1909. He went to work at the creamery. He needed to earn money to help pay for his older brother's college education. Eisenhower wanted to go to college, too, but didn't have enough money. So he applied at both the U.S. Naval Academy at Annapolis and the U.S. Military Academy at West Point, where tuition was free.

Eisenhower was accepted to West Point in 1911. Once again, he showed average ability in the classroom and talent in athletics. He was a star halfback on Army's football team until a knee injury ended his athletic career. Eisenhower graduated from West Point in 1915 and began his military career.

MARRIAGE AND FAMILY: While stationed at Fort Sam Houston in San Antonio, Texas, Eisenhower met Mamie Geneva Doud. He fell in love at first sight. Mamie was from a wealthy Denver family and was used to a life of luxury. At first, she discouraged him. But Eisenhower persisted and finally won her over. They were married on July 1, 1916, in Denver, Colorado.

First Lady Mamie Eisenhower.

Dwight and Mamie had a happy marriage. Mamie accompanied her husband as he moved from one military post to the next. They had two sons. Their first son, Doud Dwight, was born in 1917. He died of scarlet fever in 1920. A second son, John, was born in 1923. John followed in his father's footsteps. He graduated from West Point and had a successful military career. He later became U.S. ambassador to Belgium.

EARLY MILITARY CAREER: Eisenhower was promoted to captain in 1917 and was an instructor at several Army training camps.

In August 1914, Great Britain and France went to war with Germany and Austria. **World War I** began. Most Americans wanted to stay out of it. In 1917, Germany began a policy of unconditional submarine warfare. This meant that German submarines attacked any ship they saw, even if it was from a neutral country. On April 2, 1917, **President Woodrow Wilson** asked Congress to declare war on Germany.

Eisenhower was eager to go to France and join the fighting. But he was so good at training troops, he was assigned to remain in the U.S. and prepare the new recruits. He commanded Camp Colt, a tank-training center near Gettysburg, Pennsylvania. He learned a lot about armored warfare and turning civilians into soldiers.

After the war, Eisenhower spent the next several years at various military assignments and commands. In 1928, he graduated from the Army War College in Washington, D.C. In 1935, he was sent to the Philippines.

WORLD WAR II: In the late 1930s, Europe was on the brink of war. In 1939, Adolf Hitler and the German army invaded Poland. World War II began. Germany, Italy, and Japan made up the "Axis" powers. They fought against the "Allies," made up of England, France, and the Soviet Union. On December 7, 1941, Japanese planes bombed the U.S. naval base at Pearl Harbor, in Honolulu, Hawaii. **President Franklin D. Roosevelt** immediately asked Congress to declare war on Japan, and the U.S. joined the Allies to fight the Axis powers.

When the U.S. entered the war, Eisenhower was a brigadier — one star — general. He worked in the war plans department. In May 1942, he was promoted to lieutenant general and took command of the U.S. forces in Europe. Eisenhower next commanded U.S. and British forces in North Africa. The German and Italian forces surrendered in May 1943. The Allies took 250,000 Axis troops prisoner.

In 1943, Eisenhower was appointed Supreme Commander of the Allied forces. He returned to England to begin planning the invasion of France.

D-DAY: By 1944, Germany and the Axis powers had taken control of much of Europe, including France. The Allies planned a massive invasion to retake control of Europe. The Normandy Invasion, known as "D-Day," was the largest military operation ever attempted. Eisenhower organized a combined force of 160,000 soldiers, 6,000 ships, and thousands of airplanes. They crossed the English Channel and landed on the Normandy Beaches in France on June 6, 1944. The invasion was a great success. By September 1944, German troops had been driven out of France.

THE END OF WORLD WAR II: In late 1944, Eisenhower began his final push into Germany. British and American political and military leaders disagreed on how the invasion should proceed. Eisenhower's tactful leadership kept them working together as a team. The British and U.S. forces swept through Germany from the west. The Soviet Army attacked from the east. On May 7, 1945, the German military command signed an unconditional surrender at Eisenhower's headquarters. The war in Europe was over.

POSTWAR YEARS: Eisenhower returned home to a hero's welcome. He became Army Chief of Staff in November 1945. In 1948, Eisenhower retired from active service. He wrote a book about his wartime experiences, titled *Crusade in Europe*. In 1949 he became president of Columbia University, in New York City.

THE COLD WAR: After World War II, the Soviet Union invaded many of the countries of Eastern Europe. They controlled the people and the governments of these nations. The U.S. was opposed to the Communist policies of the Soviet Union. **President Harry Truman** decided to commit the U.S. to a policy of containing Soviet expansion to prevent Communism from spreading to even more countries. The U.S. joined the North Atlantic Treaty Organization (NATO). NATO is an alliance that provides military protection to nations in Europe. Eisenhower was appointed Supreme Commander of NATO military forces in 1950.

GETTING INVOLVED IN POLITICS: While Eisenhower was in the military, he didn't belong to a political party. Both the **Democratic** and **Republican** parties tried to get him to run for President in 1947, but he refused. Later, he became a Republican.

In 1952, Eisenhower resigned his NATO command and campaigned for the Republican Presidential nomination. He won easily.

Eisenhower with American troops in World War II.

His campaign slogan, "I like Ike," reflected the war hero's popularity with most voters. He defeated his Democratic opponent, Adlai E. Stevenson, by 442 to 89 **electoral votes**.

PRESIDENT OF THE UNITED STATES: When Eisenhower took office, the U.S. was involved in the **Korean War.** In 1950, Communist forces from North Korea invaded South Korea. The U.S. sent troops to defend South Korea. Eisenhower worked out a truce with the Communist forces and ended the fighting in 1953.

REELECTION: In September 1955, Eisenhower suffered a serious heart attack. He recovered and was back to work full time after a few months. Despite his health problems, he decided to run for reelection in 1956. Once again his Democratic opponent was Adlai Stevenson. Eisenhower won reelection with 457 electoral votes; Stevenson got 73. He received almost 35,590,000 popular votes. That was the largest number of votes received by a U.S. President up to that time.

In his second term, Eisenhower continued to focus on the fight against the spread of Communism. In 1957, he offered to send U.S. troops to any country in the Middle East that asked for help to resist the Communists. This was known as the Eisenhower Doctrine. Under this policy, he sent troops to Lebanon in 1958 to stop a Communist takeover of the government. In 1960, Eisenhower retired from politics.

LIFE AT THE WHITE HOUSE: Mamie was a shy person who avoided public attention. Even so, she was a gracious and active hostess. The U.S. had become a leading nation after World War II. She and Dwight spent a lot of time entertaining leaders of foreign governments at the White House.

Eisenhower loved to golf. He had a putting green built on the White House lawn so he could practice. He was also an excellent cook, and was famous for his vegetable soup, steaks, and cornmeal pancakes.

RETIREMENT TO PENNSYLVANIA: In 1961, the Eisenhowers retired to a farm in Gettysburg, Pennsylvania. Ike wrote several books about political issues. **Presidents John F. Kennedy** and **Lyndon B. Johnson** often asked his advise on foreign affairs.

Eisenhower suffered another serious heart attack in August 1965. During the next three years his health continued to get worse. He died on March 28, 1969, in Washington D.C., and was buried in Abilene, Kansas.

President Dwight D. Eisenhower.

Mamie lived on at the Gettysburg farm for several years after her husband's death. She lived quietly, devoted to her family and friends. She died on November 1, 1979, and was buried beside her husband in Abilene.

WHAT DID HE LOOK LIKE? Eisenhower was 5 feet 10 fi inches tall and weighed 168 pounds. He was bald, with a fringe of gray hair. He had blue eyes and a ruddy complexion.

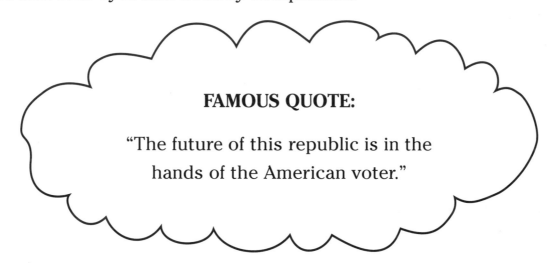

FAMOUS QUOTE:

"The future of this republic is in the hands of the American voter."

FOR MORE INFORMATION ON DWIGHT D. EISENHOWER:

Historic Sites:

Eisenhower Birthplace State Historical Park
609 S. Lamar Ave.
Denison, TX 75021
Phone: 903-465-8908

Dwight D. Eisenhower Library and Museum
200 SE 4th St.
Abilene, KS 67410
Phone: 785-263-6700

Eisenhower National Historic Site
250 Eisenhower Farm Lane
Gettysburg, PA 17325
Phone: 717-338-9114

WORLD WIDE WEB ADDRESSES:

The White House offers young readers information on the U.S. government and the Presidents on a Web site called **"White House 101."** The address is:
http://www.whitehouse.gov/about/white_house_101/

The Internet Public Library has a site on the Presidents. The address is:
http://www.ipl.org/div/potus

American Memory is a site maintained by the Library of Congress that contains biographical and historical information on the Presidents. It also provides links to Presidential portraits.
For Dwight D. Eisenhower:
http://memory.loc.gov/learn/

Dwight D. Eisenhower Presidential Library
http://www.eisenhower.archives.gov/

Eisenhower National Historic Site
http://www.nps.gov/eise/

John F. Kennedy
1917-1963
35th President of the United States (1961-1963)
"J.F.K."

JOHN F. KENNEDY WAS BORN May 29, 1917, in Brookline, Massachusetts, near Boston. His full name was John Fitzgerald Kennedy. His father was Joseph Kennedy, and his mother was Rose Fitzgerald Kennedy. Joseph Kennedy was a wealthy businessman who was once Ambassador to Britain. Rose Kennedy was a homemaker. Both of their fathers had been involved in Boston politics.

John was the second of nine children. He had three brothers and five sisters. His brothers were named Joseph Jr., Robert, and

Edward. His sisters were named Rosemary, Kathleen, Eunice, Patricia, and Jean.

JOHN F. KENNEDY GREW UP first in Boston, then in New York City. His family moved to New York City when he was ten. The Kennedys also had a home on Cape Cod in Massachusetts, where they spent summers. John, called Jack by his family, loved sports of all kinds. He liked to swim, sail, and play football with his brothers. The boys were encouraged by their father to be close but competitive.

JOHN F. KENNEDY WENT TO SCHOOL at local public and private schools in Massachusetts and New York. He spent his high school years at Choate, a famous private school in Connecticut. Kennedy started college at Princeton, in New Jersey. His first semester there, he became ill and had to return home. The next fall, he decided to go to Harvard. His first years at Harvard he got only fair grades. Then he became more interested in his studies and got better grades.

Kennedy traveled to Europe while still in college. **World War II** had begun in Europe in 1939. Kennedy, who loved history and politics, studied what had caused the war. Returning to Harvard, he wrote a long essay on the war. In 1940, he

John F. Kennedy at about 8 years old.

Lt. John F. Kennedy aboard PT-109, in 1943.

graduated from Harvard with honors. After college, he published a book based on his college paper.

WORLD WAR II AND PT-109: In 1941, the U.S. officially entered World War II. Kennedy wanted to join the army, but he was rejected. He had injured his back playing football in college, and his body was still weak. Kennedy did exercises to build up his strength. In 1941, he was accepted into the Navy.

In World War II, Americans and their allies—England, France, and the Soviet Union—were fighting in two places. In Europe they fought the Germans, and in the Pacific they fought the Japanese. As a Navy lieutenant, Kennedy was sent to fight in the Pacific. He commanded a "PT" boat—a torpedo boat—called PT-109.

In August 1943, PT-109 was struck by a Japanese destroyer and torn in half. Kennedy's men were stranded in the ocean. One man was badly burned. Kennedy led his men to safety, swimming three miles while towing the injured man. The men nearly starved while waiting to be rescued. Kennedy found some friendly natives and carved a message on a coconut. He told them to take the coconut to the nearest island with American soldiers. He and his men were finally rescued.

GETTING INVOLVED IN POLITICS: After the war ended in 1945, Kennedy returned to the U.S. He worked briefly as a newspaper reporter. Deciding he didn't want to make that his career, he got involved in **Democratic** politics.

Kennedy returned to Massachusetts, where he ran for the U.S. **House of Representatives** in 1946. He was elected and served in the House for three terms, from 1946 to 1952. In 1952, he ran for the U.S. **Senate**. He won that race, and spent the next eight years as a U.S. Senator.

MARRIAGE AND FAMILY: Kennedy met the glamourous Jacqueline Bouvier in the early 1950s. A beautiful, elegant woman, she was a photographer when they met. They married on September 12, 1953. Their first child, Caroline, was born in 1957. A son, John Jr., called was born in 1960. A third child, Patrick, died a few days after his birth in 1963.

First Lady Jacqueline Kennedy.

Shortly after his marriage, Kennedy had to have serious surgery. His back had never fully healed from his football injury, and he had reinjured it during World War II. While he was recovering from back surgery, he wrote a book called *Profiles in Courage*. It was a collection of biographies of famous U.S. Senators. The book was a great success and won the Pulitzer Prize, one of the most important prizes in publishing.

In 1956, Kennedy thought he was ready for a higher political post. That year, he tried to win the Democratic Vice Presidential nomination. He didn't win, but he was noticed. When the elections came around in 1960, Jack Kennedy won the Democratic Party's nomination for President. He chose **Lyndon Johnson**, a Democrat from Texas, as his running mate.

Kennedy waged a lively campaign. He was young and vigorous and seemed at ease in the world of politics. He debated his **Republican** opponent, **Richard Nixon,** on television. It was the first time Presidential debates had appeared on TV. Kennedy looked relaxed and prepared. Nixon looked nervous and seemed uneasy. When the vote was counted in November 1960, Kennedy had won by a very narrow margin. He defeated Nixon with 303 **electoral votes** to Nixon's 219. At 43, he was the youngest man ever elected President.

PRESIDENT OF THE UNITED STATES: Kennedy became President during a time known as the **"Cold War."** After World War II, the Soviet Union and the U.S. became the two strongest nations in the world. They represented two very different political systems. The U.S. was a democracy; the Soviet Union was a Communist state. The two "superpowers" also had powerful nuclear weapons. These weapons could destroy entire cities. The relationship between the two nations was very important — and very tense.

THE CUBAN MISSILE CRISIS: In October 1962, President Kennedy learned of a buildup of Soviet missiles in Cuba, an island nation in the Caribbean just south of Florida. These missiles carried nuclear bombs that could reach the United States. Kennedy confronted the Soviet leader, Nikita Khrushchev, about the missiles. He said that all Soviet ships in the area of Cuba would be stopped and searched for weapons. For a number of days, the world was on the brink of war. Finally, the Soviets backed down. They removed the missiles from Cuba. Nuclear war had been avoided.

Kennedy knew the enormous risks of nuclear war. He began talks with the Soviet leaders to draw up a treaty to stop nuclear testing. They agreed to restrict nuclear tests.

THE PEACE CORPS: In 1961, President Kennedy created the Peace Corps. Its purpose was to encourage young Americans to share their skills in countries less fortunate than the U.S. Kennedy wanted them to help bring a "decent way of life which is the foundation of freedom and a condition of peace." Over the years, thousands of young Americans served all over the world. They helped to build roads, schools, and farms in many of the poorest nations.

Kennedy also fought for civil rights for African-Americans. He encouraged Congress to write laws to guarantee equality for all Americans.

ASSASSINATION: On November 22, 1963, Kennedy was visiting Dallas, Texas, with his wife and Vice President Johnson. As they rode in an open car, someone shot the President. He died one hour later. The youngest man ever elected President, Kennedy was now the youngest ever to die in office. Vice President **Lyndon Johnson** became the next President.

Police arrested a man named Lee Harvey Oswald and charged him with the crime. Two days after he was arrested, Oswald was shot and killed by a man named Jack Ruby. Although Kennedy's assassination has been investigated for years, no one is absolutely sure if Oswald acted alone in shooting the President or if he had help from someone else.

The nation, and the world, mourned the death of the President. Heads of state from more than 90 nations came to his funeral in Washington, D.C. Millions of Americans watched the ceremonies on television. Kennedy was buried in Arlington Cemetery in Washington. His wife, Jackie, lit an eternal flame at his grave.

Jackie Kennedy remarried in 1968. She died in New York City in 1994.

LIFE AT THE WHITE HOUSE: The Kennedys were the first White House residents with young children in 50 years. Jackie was very stylish, and American women copied her hairstyle and clothing. She was one of the most popular First Ladies. She redecorated the White House, choosing fabrics and designs from different eras of American

President and Mrs. Kennedy with John Jr. and Caroline, 1962.

history. When the redecoration was complete, she invited a TV crew into the White House to share it with the American people.

Both the President and First Lady loved the arts. They invited some of the most famous musicians of the era to perform at the White House. They also promoted funding for the arts.

To preserve their privacy, Jackie Kennedy set up a kindergarten in the White House when Caroline was five. She was a devoted mother. She once said that "if you bungle raising your children, I don't think whatever else you do well matters very much."

Caroline was a spirited little girl. She had a pony named Macaroni, a canary named Robin, and a dog named Pushinka. Once, news reporters asked where her father was. "Oh," she said, "he's upstairs with his shoes and socks off. He's not doing anything."

WHAT DID HE LOOK LIKE? Kennedy is considered one of the most handsome Presidents. He was six feet tall and slim, with red hair and blue eyes.

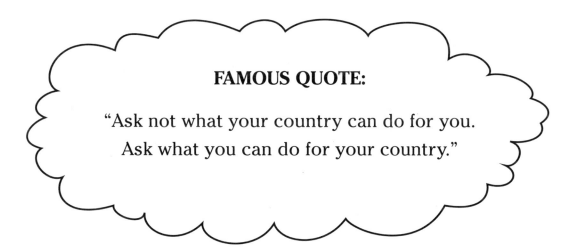

FAMOUS QUOTE:

"Ask not what your country can do for you.
Ask what you can do for your country."

FOR MORE INFORMATION ABOUT JOHN F. KENNEDY:

Historic Sites:

John F. Kennedy National Historic Site
83 Beals St.
Brookline, MA 02446
Phone: 617-566-7937

John F. Kennedy Library and Museum
Columbia Point
Boston, MA 02125
Phone: 617-514-1600

WORLD WIDE WEB ADDRESSES:

The White House offers young readers information on the U.S. government and the Presidents on a Web site called **"White House 101."** The address is:
http://www.whitehouse.gov/about/white_house_101/

The Internet Public Library has a site on the Presidents. The address is:
http://www.ipl.org/div/potus

American Memory is a site maintained by the Library of Congress that contains biographical and historical information on the Presidents. It also provides links to Presidential portraits.
For John F. Kennedy:
http://memory.loc.gov/ammem/today/nov22.html

John F. Kennedy Presidential Library
http://www.jfklibrary.org/

John F. Kennedy National Historic Site
http://www.nps.gov/jofi

Lyndon B. Johnson
1908-1973
36th President of the United States (1963-1969)
"L.B.J."

LYNDON B. JOHNSON WAS BORN August 27, 1908, near Stonewall, Texas. His full name was Lyndon Baines Johnson. His parents were Sam Ely Johnson and Rebekah Baines Johnson. Sam worked as a farmer, teacher, and state legislator. Rebekah was a homemaker. Lyndon was the oldest of five children. He had one brother, Sam, and three sisters, Rebekah, Josefa, and Lucia.

LYNDON B. JOHNSON GREW UP in Stonewall and in Johnson City, which had been founded by his grandfather. His father never made a lot of money. The Johnsons weren't poor, but they weren't well off. The family always had food and clothes, but nothing for extras. Lyndon worked at odd jobs as a youngster, shining shoes and delivering papers.

When Lyndon was young, his father served in the Texas legislature. He liked to attend the sessions with his father. He was fascinated by politics. He knew early on he would make it his life.

LYNDON B. JOHNSON WENT TO SCHOOL at the local public schools in Johnson City. He had been raised to value education, and he did well. He graduated from high school in 1924, at just 15.

After high school, Johnson wanted to travel. He went to California with some friends and worked at different jobs for a few years. When he returned to Texas, he was ready for college. He attended Southwest Texas State Teachers College in San Marcos, Texas. He studied history, edited the school paper, and took part on the debate team. He worked his way through school, first as a janitor, then as a secretary. He graduated in just three years, in 1930.

After college, Johnson taught debate at Sam Houston High School in Houston, Texas. Then he began his political career.

GETTING INVOLVED IN POLITICS: Johnson got his chance to enter politics in 1931. A **Democrat,** he campaigned for a fellow Democrat from Texas, Richard Kleberg, who was running for U.S. **Congress**. Kleberg won his race, and he hired Johnson to work for him. Johnson moved to Washington, D.C.

Johnson was known as an energetic, hard worker. He got to know most of the leading Democratic politicians in Washington, and he impressed them. He even came to the attention of **Presi-**

Lyndon Johnson at about age 5.

dent **Franklin D. Roosevelt**. Johnson was a young man with a bright political future.

MARRIAGE AND FAMILY: While home in Texas in the fall of 1934, Johnson met Claudia Alta Taylor, who had been called "Lady Bird" since she was a child. She was the daughter of a wealthy businessman and loved the arts and the outdoors. Johnson fell in love with her and proposed. She said yes, and they were married on November 17, 1934, in San Antonio, Texas.

Lady Bird was intelligent, charming, and helpful to her husband's political career. Over the years the Johnsons had two daughters, Lynda Bird and Luci Baines.

U.S. HOUSE OF REPRESENTATIVES: Johnson worked as an aide in Congress for several years. Then, is 1935, he became head of the Texas National Youth Administration. This organization helped young people get an education and find jobs. In 1937, he decided to run for office. That year, he won a seat in the U.S. **House of Representatives**.

Now an elected official, Johnson continued his rise in politics. He was a good friend of Sam Rayburn of Texas. Rayburn was the Speaker of the House and one of the most powerful men in politics.

He helped Johnson get positions on important committees. Johnson showed his ability to work hard and to find compromises between political foes.

Johnson served in the House for most of the next 10 years. When **World War II** began, Johnson left Washington to join the Navy. He served in the Pacific and won a Silver Star for bravery. When President Roosevelt recalled all Congressman serving in the war, Johnson returned to Washington.

U.S. SENATE: Johnson ran for the U.S. **Senate** in 1941, but didn't win. In 1948, he ran again. This time he won. He became part of the Armed Service Committee, where he supported the **Korean War** policies of **President Harry Truman.** Over the next several years, Johnson won reelection and became head of the Democrats in the Senate.

His title was Senate Majority Leader, and in that position he worked to pass legislation favored by his party. He was still known as a skilled politician who could work out tough compromises.

In 1960, Johnson thought he was ready to run for President. His competitor for the Democratic nomination was **John F. Kennedy.** Kennedy won the nomination from the party, and he chose Johnson to be his running mate. In the election Kennedy ran against **Richard Nixon**, a **Republican.** It was one of the closest elections in history, but Kennedy won. Johnson was now Vice President.

VICE PRESIDENT OF THE UNITED STATES: Johnson was a very active Vice President. He traveled around the country and the world representing the Kennedy administration. Johnson believed in the importance of the U.S. space program. Kennedy named him head of NASA, the National Aeronautics and Space Administration. Johnson also headed the President's Equal Employment Opportunity committee.

KENNEDY'S ASSASSINATION: On November 22, 1963, Kennedy and Johnson were traveling together in Dallas, Texas. While riding in an open car, Kennedy was assassinated by a sniper, or gunman. Johnson was the new President.

PRESIDENT OF THE UNITED STATES: Johnson became President at a time when the country was mourning the loss of Kennedy. In his first years, Johnson worked to pass laws in areas that were important to him and Kennedy. Some of the most important laws guaranteeing equal rights to blacks were passed at this time. He also lowered taxes.

In 1964, Johnson ran for election as President. He defeated his Republican opponent, Barry Goldwater, with 61% of the vote. It was one of the greatest landslides in history. Johnson received 486 **electoral votes**; Goldwater got 52.

"THE GREAT SOCIETY": In his first full term, Johnson announced his program for the nation. He called it the "Great Society." He wanted to create "a place where the meaning of man's life matches the marvels of man's labor." He wanted to guarantee health care to older Americans through a program called Medicare. He wanted to guarantee voting rights to blacks. He wanted to increase money to education for better schools. Johnson created "Head Start," the early education program for preschool children that still exists today. He declared a "war on poverty" to help poor people find jobs and housing. These were the goals of his Presidency.

President Lyndon B. Johnson.

Johnson's commitment to equal rights also showed in his choices of people for office. He appointed several blacks to key jobs in the government. And he made history in 1967 by appointing Thurgood Marshall as of the first black **Supreme Court** Justice.

Yet even with these positive goals, there were severe problems in the nation. In the late 1960s, race riots broke out in several large cities. In Los Angeles, Detroit, and other cities people were killed and property was destroyed. Johnson sent in federal troops to stop the rioting, but the problems continued.

THE VIETNAM WAR: The U.S. had gotten involved in a war in the Southeast Asian nation of Vietnam in the early 1960s. Vietnamese people in the North and South parts of their country were fighting against each other. While Kennedy was President, there were 16,000 U.S. troops in the country. The U.S. forces at that time were mainly observers.

First Lady, Lady Bird Johnson.

Johnson expanded U.S. involvement in Vietnam. The number of soldiers increased to 500,000. U.S. forces took an active, aggressive role. American planes bombed North Vietnam. In the U.S., many Americans disagreed with Johnson. They didn't want U.S. soldiers fighting and dying in a war in another nation. They wanted the U.S. out of Vietnam.

The lack of support for his policy upset Johnson. He decided to get out of politics. In a decision that surprised many, he chose not to run for reelection in 1968. Instead, he retired to his ranch in Texas.

LIFE AT THE WHITE HOUSE: Lady Bird Johnson was known as a gracious White House hostess. As First Lady, she took part in the Head Start program for children that Johnson had developed. She also created a plan to beautify Washington, D.C., and the country.

She took an active role in planting trees and flowers all over the nation's capital. She also worked to beautify the nation's highways.

The Johnsons also hosted a White House wedding. Their daughter Lynda Bird married Charles Robb on December 9, 1967, in the White House.

One of Johnson's favorite foods was pancakes. He ate them with Mrs. Johnson's homemade peach preserves. He also liked to host big Texas-style barbeques at the White House. As pets, the Johnson's had two beagles named Him and Her. They attended Johnson's inauguration.

RETIREMENT TO TEXAS: Lyndon and Lady Bird Johnson returned to their home in Johnson City, Texas, in 1969. There, Johnson wrote a book about his life in politics. He also planned the Lyndon Baines Johnson Library, where his Presidential papers are kept. Johnson died of a heart attack on January 22, 1973, at his home in Texas. He was 64.

Lady Bird Johnson lived on the Johnson ranch in Texas until her death on July 11, 2007. She was involved with beautification and conservation programs.

FAMOUS QUOTE: Johnson was a strong supporter of the space program. Just before he left office, in December 1968, he congratulated the Apollo 8 astronauts as they orbited the moon:

"You've taken all of us, all over the world, into a new era."

WHAT DID HE LOOK LIKE? Johnson was 6 feet 3 inches tall and weighed 200 pounds. He had gray hair and glasses.

FOR MORE INFORMATION ON LYNDON B. JOHNSON:

Historic Sites:

Lyndon B. Johnson National Historical Park
P.O. Box 329
Johnson City, TX 78636
Phone: 830-868-7128

Lyndon Baines Johnson Library and Museum
2313 Red River St.
Austin, Tex. 78705
Phone: 512-712-0200

Lyndon B. Johnson State Historical Park
P.O. Box 238
Stonewall, TX 78671
Phone: 830-644-2252

WORLD WIDE WEB ADDRESSES:

The White House offers young readers information on the U.S. government and the Presidents on a Web site called **"White House 101."** The address is:
http://www.whitehouse.gov/about/white_house_101/

The Internet Public Library has a site on the Presidents. The address is:
http://www.ipl.org/div/potus

American Memory is a site maintained by the Library of Congress that contains biographical and historical information on the Presidents. It also provides links to Presidential portraits. For Lyndon B. Johnson:
http://memory.loc.gov/learn/

Lyndon Baines Johnson Library and Museum
http://www.lbjlib.utexas.edu/

Lyndon Baines Johnson National Historic Park
http://www.nps.gov/lyjo

Richard M. Nixon
1913-1994
37th President of the United States (1969-1974)
"Tricky Dick"

RICHARD M. NIXON WAS BORN January 9, 1913, in Yorba Linda, California. His full name was Richard Milhous Nixon. His parents were Francis Anthony Nixon and Hannah Milhous Nixon. Francis was a farmer and store owner. Hannah was a homemaker who later helped out in the family store.

Richard was the second of five boys. His brothers were named Harold, Francis, Arthur, and Edward. Two of the Nixon boys died young. Arthur died at age seven of meningitis, and Harold died at 23 of tuberculosis.

RICHARD M. NIXON GREW UP in Yorba Linda. After the family lemon farm failed when he was nine, the family moved to Whittier, California. The Nixons were Quakers. The Quakers are a religious group that believes in a simple, peaceful way of life. Much of the Nixon family's social life centered on the church.

Young Richard Nixon didn't have a lot of hobbies, but he loved to read. By the time he was five, he was reading all the time. He also took piano lessons and played the instrument all his life.

In Whittier, Nixon's father ran a gas station and store. Richard, his mother, and brothers helped out any way they could. Money was always tight. He remembered later, "We had very little. I wore my brother's shoes and my brother below me wore mine. We never ate out — never. We certainly had to learn the value of money."

RICHARD M. NIXON WENT TO SCHOOL at the local public schools in Whittier. He did very well in school. In high school, he was an outstanding member of the debate team. Although he won most of his debates, his coach was upset with his attitude. "There was something mean in the way he argued his points," the coach remembered. "He cared too much about winning."

Nixon graduated from Whittier High School in 1930 and went on to Whittier College. Again, he did well in school and in debate. He was also elected president of his class in his senior year. After graduating in 1934, Nixon went to law school at Duke University in North Carolina, where he had won a scholarship. He graduated at the top of his class in 1937 and returned to California to practice law.

MARRIAGE AND FAMILY: Back in Whittier, Nixon worked for a law firm. He also joined a local theater group. At play practice, he met a teacher named Thelma Catherine Ryan, nicknamed Pat. He asked her immediately for a date. They were married on June 21, 1940. Throughout Nixon's career, Pat was a tireless, ambitious campaigner. The Nixons had two daughters, Patricia, called Tricia, and Julie.

WORLD WAR II: In 1941, the U.S. entered **World War II**. Nixon took a job in Washington, D.C., with the Office of Price Administration. Shortly after, he joined the Navy. He served until the war was over in 1945.

GETTING INVOLVED IN POLITICS: In 1946, Nixon decided to run for political office. Running as a **Republican,** he challenged a **Democrat** from California who had served in **Congress** for many terms.

In his first political race, Nixon used questionable methods to win. He suggested that his opponent, Jerry Voorhis, was a Communist. At that time, the U.S. and the Communist Soviet Union were the major world powers and were enemies. Most Americans were afraid of Communism and its spread. To label someone a Communist was to ruin him or her in politics. Later, Nixon said, "Of course I knew Jerry Voorhis wasn't a Communist, but I had to win."

U.S. HOUSE OF REPRESENTATIVES: Nixon defeated Voorhis and went to Washington to serve in the **House of Representatives**. He was reelected in 1948. In his second term, he became part of a powerful committee investigating possible spying by Americans.

U.S. SENATE: In 1950, Nixon decided to run for the U.S. **Senate**. His opponent was a California Congresswoman named Helen Douglas.

Richard Nixon, left, at age 14, with his brother Donald.

Once again, Nixon suggested his opponent was a Communist. He won by a huge margin. Douglas labeled Nixon "Tricky Dick" for his methods. The name stuck with him all of his life.

Nixon served only two years in the Senate. He had attracted the attention of the national Republican Party. They chose Nixon to run as Vice President with Presidential candidate **Dwight Eisenhower** in 1952. Eisenhower was a popular hero of World War II. Eisenhower and Nixon easily defeated Democratic opponent Adlai Stevenson.

VICE PRESIDENT OF THE UNITED STATES: Nixon served as Vice President for two terms, from 1952 to 1960. He traveled often in his new role, visiting 56 countries in all. He was a loyal Republican and a good speaker. In 1960, Nixon won the Party's nomination for the Presidency.

RUNNING FOR PRESIDENT IN 1960: Nixon faced the young, dynamic Democratic challenger **John F. Kennedy**. Nixon and Kennedy met in a series of debates broadcast on television. It was the first time Presidential debates had appeared on TV. Kennedy looked relaxed and prepared. Nixon looked nervous and seemed uneasy. When the vote was counted in November 1960, Kennedy had won by a very narrow margin.

Nixon returned to California to consider his future. In 1962, he decided to run for Governor of California. He lost the election to Edmund Brown by a large margin. An angry Nixon met with reporters, whom he had often blamed for his political problems. He told them they "wouldn't have Nixon to kick around anymore." He had decided to retire from politics.

RUNNING FOR PRESIDENT IN 1968: For the next several years, Nixon worked as a lawyer in California and New York. He remained a loyal Republican and stayed active in the Party. By 1968, he had decided to run again for President. His Vice Presidential running mate was Spiro Agnew, the former Governor of Maryland. Nixon beat his Democratic opponent, Hubert Humphrey, in a close race. Nixon got 301 **electoral votes**; Humphrey got 191.

PRESIDENT OF THE UNITED STATES: When Nixon took over as President, the nation was concerned about a number of problems. **The Vietnam War** was still raging, and many Americans wanted the

The Nixon family around 1972.
Left to right, Dwight Eisenhower II, Julie Nixon Eisenhower, President Richard
Nixon, Pat Nixon, Tricia Nixon Cox, and Edward Cox.

U.S. to get out of the war. Americans protested the war across the nation. Nixon began a program to reduce the number of American troops fighting in Vietnam. He also created the Environmental Protection Agency.

Nixon made an important trip to China in 1972. He was the first President to visit the country since it became Communist in 1949. He met with Chinese leaders and started talks on trade and other matters.

REELECTION: In 1972, Nixon won reelection in a landslide victory over Democrat George McGovern. Nixon received 520 electoral votes; McGovern got just 17. But during the course of the 1972 campaign, Nixon aides had been involved in "dirty tricks" to hurt the Democrats.

WATERGATE: Richard Nixon's name will always be tied to the word "**Watergate**." It was the scandal that ended his Presidency. During the 1972 campaign, five men were caught burglarizing the Democratic headquarters, located in the "Watergate" building complex in Washington.

When the burglars were tried for their crime, it came out that they were working for the reelection committee for Nixon.

The story reached the newspapers. Nixon denied having anything to do with the burglars or any illegal activity. But over the next two years, more information became known about the illegal operations of his reelection committee. Nixon believed he had many "enemies" in politics and in the press. He ordered his aides to gather information to ruin them. The aides broke the law. They recorded private phone calls of people Nixon thought were enemies. They stole documents Nixon could use to hurt them.

Nixon broke the law by "covering up" these activities. He used his powers as President to stop any investigation that could prove he was guilty of ordering illegal acts or covering up what had been done. He had even used the F.B.I. to assist in the coverup.

The Congress ordered a special investigation into the Watergate matter. The Congressional committee found out that Nixon taped all his White House conversations. By listening to those tapes, the Congressional committee could tell "what the President knew and when he knew it." Congress ordered Nixon to turn over the tapes.

But Nixon wouldn't release the tapes. The Congress went to court to force Nixon to release the recordings. The case went all the way to the **Supreme Court**. The Court ruled that Nixon had to give up the tapes. When the tapes were made public they showed clearly that Nixon had known about illegal activities in his reelection campaign and had authorized a coverup of those activities.

Up to this point, Nixon still had support in his party and among some Americans. But when it was obvious that he had lied to the American people, he lost their trust.

While Nixon was fighting his Watergate problems, Vice President Agnew was charged with not paying taxes while he was Governor of Maryland. Agnew resigned as Vice President in October 1973. Nixon appointed **Gerald Ford**, a Congressman from Michigan, to be his new Vice President. The Watergate scandal raged on.

The Congress began the process of **"impeachment"** against Nixon.

IMPEACHMENT: The U.S. **Constitution** states that if the U.S. House of Representatives thinks that a President has broken a law, it can accuse him of wrongdoing. That is called "impeachment." After a President is impeached, he is tried in the Senate for breaking the law. The Senate listens to the evidence, then votes to decide if the President should be removed from office.

Rather than face impeachment, Nixon chose to resign.

RESIGNATION: Richard Nixon resigned as President on August 8, 1974. He is the only President ever to resign. Gerald Ford became the next President. One month later, President Ford granted Nixon a pardon. That means that Nixon was never charged or tried for any of the offenses associated with Watergate. He always denied that he had done anything wrong, but he accepted the blame for how Watergate had affected the country.

First Lady Pat Nixon.

The American people were shocked at the revelations of Watergate. The scandal affected the way Americans felt about the President and politics for years. It has made Richard Nixon the most controversial President in our history.

LIFE AT THE WHITE HOUSE: Pat Nixon was a very active First Lady. She traveled around the world with her husband. She also was a very busy White House hostess. In three years, the Nixons had more than 110,000 guests at the White House. As a pet, the Nixons had an Irish setter named King Timahoe.

The Nixons hosted a White House wedding during their years there. On June 12, 1971, Tricia Nixon married Edward Cox at the White House.

RETIREMENT TO CALIFORNIA: After resigning, Nixon moved back to California. He spent the next several years out of the public eye. He worked on a number of books about his Presidency and his achievements. In his last years, he lived in New Jersey and continued writing and traveling. Richard Nixon died in New York City on April 22, 1994, after a stroke. Pat Nixon had died the year before, in 1993.

WHAT DID HE LOOK LIKE? Richard Nixon was 5 feet 11 inches tall and slim. He had a large nose and jaw.

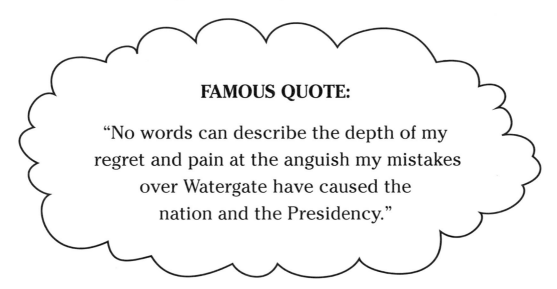

FAMOUS QUOTE:

"No words can describe the depth of my regret and pain at the anguish my mistakes over Watergate have caused the nation and the Presidency."

FOR MORE INFORMATION ON RICHARD M. NIXON:

Historic Sites:

Birth Site:
18001 Yorba Linda Blvd.
Yorba Linda, CA 92686
Phone: 714-993-5075

Richard Nixon Library
18001 Yorba Linda Blvd.
Yorba Linda, CA 92686
Phone: 714-993-5075

WORLD WIDE WEB ADDRESSES:

The White House offers young readers information on the U.S. government and the Presidents on a Web site called **"White House 101."** The address is:

http://www.whitehouse.gov/about/white_house_101/

The Internet Public Library has a site on the Presidents. The address is:

http://www.ipl.org/div/potus

American Memory is a site maintained by the Library of Congress that contains biographical and historical information on the Presidents. It also provides links to Presidential portraits.
For Richard M. Nixon:

http://memory.loc.gov/learn/

Richard Nixon Library and Birthplace

http://www.nixonlibraryfoundation.org/

Gerald R. Ford
1913-2006
38th President of the United States (1974-1977)

GERALD R. FORD WAS BORN July 14, 1913, in Omaha, Nebraska. His name when he was born was Leslie Lynch King, Jr. His father was Leslie Lynch King and his mother was Dorothy Gardner King. His parents were divorced when he was two years old. He and his mother moved to Grand Rapids, Michigan. There, his mother met and married a man named Gerald Rudolph Ford. Ford adopted young Leslie and changed his name to Gerald Rudolph Ford, Jr. Young Gerald's nickname was Jerry.

Gerald Ford at about age 10.

Jerry Ford had three half-brothers from his mother's second marriage. Their names were Thomas, Richard, and James. His father also remarried and had children. These three half-siblings were named Marjorie, Leslie, and Patricia.

GERALD R. FORD GREW UP in Grand Rapids. He was a large, strong boy and he loved sports. He was especially good at football.

GERALD R. FORD WENT TO SCHOOL at the local public schools in Grand Rapids. He did very well in school. At Grand Rapids South High School, Ford played on the football team. He graduated in 1931.

In 1931, Ford went on to college at the University of Michigan. He studied economics and political science. Ford also played center on the Michigan football team. He played on two national championship teams. In 1934, he was named Most Valuable Player. Ford graduated from Michigan with honors in 1935.

Ford went on to Yale University to study law. To make extra money, he worked as an assistant football coach. After graduating from law school in 1941, Ford returned to Grand Rapids to practice law.

WORLD WAR II: When the U.S. entered **World War II** in 1941, Ford joined the Navy. He spent three years in the Pacific aboard the USS *Monterey.* Ford earned ten medals for bravery during the war. He was discharged in 1946 and returned to Grand Rapids.

GETTING INVOLVED IN POLITICS: Ford returned to Michigan and began to practice law again. He also got involved in local **Republican** politics. By 1948, he was ready to run for office. He ran for a seat in the U.S. Congress and won.

MARRIAGE AND FAMILY: Ford had met Elizabeth Bloomer when he returned from the war. She was a former dancer and model who was living in Grand Rapids. She had recently been divorced and was working in a department store. She and Ford started dating, and soon fell in love. They were married on October 15, 1948, while Ford campaigned in his first Congressional race. According to reports, Ford was so nervous that he wore one brown shoe and one black shoe to the wedding. The Fords had four children, three boys and one girl. Their names are Michael, Jack, Steven, and Susan.

U.S. HOUSE OF REPRESENTATIVES: Ford went to Washington in 1948 to serve in the **House of Representatives**. He spent the next 25 years there. He was reelected 12 times, and over the years gained a reputation as a man of honesty and integrity.

In 1963, Ford became chairman of the House Republican Conference. He gained national attention in that position. In 1965, he became the leader of the House Republicans. A conservative, loyal Republican, he supported Republican Presidents **Dwight D. Eisenhower** and **Richard Nixon.** He also rallied his fellow

Republicans in the House to vote for conservative Republican measures.

WATERGATE: In 1973, the Presidency of **Richard Nixon** was threatened with two big scandals. One was the **Watergate** scandal. Nixon was accused of covering up illegal activities that took place during his reelection campaign of 1972. [Please read the Nixon entry for more information.]

The other scandal focused on Vice President Spiro Agnew. Agnew was charged with not paying taxes. He was forced to resign as Vice President in October 1973. Nixon appointed Ford to be the new Vice President.

VICE PRESIDENT OF THE UNITED STATES: Ford took over as Vice President when many Americans had lost respect for the President. A loyal Republican, Ford spoke all over the country trying to win support for Nixon.

In July 1974, a House committee voted to recommend that Nixon be "impeached." The U.S. Constitution states that if the U.S. House of Representatives thinks that a President has broken a law, they can accuse him of the crime. That is called **"impeachment."**

Rather than face impeachment, Nixon resigned on August 8, 1974. Gerald Ford became President. He was the first man to serve as both Vice President and President without being elected to either position.

PRESIDENT OF THE UNITED STATES: Gerald Ford took office at a difficult time in our nation's history. Watergate had deeply affected the way the American people felt about government. Ford was a

The Ford family in The White House, 1974. Left to right, Jack, Steve, Mrs. Ford, President Ford, Susan, daughter-in-law Gayle, and Mike.

man of honesty and integrity. He tried to regain the nation's confidence in the Presidency.

Within one month of taking office, Ford made a controversial decision. He granted Nixon a full pardon. That meant that Nixon would not be accused or tried for anything he had done involving Watergate. Many Americans were outraged at the decision. They wanted Nixon to stand trial for what he had done. Ford explained that he wanted to help the nation to get over the scandal and focus on the future.

Ford appointed Nelson Rockefeller to be his new Vice President. They faced a country going through difficult economic times. There was high inflation—a period when prices for most goods are rising all the time. There was also high unemployment, and many Americans couldn't find jobs. As President, Ford worked for legislation that would help the economy. He vetoed many bills he thought would only add to the nation's economic problems.

Ford also dealt with problems outside the U.S. In 1975, the last American troops left Vietnam. Around the same time, Cambodians seized a U.S. boat called *Mayaguez* with its crew. Under Ford's order, U.S. Marines freed the ship and crew. Ford also met with the leader of the Soviet Union, Leonid Brezhnev, to discuss limiting nuclear weapons.

ELECTION OF 1976: In 1976 Ford ran for President. Because he had been appointed President, not elected, it was his first race for the Presidency. He won the Republican Party's nomination, and faced Democrat Jimmy Carter. After a long, hard campaign, Carter defeated Ford in a close race. Carter won the popular vote by 1.7 million votes. He gained 297 electoral votes to Ford's 240. Most observers believe that it was the pardon of Nixon that cost Ford the election. Yet throughout the rest of his life, he maintained he had done the right thing for the nation.

LIFE AT THE WHITE HOUSE: As a former dancer with the famous Martha Graham company, Betty Ford welcomed arts groups to the White House.

Betty Ford was admired for her remarkable openness about her own personal problems. She had to have surgery for breast cancer in 1974. She told the American people about her illness. She urged women to get the medical and emotional help they needed to fight breast cancer. She said, "Maybe if I as First Lady could talk about it candidly and without embarrassment, many other people would be able to as well."

The Fords were a close, loving family. As a pet, they had a golden retriever named Liberty who gave birth to puppies in the White House.

RETIREMENT: The Fords retired to California in 1977. Gerald Ford remained an advisor to Presidents and served on boards of several companies. After leaving the White House, Betty Ford admitted

First Lady Betty Ford.

that she was addicted to drugs and alcohol. She got help for her addictions and is now doing fine. By admitting her problems, she helped many Americans to confront their own. She also helped to start the Betty Ford treatment center for people with addictions.

DEATH: Gerald R. Ford died at his home in Palm Desert, California on December 26, 2006. He was 93 years old. At the time of his death, he was the oldest living former President.

Ford's coffin was displayed for public viewing in California, Washington, D.C., and Grand Rapids, Michigan. Tens of thousands of people paid their personal respects to the 38th President. His state funeral at the National Cathedral in Washington was watched by millions on television.

At his funeral and in published tributes, Ford was remembered as a man of honor, integrity, and humility. Many Americans, reflecting on his legacy, now consider his pardon of Nixon to have been in the nation's best interest, because it spared the country months of political and legal turmoil. For many, it reflected the quiet courage and decency of a humble man.

WHAT DID HE LOOK LIKE? Gerald Ford was 6 feet tall, with a slim, athletic build. When he was a young man, he had worked as a model. He was still an active athlete while in the White House. He enjoyed swimming and golfing especially.

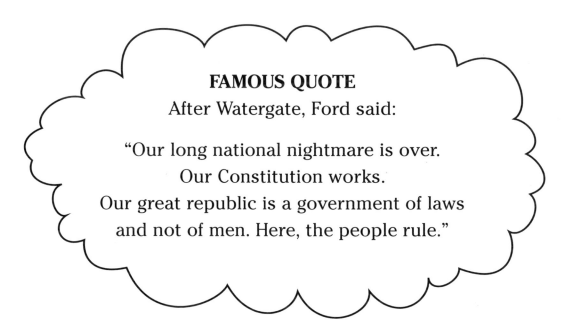

FAMOUS QUOTE
After Watergate, Ford said:

"Our long national nightmare is over.
Our Constitution works.
Our great republic is a government of laws
and not of men. Here, the people rule."

FOR MORE INFORMATION ON GERALD R. FORD

Historic Sites:

Birth Site:
Birth Site Park
3202 Woolworth Ave.
Omaha, NE 68105
Phone: 402-444-5900

Gerald R. Ford Library
University of Michigan
1000 Beal Ave.
Ann Arbor, MI 48109
Phone: 734-205-0555

Gerald R. Ford Museum
303 Pearl St., N.W.
Grand Rapids, MI 49504
Phone: 616-254-0400

WORLD WIDE WEB SITES:

The White House offers young readers information on the U.S. government and the Presidents on a Web site called **"White House 101."** The address is:
http://www.whitehouse.gov/about/white_house_101/

The Internet Public Library has a site on the Presidents. The address is:
http://www.ipl.org/div/potus

Gerald R. Ford Presidential Library and Museum:
http://www.ford.utexas.edu

Jimmy Carter
1924-
39th President of the United States (1977-1981)

JIMMY CARTER WAS BORN October 1, 1924, in Plains, Georgia. His full name is James Earl Carter, Jr., but he has always been called Jimmy. His parents were James Earl Carter, Sr., and Lillian Gordy Carter. James, Sr., was a farmer and businessman. Lillian was a nurse and homemaker.

Jimmy was the oldest of four children. He had two sisters, Ruth and Gloria, and a brother, William, called Billy. The family was very close, and spent a good deal of time at their Baptist church.

JIMMY CARTER GREW UP in Archery, near Plains. He often helped out on the family peanut farm. He sold peanuts for extra money. He remembered it well. "The early years of my life on the farm were full and enjoyable. We always had enough to eat, but no money to waste."

JIMMY CARTER WENT TO SCHOOL at the local public schools in Plains. He loved to read and was an excellent student. Even though he was small, he played sports. He liked basketball especially. Carter graduated from Plains High School in 1941. He went on to one year of college at Georgia Southwestern College. He then took math courses at Georgia Institute of Technology.

In 1942, he realized a life-long dream when he was accepted at the Naval Academy. He studied science and graduated in 1946. He got married soon after graduation.

MARRIAGE AND FAMILY: Jimmy Carter fell in love with Rosalynn Smith, a friend of his sister Ruth, when they first met. After their first date in 1945, he told his mother, "she's the girl I want to marry." They married on July 7, 1946, in Plains. The Carters had four

Jimmy Carter at about age 10, with his pet dog.

children, three boys and a girl. Their sons are named John (called Jack), James Earl 3rd (called Chip), and Donnel Jeffrey (called Jeff). Their daughter's name is Amy.

JOINING THE NAVY: Graduates of the Naval Academy go directly from school into the Navy, and that's what Carter did. From 1946 to 1953, he worked as a naval officer all over the world. He worked on some of the earliest nuclear submarines. Carter had planned a Navy career, but when his father died in 1953, he went home to Plains to take over the farm.

LIFE AS A FARMER: In 1953, Carter began his career as a farmer and businessman. He grew peanuts and also developed other farm products. Rosalynn worked closely with him. She was in charge of keeping the records of the company. Within a few years, the farm was making a comfortable income.

GETTING INVOLVED IN POLITICS: Carter began to get more involved in local politics. He served on the local school board. He was part of the state planning commission, a group that helps areas develop land and businesses.

In 1962, Carter decided to run for office. He ran as a **Democrat** for a seat in the Georgia State **Senate**. He won, and was reelected two years later. In 1966, he decided to run for Governor. He didn't win, but he made up his mind to try again. He ran again in 1970, and this time he won.

GOVERNOR OF GEORGIA: As Governor of Georgia, Carter made some important changes. The South denied blacks equal rights for years. Carter wanted an end to racial discrimination. He hired

The Carter family in 1977.

many blacks for state jobs. He also helped improve the environment and to make the state government more efficient.

In 1975, Carter decided he wanted to run for President. It was a difficult time in the nation. In 1974, **President Richard Nixon** had been forced to resign because of the **Watergate** scandal. Many Americans distrusted politicians with links to Nixon and Washington, D.C. Carter had never held a political job in Washington. He was an "outsider." He was at first an unknown candidate for President. But people began to recognize the "outsider" from Georgia. He won the Democratic nomination in 1976.

Carter beat **President Gerald Ford** in a narrow race. He won with just over 50% of the vote, getting 297 **electoral votes** to Ford's 240.

PRESIDENT OF THE UNITED STATES: Carter took over as President when the nation was facing tough economic times. There was high inflation—a period when prices for most goods were rising. There was also high unemployment, and many Americans couldn't find jobs. Carter was also concerned because Americans were very dependent on foreign oil to run cars and heat their homes. He tried to introduce legislation to limit oil imports and conserve energy.

Carter had never worked in the federal government. He didn't know how to work with the **Congress**. His assistants, too, didn't know the ways of Washington. Many of the changes Carter wanted to make didn't take place. His relationship with Congress, even with members of his own party, remained difficult.

Carter handled many problems involving foreign countries as President. In 1979, he helped work out a peace agreement between Israel and Egypt. The two nations had been at war for years, and Carter helped make peace. He also strengthened political ties with China.

Carter was a firm believer in human rights. He stressed to the leaders of other nations that the U.S. believed in democracy and personal freedom for all peoples. This stand was very

First Lady Rosalynn Carter.

unpopular with the leaders of the Soviet Union. Still, Carter was able to work out an agreement with the Soviets to limit weapons. That agreement fell apart, however, when the Soviets invaded Afghanistan in 1979.

Carter faced his worst crisis with Iran. In November 1979, militants took over the U.S. Embassy in Tehran, the capital of Iran. They took all 52 Americans in the Embassy hostage. They threatened to kill them. For months, the Iranians kept the American hostages locked up. Carter worked hard to try to get the hostages freed. The negotiations were still going on while Carter was running for reelection.

RUNNING FOR REELECTION: When Carter ran for reelection in 1980, he wasn't a very popular President. Some Americans thought he was not an effective leader. He ran against Republican **Ronald Reagan**. Reagan won in a landslide, with 489 electoral votes to Carter's 49.

The long, painful hostage crisis in Iran ended the day Carter left office. That day, in January 1981, all the hostages were released.

LIFE AT THE WHITE HOUSE: When Carter became President, he did away some of the pomp and ceremony of the Presidency. He sold the Presidential yacht. He had fewer White House dinners, and when he did he made sure they ended early. He wanted to take a simpler, less complicated approach to life as President.

Rosalynn Carter took a very active role in her husband's Presidency. She attended Cabinet meetings. She was also Carter's official representative to Latin America. Her special areas of interest as First Lady included care for the mentally ill and elderly. She also brought a number of outstanding artists to the White House to perform.

RETURN TO GEORGIA: Jimmy and Rosalynn Carter returned to Plains, Georgia, in 1981, where they still live. Carter is a very active ex-President. He is the director of the Carter Center, an organization devoted to human rights and world peace. He is also a volunteer for Habitat for Humanity. That is a group that builds homes for the poor in the U.S. and around the world. Carter has also traveled to Haiti and North Korea to help those countries work toward peace. He has written a number of books about his life and work.

WHAT DOES HE LOOK LIKE? Carter is 5 feet 9 inches tall and slim. He has gray hair and blue eyes. He still enjoys athletics, especially jogging and tennis.

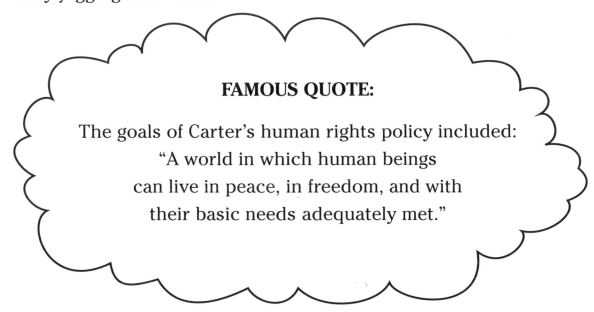

FAMOUS QUOTE:

The goals of Carter's human rights policy included:
"A world in which human beings
can live in peace, in freedom, and with
their basic needs adequately met."

FOR MORE INFORMATION ON JIMMY CARTER:

Historic Sites:

Jimmy Carter Library and Museum
441 Freedom Parkway
Atlanta, GA 30307
Phone: 404-865-7100

Jimmy Carter National Historic Site
300 North Bond Street
Plains, GA 31780
Phone: 229-824-4104

WORLD WIDE WEB ADDRESSES:

The White House offers young readers information on the U.S. government and the Presidents on a Web site called **"White House 101."** The address is:
http://www.whitehouse.gov/about/white_house_101/

The Internet Public Library has a site on the Presidents. The address is:
http://www.ipl.org/div/potus

American Memory is a site maintained by the Library of Congress that contains biographical and historical information on the Presidents. It also provides links to Presidential portraits.
For Jimmy Carter:
http://memory.loc.gov/learn/

Jimmy Carter National Historic Site
http:www.nps.gov/jica/

The Carter Center
http://www.cartercenter.org/

Jimmy Carter Presidential Library
http://www.jimmycarterlibrary.org/

Ronald Reagan
1911-2004
40th President of the United States (1981-1989)
"The Great Communicator"

RONALD REAGAN WAS BORN February 6, 1911, in Tampico, Illinois. His full name was Ronald Wilson Reagan. His parents were John Edward Reagan and Nelle Wilson Reagan. John was a shoe salesman and Nelle was a homemaker. Ronald was the youngest of two boys in the family. He had an older brother, Neil.

RONALD REAGAN GREW UP in many different small towns in Illinois. His father moved often to find work. Reagan, whose nickname was "Dutch," remembered that his family didn't have much money. "We were poor, but we didn't know we were poor," he said.

Young Reagan loved life in the countryside. He compared it to Mark Twain's stories. "My existence turned into one of those rare Huck Finn-Tom Sawyer idylls," he said. He loved to fish and swim. He also loved playing football with the neighborhood kids. "There was no field, no lines, no goal," he remembered. "Simply grass, the ball, and a mob of excited youngsters. These were the happiest times of my life."

RONALD REAGAN WENT TO SCHOOL at the public schools in several small towns in Illinois. When he was nine, the family settled in Dixon, Illinois. He went to grade school and high school there. Although he was never a great student, Reagan was a good athlete. In high school he played football, swam, and ran track. He was also in the drama club and served as class president. Reagan graduated from high school in 1928.

Reagan went on to college at Eureka College in Eureka, Illinois. He studied economics and competed in football and swimming. He worked his way through college washing dishes, finding time to act in plays and serve as class president. Reagan graduated from Eureka in 1932.

FIRST JOBS: After college, Reagan worked as a radio announcer. He broadcast sports for a station in Iowa and was very successful. In 1937, he went to California with the Chicago Cubs for spring training. While he was there, he decided to try out for an acting job with a big movie studio. Warner Brothers gave him a contract. He started a movie career that lasted until the 1950s and included 53 films.

A FAMOUS HOLLYWOOD ACTOR: Reagan was a popular star. He played a variety of characters over the years, from cowboys to college students. Two of his most famous movies were *King's Row* and *Knute Rockne—All American.* In *Knute Rockne* he played a Notre Dame football player named George Gip. The character dies in the movie, asking the coach to "win one for the Gipper." "The Gipper" became one of Reagan's nicknames. Reagan also starred in several movies with a chimp named Bonzo.

Reagan at age 18, playing football for Eureka College.

When the U.S. entered **World War II** in 1941, Reagan joined the Army. His eyesight was poor, so he couldn't be in combat. Instead, he made war training films for the Army.

After the war, Reagan became president of the Screen Actors Guild, a union for actors. He had always been a **Democrat,** but after the war he became more conservative. He became concerned with the spread of Communism. He joined the **Republican Party** in 1962.

MARRIAGE AND FAMILY: Reagan was married twice. In 1940, he married a Hollywood actress named Jane Wyman. They had one daughter, Maureen. They also adopted a son, Michael. Reagan and Wyman divorced in 1948. Reagan married actress Nancy Davis in 1952. They had two children, Patricia and Ronald.

GETTING INVOLVED IN POLITICS: In the 1960s Reagan got involved in television. He was the host of two popular shows, "General Electric Theater" and "Death Valley Days." After several years, he began to tour the country and give speeches. In his speeches he would talk about his conservative Republican views.

Reagan became a well-known Republican spokesman. In 1964, Barry Goldwater was running for President for the Republicans. Reagan gave a powerful speech at the convention that year. A group of California conservatives who heard Reagan asked him to run for Governor. He accepted.

GOVERNOR OF CALIFORNIA: In 1966, Reagan ran for Governor of California. His opponent was the current Governor, Edmund Brown. Reagan beat him in a landslide. He was also reelected in 1970.

Reagan's main ambition was to be President. In 1968, he challenged **Richard Nixon** for the Republican nomination for President. He didn't win, but he wasn't discouraged. He tried again in 1976 and almost beat **President Gerald Ford** for the nomination. Finally, in 1980, Reagan won the Republican nomination. With his running mate, **George Bush**, he won the election, beating **President Jimmy Carter**. Reagan received 489 electoral votes; Carter got 49. At 69, Reagan was the oldest man ever elected President.

PRESIDENT OF THE UNITED STATES As President, Reagan promised to cut back the size of government. He wanted to cut

Reagan riding his horse El Alamein, 1986.

government spending for social programs and increase military spending. His political views were called the "Reagan Revolution." They represented a major shift in government.

Many of Reagan's policies were controversial. Some people disagreed with Reagan strongly; some supported him just as vigorously. His defense spending program led to the greatest deficit—the amount of U.S. government debt—in history. Despite this, Reagan was a very popular President. He was known as the "Great Communicator." Some people thought it was his years in movies and television that made Reagan able to reach the American people. Whatever it was, he was a very popular President.

Reagan also made some very popular appointments. In 1981, he appointed the first woman, Sandra Day O'Connor, to the Supreme Court.

Terrorism targeted at Americans was a threat during Reagan's term. In 1983, a terrorist bomb killed 241 Marines stationed in Lebanon. Reagan learned that Libya was behind much of the terrorist activity. So in 1986, he ordered U.S. planes to bomb sites in Libya.

Reagan faced personal injury and health problems during his Presidency. Just a few months into his first term, Reagan was shot by John Hinckley, Jr. He was seriously wounded, but he survived. Several years later, he had to have surgery for cancer. Once again, he survived. He faced these challenges with optimism, and his personal popularity continued.

REELECTION: In 1984, Reagan ran for reelection and won a landslide victory over Democratic challenger Walter Mondale. The electoral count was 525 votes for Reagan and just 13 for Mondale.

During his term, Reagan cut taxes and spending for programs within the U.S. As an opponent of Communism, Reagan called the Soviet Union "the evil empire." He wanted spending for military purposes increased to fight the threat of Communism.

After several years in office, he had a series of meetings with the Soviet leader, Mikhail Gorbachev (GORE-bah-choff). Despite his belief in the evils of Communism, Reagan developed a warm relationship with Gorbachev. During their meetings, they worked out agreements to destroy some nuclear weapons and limit the building of others.

Reagan also opposed Communist governments in Central America. Countries like Nicaragua were run by Communists. They were opposed by anti-Communists in Nicaragua called "contras." Reagan wanted the U.S. to support the contras. Congress refused to fund that support. In 1986 it came out that Reagan aides had secretly sold arms to Iran, a U.S. enemy. They were trying to buy the freedom of U.S. hostages held in the Middle East. The aides also used the money from the arms sale to fund the contras. This led to a Congressional investigation that resulted in some aides being charged with wrongdoing. Reagan was never charged, but the "Iran-Contra Affair" was embarrassing to his administration.

In 1988, Reagan stepped down from the Presidency. He campaigned vigorously for his Vice President, **George Bush**, who ran for President.

LIFE AT THE WHITE HOUSE: The Reagans brought back some of the pomp and ceremony that President Carter had done away with. They gave many lavish dinner parties and enjoyed entertaining in the White House.

First Lady Nancy Reagan.

As First Lady, Nancy Reagan focused on drug abuse among teenagers. She started a campaign against drugs called "Just Say No." She was also a spokesperson for the Foster Grandparents organization. Mrs. Reagan also brought many arts groups to the White House to perform.

One of Reagan's favorite foods was jelly beans. He had jars full of them all over the White House. At his inauguration, his well-wishers ate over 40 million jelly beans.

RETIREMENT TO CALIFORNIA: Reagan retired to California in 1989. At 77, he was the oldest man to retire from the Presidency. He and Mrs. Reagan lived on their ranch in Santa Barbara, where he enjoyed hobbies like horseback riding. For several years they spent time traveling.

Reagan announced in 1994 that he had Alzheimer's disease. That disease slowly takes away the brain's ability to function properly. Reagan continued to live on his ranch, but didn't make public appearances.

DEATH: Ronald Reagan died on June 5, 2004, at the age of 93. There was an immediate outpouring of grief from the nation, and Reagan was given a full state funeral, attended by political leaders from around the world. Thousands of Americans paid their respects to the former President, and he was buried at his presidential library in Simi Valley, California.

Ronald Reagan has come to be remembered best for his confidence, hopefulness, and optimism. He helped the nation regain its sense of optimism, too, and reassured the people that the nation was still proud and strong. He remains one of the most popular of recent Presidents.

WHAT DID HE LOOK LIKE? Reagan was 6 feet tall and slim. He had reddish hair and blue eyes. By the time he was President, he wore hearing aids.

FAMOUS QUOTE

"It is not my intention to do away with government.
it is rather to make it work—
work with us, not over us;
stand by our side, not ride on our back."

FOR MORE INFORMATION ON RONALD REAGAN:

Historic Sites:

Birth Site:
119 South Main St.
Tampico, IL 61283
Phone: 815-438-2130

Childhood Home:
816 S. Hennepin Ave.
Dixon, IL 61021
Phone: 815-288-5176

Ronald Reagan Presidential Library and Museum
40 Presidential Dr.
Simi Valley, CA 93065
Phone: 800-410-8354

WORLD WIDE WEB ADDRESSES:

The White House offers young readers information on the U.S. government and the Presidents on a Web site called **"White House 101."** The address is:
http://www.whitehouse.gov/about/white_house_101/

The Internet Public Library has a site on the Presidents. The address is:
http://www.ipl.org/div/potus

American Memory is a site maintained by the Library of Congress that contains biographical and historical information on the Presidents. It also provides Presidential portraits.
For Ronald Reagan:
http://memory.loc.gov/learn/

Ronald Reagan Presidential Library:
http://www.reagan.utexas.edu/

George H.W. Bush
1924-
41st President of the United States (1989-1993)

GEORGE BUSH WAS BORN June 12, 1924, in Milton, Massachusetts. His full name is George Herbert Walker Bush. His parents were Prescott Sheldon Bush and Dorothy Walker Bush. Prescott was a banker who also served as a U.S. Senator. Dorothy was a homemaker.

George was the second of five children. He had a sister, Nancy, and three brothers, Prescott Jr., Jonathan, and William. The family was very close. George was especially close to his brother Prescott.

GEORGE BUSH GREW UP in Greenwich, Connecticut, a city close to New York City. The Bush family was wealthy and the children were raised in a large, comfortable home. They also had a home in Maine where the family spent vacations. There, George loved to sail and fish. He was very close to his grandfather, who was called "Pop." He was so close to Pop, that his own nickname, "Poppy," comes from his grandfather's.

Prescott and Dorothy Bush expected their children to achieve, but also to serve their community. They raised their children to be honest and modest. George was modest and generous as a child. In fact, he was so eager to share that he was called "Have Half."

GEORGE BUSH WENT TO SCHOOL at private schools. He went to elementary school at Greenwich Country Day School. For high school, he went to a famous prep school in Massachusetts called Phillips Andover. He was always a good student and a fine athlete. He played baseball, soccer, and basketball. He was also the president of his senior class.

WORLD WAR II: Just as Bush was graduating from high school, **World War II** was beginning. He put off college and enlisted in the Navy on his 18th birthday. He trained to be a pilot, and in 1943 became the Navy's youngest pilot. He was sent to the Pacific, where he flew 58 combat missions. In 1944, he was shot down by the Japanese. His two crew members were killed, but Bush survived and was rescued by a submarine. He earned the Distinguished Flying Cross for bravery in the war.

MARRIAGE AND FAMILY: Before he had left for the war, Bush had met Barbara Pierce, and they had fallen in love. When he returned to the U.S. after the war, he and "Bar," as he calls her, were married

First Lady Barbara Bush.

on January 6, 1945. They had six children, George, Robin, John (known as Jeb), Neil, Marvin, and Dorothy. Robin died of cancer when she was three years old. Two of the Bush children are now in politics. **George W. Bush** was elected President in 2000. Jeb is Governor of Florida.

Barbara Bush has always been an active supporter of her husband's career. His different jobs in government have required the family to move 29 times. They started their married life while Bush began college.

COLLEGE: Returning to the U.S. after the war, Bush entered Yale University. He studied economics and played on the baseball team. One of his most memorable moments came in 1948, when he met Babe Ruth. The great baseball player was donating his papers to Yale, and Bush received them as team captain. Bush graduated with honors from Yale in 1948.

MAKING A LIVING AS AN OILMAN: After graduating from college, Bush could have worked in banking with his father. He chose instead to try to make a living on his own as an oil man. He moved his family to Texas, where he sold equipment for getting oil out of the ground. Later, he started an oil company, which he sold when he got into politics.

GETTING INVOLVED IN POLITICS: Bush became involved in **Republican** politics in Texas in the 1960s. In 1964, he ran for the U.S. **Senate**, but didn't win. Two years later, he ran for a seat in the U.S. **House of Representatives**. He won that time, and was reelected in 1968. In 1970, Bush ran again for the Senate. He lost again, but stayed in politics.

REPUBLICAN APPOINTMENTS: In 1971, **President Richard Nixon** appointed Bush as U.S. representative to the United Nations. Bush served in the United Nations for two years.

In 1973, Nixon asked Bush to become head of the Republican National Committee. These were the years of the **Watergate** scandal. (Please read the entry on President Nixon for more information). They were very difficult years for the Republicans. As he always had, Bush served the party and his President loyally. But as the scandal developed, it became evident that Nixon had lied to his party and the nation. Bush wrote a letter to Nixon in August 1974 asking him to resign. Nixon resigned several days later.

President Gerald Ford took over when Nixon left office. He appointed Bush head of the U.S. office in China to develop political relations. Bush served in that job for just over a year. Then, in 1975, Ford asked Bush to return to the U.S. to become director of the Central Intelligence Agency (C.I.A.). Bush served as C.I.A. director until **President Jimmy Carter** was elected in 1976. He returned to Texas and private life for three years.

In 1979, Bush decided to run for President. He spent a year trying to get support from Republicans around the country. He needed to get the Republican nomination for President, but **Ronald Reagan** also wanted to be the Republican candidate. Reagan proved to be more popular, and he won the nomination. Reagan then asked Bush to run as his Vice President. Bush accepted. Together, Reagan and Bush beat Democrat **Jimmy Carter**.

VICE PRESIDENT OF THE UNITED STATES: Bush was an active and involved Vice President. He visited more than 60 countries and sat in on Reagan's daily meetings. Twice when Reagan was President, Bush had to step in and take over briefly. In March 1981, Reagan was shot. While he recovered, Bush handled matters. In July 1985, Reagan had surgery for cancer. Once again, Bush handled the powers of the Presidency while Reagan recovered.

The team of Reagan and Bush won reelection easily in 1984. In 1988, Reagan retired after serving two terms. Bush ran for and got the Republican nomination for President. Bush beat the **Democratic** contender Michael Dukakis. He received 426 **electoral votes**; Dukakis got 111. Bush was the first Vice President to be directly elected President since Martin Van Buren won the office in 1836.

PRESIDENT OF THE UNITED STATES: When George Bush became President, the country was going through tough economic times. Reagan's defense spending program led to the greatest deficit — the amount of U.S. government debt — in history. Yet Bush had made a campaign promise not to raise taxes. During the race he said, "Read my lips. No new taxes." But he was unable to keep that pledge. Within months of taking office, he raised taxes to help pay off the growing debt. This was one of the most unpopular decisions of his Presidency.

THE END OF THE COLD WAR: Bush was President at a time of great change in the world. He was President at the end of the "**Cold War**," the hostilities between the U.S. and the Soviets. After

The Bush family in 1992.

World War II, the Soviet Union and the U.S. became the two strongest nations in the world. They represented two very different political systems. The U.S. was a democracy; the Soviet Union was a Communist state. For more than 40 years, the hostilities between these two powers determined world politics. During Bush's term, the Soviet Union abandoned Communism and broke up into many independent states. The former Communist nations of Eastern Europe became democracies. Now, a "new world order," as Bush called it, was at hand.

THE GULF WAR: The high point of Bush's Presidency occurred in 1990. In August 1990, Iraq, led by Saddam Hussein (sah-DAHM hu-SAIN), invaded Kuwait. Kuwait is a small, oil-rich country on the Persian Gulf in the Middle East. Bush called the invasion an act of aggression. He demanded that Iraq withdraw its forces from Kuwait. Iraq refused.

Barbara Bush reads Corduroy *to young visitors.*

Bush put together a coalition of troops from the U.S. and other countries from the United Nations. Together, they challenged Hussein. The allied forces, called "Desert Storm," attacked the Iraqis on land and in bombing raids. The **Gulf War** lasted only 100 hours. The Iraqis were beaten and withdrew from Kuwait. Bush's actions were hailed throughout the world. His popularity soared.

RUNNING FOR REELECTION: At the end of Bush's term in 1992, the country faced rising unemployment and an economy that wasn't growing. When he ran for reelection, the voters were focused on the country's financial problems. In addition to Democratic challenger **Bill Clinton,** Bush faced independent candidate Ross Perot in the election. Perot was a businessman without political experience who focused on the economy and the dangers of the deficit.

In the 1992 election, Bush lost to Bill Clinton. Clinton got 370 electoral votes; Bush received 168.

LIFE AT THE WHITE HOUSE: Barbara Bush was one of the most popular First Ladies of the modern era. She said it was because people knew "I'm fair and I like children and I adore my husband." As First Lady, she devoted much of her time to fighting illiteracy in the country. She also encouraged Americans to volunteer, as she did, to help the homeless, AIDS patients, and older people.

The Bush family had a rather famous dog named Millie. Millie, a springer spaniel, had puppies while the Bushes were in the White House. Barbara Bush wrote a book as "Millie," called *Millie's Book*. All the money made from the book went to help fight illiteracy.

George Bush always loved athletics, and he continued to play golf and tennis as President. He also had a horseshoe pit dug on the White House grounds.

FAMOUS QUOTE:

"We cannot hope only to leave our children a bigger car, a bigger bank account. We must hope to give them a sense of what it means to be a loyal friend, a loving parent, a citizen who leaves his home, his neighborhood, and town better than he found it."

RETIREMENT TO TEXAS: After losing the 1992 election, George and Barbara Bush moved back to Texas. They built a home in Houston. They now divide their time between their homes in Texas and Maine. Since leaving politics, Bush has written a book, acted as an advisor to **President Clinton**, and set up his Presidential library.

WHAT DOES HE LOOK LIKE? Bush is 6 feet 2 inches tall and slim. He has brown hair and blue eyes.

FOR MORE INFORMATION ON GEORGE BUSH:

Historic Site:

George Bush Presidential Library and Museum
1000 George Bush Drive West
College Station, TX 77844
Phone: 979-691-4000

WORLD WIDE WEB ADDRESSES:

The White House offers young readers information on the U.S. government and the Presidents on a Web site called **"White House 101."** The address is:
http://www.whitehouse.gov/about/white_house_101/

The Internet Public Library has a site on the Presidents. The address is:
http://www.ipl.org/div/potus

American Memory is a site maintained by the Library of Congress that contains biographical and historical information on the Presidents. It also provides links to Presidential portraits.
For George Bush:
http://memory.loc.gov/ammem/today/jan06.html

George Bush Presidential Library and Museum
http://bushlibrary.tamu.edu/

Bill Clinton
1946-
42nd President of the United States (1993-2001)

BILL CLINTON WAS BORN August 19, 1946, in Hope, Arkansas. His name when he was born was William Jefferson Blythe IV. His father was William Jefferson Blythe III, and his mother was Virginia Blythe. William Jefferson Blythe III died in a car accident three months before his son was born, so Bill never met his father. Virginia Blythe worked most of her life as a nurse. She married again when Bill was four. Virginia's second husband was named Roger Clinton, who became Bill's stepfather. Bill had a half-brother named Roger, Jr.

BILL CLINTON GREW UP in Hope and Hot Springs, Arkansas. After the death of his father, he and his mother lived with his grandparents. When Bill was two, his mother moved to New Orleans to study nursing. Bill stayed with his grandparents and became very close to them. His grandfather owned a store, and Bill spent a lot of time listening to his grandfather and the neighbors talking. He says he learned a lot about life and love from his grandparents.

After his mother finished school, she moved back to Hope. When Virginia married Roger Clinton, the family moved to Hot Springs, Arkansas, where Roger worked as a car salesman. Bill's half-brother, Roger Jr., was born when Bill was 10. Bill changed his last name from Blythe to Clinton when he was 15.

Bill Clinton's family life was unhappy. His stepfather, Roger, was an alcoholic. He would sometimes get drunk and beat Bill's mother and brother. When he was in high school, Bill told his stepfather to leave them alone. Though he was just a boy himself, Bill wanted to protect his mother and brother.

The experience of growing up in such a troubled house was very painful for Clinton. He didn't talk about it to friends or teachers. Very few people knew about it until he was an adult and running for President.

BILL CLINTON WENT TO SCHOOL at the public schools in Hope and Hot Springs. He was an excellent student. He was also involved in many other activities, including church groups, the school band, and the Boy Scouts. He loved to play the saxophone, and he played in a trio called the "Three Blind Mice." They wore dark glasses and played jazz.

Clinton's interest in government started when he was in high school. He took part in school government groups and learned about the world of politics. As a high school student, he met **President John F. Kennedy**. It was a meeting he never forgot.

First Lady Hillary Clinton.

After graduating from high school in 1964, Clinton went to Georgetown University in Washington, D.C. At Georgetown, he studied international politics. After college, he went to school in England at Oxford University. Then he went to Yale University to study law.

MARRIAGE AND FAMILY: Bill Clinton met his future wife, Hillary, when they were both law students at Yale. They got married in 1975. The Clintons have one daughter, Chelsea. Hillary Rodham Clinton is a very successful lawyer who is now a U.S. Senator representing New York.

GETTING INVOLVED IN POLITICS: After graduating from law school in 1973, Clinton worked as a lawyer in Arkansas. He also taught law school classes.

In 1974 Clinton ran for office for the first time. He ran as a **Democrat** for a seat in the U.S. **House of Representatives**. He lost the election, but he didn't give up his dream of a career in politics.

In 1976, he ran again, this time for the job of Attorney General for the state of Arkansas. (A state Attorney General is the head lawyer for a state government.) He won the election.

GOVERNOR OF ARKANSAS In 1978, Clinton was elected Governor of Arkansas. At 32, he was the youngest Governor in the U.S. He held the job for two years, then lost when he ran for reelection. When he ran again in 1982, he won. He was reelected Governor every two years until 1991. That year, he decided to run for President.

PRESIDENT OF THE UNITED STATES: In 1992, Clinton ran for President against **George Bush**, a **Republican** who was then the President. It was a three-way race in 1992, with Bush and Clinton facing independent candidate Ross Perot. Clinton and his Vice Presidential candidate, Al Gore, promised to help improve the economy and create more jobs. Clinton beat Bush, with 370 **electoral votes** to Bush's 168. Although Perot didn't receive any electoral votes, he received almost 20,000,000 popular votes.

When Clinton took over as President, the nation was concerned about the economy and unemployment. In his first term, he presented reforms in welfare and education. He also proposed major changes in the health care system. First Lady Hillary Clinton took on a large role in trying to improve health care. The Clintons were unsuccessful in trying to change the system, but they did bring attention to the problems.

During Clinton's first term, his administration faced problems in warring areas of the world, including Bosnia. As different ethnic groups battled for control of the country, many people looked to the United States to help solve Bosnia's problems. The U.S. sent

President Clinton with his daughter Chelsea on her first day of college.

troops to Bosnia to stop the fighting. Clinton also sent U.S. troops to Haiti to restore the elected president to power. He also hosted a historic peace conference between the people of Israel and the Palestinians.

REELECTION: In 1996, Clinton decided to run for reelection. The economy and unemployment had improved in the U.S. during his

Bill and Hillary Clinton

first term. Clinton had little trouble defeating his Republican opponent, Bob Dole, with 379 electoral votes to Dole's 159.

In his second term, Clinton continued to work for reforms in welfare and education. Through a National Service program, he encouraged young people to work for better communities. He also worked with the Congress to develop a plan to limit government spending and balance the federal budget.

Clinton's Presidency was also the target of investigations into possible wrongdoing. His financial dealings in a land-development deal known as "Whitewater" were investigated by Kenneth Starr, a lawyer working as an independent counsel, for several years. In addition, the fundraising practices of Clinton and his reelection campaign were investigated. And, in his last years in office, Clinton faced impeachment.

IMPEACHMENT: The U.S. **Constitution** states that if the U.S. House of Representatives thinks that a President has broken a law, it can accuse him of wrongdoing. That is called "**impeachment**." After a President is impeached, he is put on trial in the Senate for breaking the law. The Senate listens to the evidence, then votes to decide if the President should be removed from office.

During his term, Clinton had an inappropriate personal relationship with a young woman working at the White House. Her name was Monica Lewinsky. In 1998, Clinton gave testimony in a court case in which he denied that the relationship had taken place. Clinton gave his testimony while under oath, meaning that he had sworn to tell the truth.

The independent counsel in charge of the Whitewater investigation, Kenneth Starr, began an examination into Clinton's relationship with Lewinsky. The investigation revealed evidence that Clinton had not told the truth while under oath. He had lied about his relationship with Lewinsky. Not telling the truth under oath is called "perjury." Perjury is against the law.

When news of the case reached the press, it became a scandal. For months the press followed every aspect of the investigation; for months Clinton denied any wrongdoing. Finally, in August 1998, he admitted the relationship.

The Lewinsky case made Clinton a figure of scandal and scorn for many Americans, particularly conservative Republicans. In December 1998, the House of Representatives, led by Republicans, began impeachment proceedings against Clinton. They accused him of perjury and "obstruction of justice." That is trying to block lawyers and courts from finding out the truth in an investigation. Like perjury, obstruction of justice is against the law. After he was accused, Clinton was tried in the Senate. The Senate found him not guilty of the charges. Clinton is only the second President to be impeached. The first was **Andrew Johnson,** who was impeached in 1868.

While many Americans disapproved of Clinton's personal behavior in the Lewinsky scandal, most thought that what he had done, while it was wrong, did not warrant impeachment. Many thought that he was still an effective President, and he continued to receive high approval ratings in his last year in office. But his reputation had been damaged by the scandal. For many Americans, his legacy will be overshadowed by the fact that he did not tell the truth, to the court or to the American public, until the damage to his administration, and perhaps to the office itself, had been done.

After he left office, Clinton moved to New York. His wife, Hillary, was elected U.S. Senator from New York in 2000. He is currently working on his memoirs and is also involved with building his Presidential library.

HILLARY CLINTON'S HISTORIC RUN FOR THE WHITE HOUSE: In 2007, Hillary Clinton decided to run for President. She ran for the Democratic nomination, and her main opponent was **Barack Obama**. Soon it was clear that they were the frontrunners. It was an historic race. It was the first time that a woman and an African-

American were fighting for the nomination of a major party. Clinton won several early primaries and many dedicated delegates. By June 2008, Obama had won enough delegates to win the nomination, and Clinton campaigned for him vigorously.

After Obama won the election in November 2008, he chose Hillary Clinton to be his Secretary of State. In that role, she is traveling the world and working with President Obama to determine U.S. foreign policy.

LIFE AT THE WHITE HOUSE: Chelsea Clinton spent four years growing up in the White House. Her parents tried very hard to protect her privacy. Even with the extra publicity, Chelsea managed to grow up like a normal kid. She even had sleepovers at the White House.

While in the White House, the Clintons had a cat, Socks, and a dog, Buddy.

WHAT DOES HE LOOK LIKE? Bill Clinton is 6 feet 2 inches tall and weighs 220 pounds. He has gray hair and blue eyes.

FAMOUS QUOTE

"In the years ahead I will never hold a position higher or a covenant more sacred than that of President of the United States. But there is no title I will wear more proudly than that of citizen."

FOR MORE INFORMATION ON BILL CLINTON:

Historic Site:
Clinton Birthplace Foundation, Inc.
P.O. Box 1925
Hope, Arkansas 71801
Phone: 870-777-4455

WORLD WIDE WEB ADDRESSES:

The White House offers young readers information on the U.S. government and the Presidents on a Web site called **"White House 101."** The address is:
http://www.whitehouse.gov/about/white_house_101/

The Internet Public Library has a site on the Presidents. The address is:
http://www.ipl.org/div/potus

American Memory is a site maintained by the Library of Congress that contains biographical and historical information on the Presidents. It also provides links to Presidential portraits.
For Bill Clinton:
http://memory.loc.gov/learn/

Clinton Birthplace Foundation
http://www.clintonbirthplace.com/

Clinton Presidential Center
http://www.clintonpresidentialcenter.org

George W. Bush
1946 -
43rd President of the United States (2001-   )

GEORGE W. BUSH WAS BORN on July 6, 1946, in New Haven, Connecticut. His father is **George Bush** and his mother is Barbara Bush. His father was a student at Yale at the time of George's birth. He would go on to become the 41st President of the United States. His mother was a homemaker while he was growing up. Later, she became First Lady of the United States. She is also a well-known supporter of literacy in the U.S.

George W. Bush at age four, with his mother, Barbara Bush, father George Bush, and grandparents, Dorothy and Prescott Bush, Midland, Texas, 1950.

George was the oldest of six children. He had two sisters, Robin and Dorothy. His three brothers are Jeb (a nickname for John Ellis Bush), Neil, and Marvin.

GEORGE W. BUSH GREW UP in Midland, Texas. His family had moved there when he was two. His dad was starting out in the oil business. There were many young families in Midland. George spent a lot time playing with friends, especially playing baseball.

He was a spunky, spirited kid. His dad wrote to a friend about him. "Georgie has grown to be a near-man, talks dirty once in while, and occasionally swears, aged four-and-a-half."

When he was just seven years old, George and his family faced a terrible tragedy. His sister Robin, just three, died of cancer. It was a painful time for all of them. Barbara Bush remembers that her son refused to play with friends. He wanted to take care of his mom. "That started my cure," she recalls. "I realized I was too much of a burden for a little seven-year-old boy."

GEORGE W. BUSH WENT TO SCHOOL at the local public schools in Midland. He attended Sam Houston Elementary School. He was a good student, and a good athlete, too.

George went to San Jacinto Junior High in Midland for seventh grade. When he was in eighth grade, his family moved to Houston. There, he went to a private school called Kincaid.

For high school, Bush went to an elite private school in New England, Phillips Academy, in Andover, Massachusetts, called "Andover." Like his father, Bush went to Yale University for college. He wasn't a great student, but one friend remembers that "he was a serious student of people." Bush graduated from Yale in 1968 with a degree in history. He returned to Texas and served in the Texas Air National Guard for the next several years.

Bush at Yale in the mid-1960s.

407

Bush in the Texas Air National Guard, late-1960s.

THE TEXAS AIR NATIONAL GUARD: As a member of the National Guard, Bush flew an F-102, a single-seat jet fighter. After one year of active duty, he continued his military service on weekends.

Over the next several years, he worked at a number of different jobs. He worked for a farming business, but found it boring. He also worked in a mentoring program for poor boys.

In 1973, he decided to go back to school. He went to Harvard and got a degree in business. Then, it was back to Texas.

AN OIL MAN: Like his dad, Bush decided to try the oil business. He started out trying to learn all he could. He started his own company, and he had a little success.

In the late 1970s, he decided to try politics. He ran for a seat in the Texas House of Representatives. He lost. The man who won called him a rich snob from the East. He claimed that Bush had a famous father and lots of money, but no experience. But Bush thought of himself as a hard-working Texan. He learned a hard lesson from the experience.

In 1988, Bush moved his family to Washington. His dad, after serving as Vice President for eight years, was running for President.

Bush was one of his father's closest advisors. The campaign was successful. His father was elected President.

Back in Texas, Bush sold his shares in his oil company and bought into another business. He'd always loved baseball. Now he would become an owner.

THE TEXAS RANGERS: Bush put together a group of investors who bought the Texas Rangers. He loved to go to the ballpark. He'd talk to players, like the famous Nolan Ryan. He'd also talk to fans. And he didn't sit in a special owner's box. He sat in the general admission seats. He got to be a well-known and popular Texan.

GETTING INVOLVED IN POLITICS: In 1994, Bush decided to run for Governor. Like his father, Bush ran as a **Republican**. The Governor of Texas was a popular **Democrat** named Ann Richards. She attacked Bush for being inexperienced and using his father's name. Bush never counter-attacked. Instead, he ran on a promise to reform the Texas government. Much to the surprise of many people, he won.

GOVERNOR OF TEXAS: As the Governor of Texas, Bush focused on several issues. He wanted to reform education, welfare, juvenile crime, and law. He was a very popular governor. He was reelected in 1998.

Bush was able to work well with Democrats as well as Republicans. He became well-known as a successful Republican Governor throughout the country. Some Republicans suggested that he would be a good candidate for President in 2000.

Bush formed a committee to look into running for President. He started to raise money for his campaign. In April 1999, he declared that he would run for the Republican nomination.

RUNNING FOR PRESIDENT: In July 2000, Bush was formally nominated at the Republican Convention. He accepted, and the presidential race was off. Bush's running mate was Dick Cheney. Their Democratic challengers were former Vice President Al Gore and Senator Joe Lieberman. The key issues in the campaign included education, taxes, the environment, health care, and crime.

THE ELECTORAL COLLEGE AND THE ELECTION OF 2000: The Presidential Election of 2000 was one of the most hotly contested in U.S. history. On election day, almost 100 million voters cast their ballots. But the contest was so close that by the next day, Americans still didn't know who the next President was. It would take five more weeks to determine who won.

Americans vote for President in a different way than they do for any other elected official. The President is *not* elected by direct vote of the people. Instead, he is elected by members of the **Electoral College**. When a voter casts a vote for a Presidential candidate, he or she is really voting for an "elector." That is someone who is pledged to vote for one of the Presidential candidates. After the Presidential election, the electors meet and cast their ballots for the candidates they are pledged to.

The number of electors is equal to the total number of U.S. Representatives and Senators. Right now, that number is 538. To win the election, the Presidential candidate must get a majority of all the possible electoral votes. Today, that number is 270 (one more than half of 538).

Al Gore had won the popular vote. But he hadn't won the electoral vote. He had 255 electoral votes and Bush had 246. Either man needed 270 to win. The 25 electoral votes from Florida turned out to be the key to the election. By November 9, the Florida count showed Bush leading by 1,784 votes. Florida voting rules state that if the vote is very close, there must be a recount. So Florida's votes were recounted by machine. This recount showed Bush still in the lead.

But Gore's supporters charged that the ballots used in some counties were badly designed. Gore requested a "manual recount." In a manual recount, ballots are counted by hand. Election officials examine each ballot. If a ballot is not clearly marked, they try to determine the intent of the voter. Bush went to court to stop the manual recount. He argued that manual recounts didn't treat all ballots — and therefore voters — equally and fairly.

Over the next five weeks, lawyers for Bush and Gore argued their cases in court. A Florida court ordered a deadline for the recounts to be completed. On November 26, the Florida Secretary of State declared the results. Bush had won Florida by 537 votes.

Gore sued to challenge the election results. Bush decided to take his case to the **Supreme Court**. His lawyers argued that treating the votes differently was unconstitutional. They stated that not treating all votes equally violated the Constitutional right to equal protection under the law. The Supreme Court ruled, 5-4, in favor of Bush. They ordered the recounts to stop. With the recount stopped, Florida's 25 electoral votes went to Bush.

PRESIDENT OF THE UNITED STATES: On December 13, 2000, George W. Bush was declared the winner of the 2000 election. He became the 43rd President of the United States. And he and his dad became only the second father and son to be elected President. (**John Adams** and **John Quincy Adams** were the first father and son to both serve as President.)

President Bush puts his arm around New York City firefighter Bob Beckwith while standing in front of the site of the terrorist attack on the World Trade Center, September 14, 2001.

President Bush faced many important tasks in his first months in office. His plan to cut taxes became law in Spring 2001. He also planned to improve education in the U.S.

A TERRORIST ATTACK: On September 11, 2001, Bush faced one of the gravest threats to the nation in modern times. That day, terrorists attacked New York City and Washington, D.C. Hijackers forced two commercial airplanes to crash into the twin towers of the World Trade Center. Less than an hour later, hijackers forced a plane to crash into the Pentagon, the home of the Department of Defense.

For the first time since **World War II**, the U.S. had been attacked. And for the first time the targets were civilian, rather than military.

The damage to the World Trade Center was devastating. An hour after the attack, the twin towers collapsed. Almost 3,000 people died. At the Pentagon, the death toll reached 189.

Within hours of the attack, the Bush administration stated that they thought the terrorists were acting under the direction of Osama bin Laden and his terrorist network, Al Qaeda. Bin Laden is a Saudi Arabian extremist who has been linked to other terrorist attacks against the U.S.

The President spoke to the nation and outlined the U.S. response. He told the American people that "On September 11, enemies of freedom committed an act of war against our country." He said the U.S. would root out and destroy terrorism all over the world. He asked Americans to be firm in their support. "I ask you to be calm and resolute, even in the face of continuing threats."

Bush said the war would be long, and unlike any the U.S. had fought before. The response to Bush's leadership was immediate and positive, with Americans showing their support for the admin-

First Lady Laura Bush.

istration's plan. In the months following the attack, he continued to lead the military response in Afghanistan and elsewhere, and to encourage the American people to return to their normal lives.

THE POST-9/11 PRESIDENCY: After the disaster of 9/11, Bush focused his presidency on fighting terrorism. In March 2003, the U.S. invaded Iraq, as part of an international coalition. Bush's purpose was to find weapons of mass destruction, which he believed the Iraqi government had hidden. He also wanted to find the terrorists responsible for 9/11 and to prevent them from planning additional attacks. Within months, U.S. forces had taken control of most of the country and captured Saddam Hussein, the dictator of Iraq. Hussein was tried in an Iraqi court and executed in 2006.

Bush pledged to bring democracy to Iraq, but the various factions within the country were soon fighting both U.S. forces and each other. U.S. casualties began to mount, and Bush's popularity fell at home and around the world.

REELECTION: In 2004, Bush ran for reelection. His opponent was John Kerry, a senator from Massachusetts. With the war in Iraq as the major focus, the voters were sharply divided. Bush won the election, with 286 electoral votes; Kerry received 251.

After his reelection, Bush continued to concentrate on fighting terrorism. With casualties continuing to rise in Iraq, Bush made a change in war policy in 2007. He ordered what was called the "surge," an increase in troops in Iraq. The surge began to work, casualties began to drop, and U.S. forces began to train Iraqis to run their military and government.

In 2008, as Bush began his final year in office, there were signs of strain in the U.S. economy. Some large banks and other financial institutions went out of business. In some cases, they had made bad investments. In others, they had lent money to people to buy houses, and the people were unable to pay. Some people lost their homes. Many Americans lost money they had invested in the stock market, too.

As the economy continued to weaken, people began to lose their jobs. Bush tried to develop plans to help the economy in his final months in office. When he left the White House in January 2009, he and Mrs. Bush moved to a home in Dallas, Texas. He is spending time writing and working on his presidential library.

MARRIAGE AND FAMILY: Bush met his future wife, Laura Welch, in 1977. He claims it was "love at first sight." They were married just three months after they met. Laura Bush used to be an elementary school librarian. She is a strong supporter of reading and literacy.

In her role as First Lady, Laura Bush helped Americans, especially children, deal with the terrorist attacks on the country. She also hosted a National Book Festival every year, with the Library of Congress.

LIFE AT THE WHITE HOUSE: The Bushes have twin daughters, Barbara and Jenna. They were in college for most of their father's presidency.

The Bushes had several pets. They had two dogs, Spot and Barney, and a cat, India. Spot is the daughter of former President George Bush's dog, Millie. Spot is the only second-generation presidential pet.

WHAT DOES HE LOOK LIKE? Bush is 6 feet tall and has a slim build. He has graying brown hair and blue eyes.

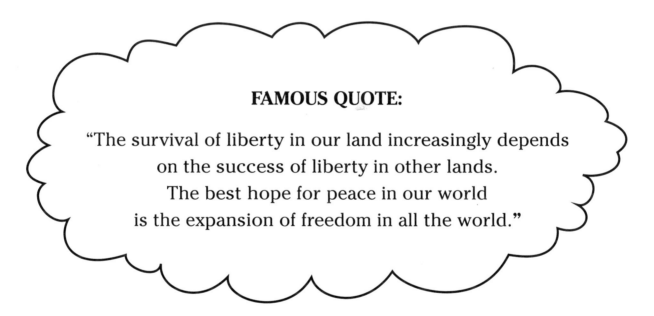

FAMOUS QUOTE:

"The survival of liberty in our land increasingly depends on the success of liberty in other lands. The best hope for peace in our world is the expansion of freedom in all the world."

WORLD WIDE WEB ADDRESSES:

The White House offers all Americans information on the U.S. government and the Presidents on a Web site called: **White House 101.** The address is:

http://www.whitehouse.gov/about/white_house_101/

The **Internet Public Library** has a site on the Presidents. The address is:

http://www.ipl.org/div/potus

American Memory

The Library of Congress maintains a Web site with biographical and historical information on the Presidents. It also provides links to Presidential portraits.

For George W. Bush:

http://memory.loc.gov/learn

George W. Bush Presidential Center

http://www.georgewbushlibrary.com

Barack Obama
1961-
44th President of the United States (2009-)

BARACK OBAMA WAS BORN on August 4, 1961, in Honolulu, Hawaii. His full name is Barack Hussein Obama Jr. He is biracial. His father, Barack Obama Sr., was black, from the African nation of Kenya. His mother, Ann Dunham, was white, and born in Kansas. They met when Barack Sr. won a scholarship to the University of Hawaii to study.

Obama has several siblings. He has a half-sister named Maya, from his mother's second marriage. His father also remarried, and Obama has another half-sister, Auma, and half-brothers named

Roy, Bernard, George, Abo, and Mark. Another half-brother, David, died in a motorcycle accident.

BARACK OBAMA GREW UP in Hawaii. His father left the family when he was two, and his parents divorced. Barack and his mother lived with his mother's parents. Barack was very close to his grandparents, who had moved to Hawaii after World War II.

When he was six, Barack and his mother moved to Indonesia. His mother had married an Indonesian man named Lolo Soetoro. He became Barack's stepfather. The family lived near the main city of Jakarta. It was a very exotic place, and Barack remembered monkeys, a cockatoo, and even baby alligators living in the garden.

BARACK OBAMA WENT TO SCHOOL first in Indonesia. He recalls that he spent two years in a Muslim school, and two years in a Catholic school. But his mother wasn't sure he was getting the education he needed in Indonesia. She wanted him to go back to Hawaii for school. He applied to and got into a private school in Honolulu.

So at the age of 10, Barack moved back to Hawaii. He lived with his grandparents, and attended the Punahou School, a prestigious prep school in Honolulu. That same year, his father came to visit. It would be the last time they would see each other, although they did write letters over the years.

Barack did very well in school, and was a basketball star, too. He graduated from high school in 1978 and went on to Occidental College in Los Angeles. After two years at Occidental, he transferred to Columbia University in New York. He graduated from Columbia in 1983. He worked briefly for a large company, but he knew he wanted more.

Obama on the campaign trail, 2008.

By this time, he was getting interested in community organizing. He knew that there were major problems in America, especially in the big cities, and especially among African-Americans. He wanted to make a difference, to get involved and help improve their lives.

GETTING INVOLVED IN COMMUNITY ORGANIZING: In 1985, Obama got a job in Chicago with an organization called the Calumet Community Religious Conference. Over the next three years, he threw himself into organizing the community to fight the problems that poverty and discrimination had brought to the city's South Side.

He got to know the people of the community, and what their problems were. Together, they tried to improve housing, education, employment, and to fight crime. He learned a tremendous amount about the problems of urban America. He got to see first-hand the problems of African-Americans who lived without hope for a better future for themselves and their families. He also learned a lot about himself.

In 1988, Obama decided he needed more education. He wanted to go to law school, to learn more about how law and politics can help change lives. But first, he began a more personal journey. He went to Africa, to learn about his African heritage.

In Africa, he met several of his half-siblings, from his father's remarriage. He also met his grandmother, and aunts and uncles.

LAW SCHOOL: Obama began law school at Harvard in 1988. He was a great student, and he became president of the Harvard Law Review. The Law Review is a very important and prestigious publication. It is written by lawyers, professors, and students, and edited by the law students themselves. Obama was the first African-American ever to be chosen for the position.

PRACTICING AND TEACHING LAW: After graduating from law school, Obama moved back to Chicago. He started working as a civil rights attorney. He also started teaching law classes at the University of Chicago. Obama taught constitutional law. That is the study of how the federal court system, including the **Supreme Court,** has interpreted the **Constitution of the United States.**

BECOMING AN AUTHOR: Obama also published his first book in 1995. It's called *Dreams of My Father*. It is a very personal look at his life, and his journey to manhood. He explores what he learned from both his mother and father, and what his heritage means to him. He also writes about how he came to understand the problems of modern America, and what he could do to help solve them.

RUNNING FOR OFFICE: In 1996, Obama decided to run for the Illinois State Senate. He won, and served for eight years. While in the Illinois congress, he worked on many issues. He championed tax cuts for working families and early childhood education.

In 2004, Obama decided to run for national office. He ran for the job of U.S. Senator from Illinois. He won, and became only the third African-American to hold the office of Senator.

That same year, he gave a speech at the Democratic National Convention. It was a moving and inspiring speech. He talked about America's problems. He also talked about how government can, and should help. Most of all, he talked about his hope for America, "the audacity of hope." Viewers were impressed with the young man from Illinois. They knew he had a bright future.

As a Senator, Obama served on several special committees. They included Health, Education, Labor and Pensions; Foreign Relations; Veterans' Affairs; and Environment and Public Works.

RUNNING FOR THE DEMOCRATIC NOMINATION: In 2007, Obama decided to run for President. Virtually unknown to most Americans, he first needed to win the nomination of the Democratic Party. His main opponent was Hillary Clinton, wife of former President **Bill Clinton** and a Senator from New York.

Obama and Clinton were soon the frontrunners in the race. It was an historical contest. It was the first time that a woman and an African-American were running for the nomination of a major party. Many states had the highest voter turnout in their history. Many Americans became engaged in the election. Young voters especially were drawn to Obama's message of hope and change.

Obama with his family: wife Michelle, and daughters Sasha and Malia.

RUNNING FOR PRESIDENT: By June 2008, Obama had won enough delegates to be declared the Presidential nominee of the Democratic Party. It was another historical moment. No black candidate had ever won the nomination of a major party before. He chose Joe Biden, Senator from Delaware, as his running mate.

Obama and Biden ran against Republican Senator John McCain and Alaskan Governor Sarah Palin. The opponents traveled the country and held town meetings and debates. The key issues in the campaign included the war in Iraq, the troubled economy, health care, education, and energy.

On November 4, 2008, Barack Obama became the first African-American President. He won the presidency with 365 electoral votes; John McCain received 251. It was the largest voter turnout in the nation's history, with almost 130 million Americans casting ballots.

PRESIDENT OF THE UNITED STATES: Obama took the oath of office on January 20, 2009. More than one million people turned out to see the event in Washington, DC, and millions more watched at home.

First Lady Michelle Obama

Obama outlined the problems the nation faces, including rebuilding the economy, creating jobs, improving education and health care, finding new energy sources, the continuing war in Iraq, and the threat of terrorism. He said the nation would respond with hope and willingness to work hard, together, to solve the problems.

Within the first month of his administration, Obama signed bills creating several programs to help the economy. These included a "stimulus" package to repair schools, roads, bridges, and other building projects, while creating new jobs. He also has outlined programs to help banks and financial institutions, and to help people having problems paying their mortgages.

MARRIAGE AND FAMILY: Obama met his future wife, Michelle, in Chicago, when they worked for the same law firm. They have two daughters, Malia, who is 10, and Sasha, who is 7.

LIFE AT THE WHITE HOUSE: The Obamas live in the White House, along with Michelle's mother, Marian Robinson. Malia and Sasha go to school at the Friends' School in Washington, DC. After spending six years in the Senate and only getting home to Chicago on weekends, President Obama is delighted to spend as much time as he can with his family every day. The First Family hopes to get a puppy soon.

FAMOUS QUOTE

"Our challenges may be new. The instruments with which we meet them may be new. But those values upon which our success depends—honesty and hard work, courage and fair play, tolerance and curiosity, loyalty and patriotism—these things are old. These things are true. They have been the quiet force of progress throughout our history. What is demanded, then, is a return to these truths. What is required of us now is a new era of responsibility: a recognition on the part of every American that we have duties to ourselves, our nation, and the world, duties that we do not grudgingly accept but rather seize gladly, firm in the knowledge that there is nothing so satisfying to the spirit, so defining of our character, than giving our all to a difficult task. This is the price and the promise of citizenship."

WHAT DOES HE LOOK LIKE: President Obama is 6 feet 3 inches tall and slim. He enjoys exercising, especially playing basketball.

FOR MORE INFORMATION BARACK OBAMA:

Write:
The White House
1600 Pennsylvania Ave.
Washington, DC 20500

WORLD WIDE WEB ADDRESSES

The White House offers all Americans information on the U.S. government and the Presidents on a Web site called: **White House 101.** The address is:
http://www.whitehouse.gov/about/white_house_101/

The **Internet Public Library** has a site on the Presidents. The address is:
http://www.ipl.org/div/potus

American Memory
The Library of Congress maintains a Web site with biographical and historical information on the Presidents. It also provides links to Presidential portraits.
For Barack Obama:
http://memory.loc.gov/learn

Photo and Illustration Credits

George Washington: Courtesy of the Library of Congress

John Adams: Courtesy of the Library of Congress; Courtesy of the National Park Service, Adams National Historic Site

Thomas Jefferson: Courtesy of the Library of Congress; Courtesy of Monticello/Thomas Jefferson Memorial Foundation, Inc.

James Madison: Courtesy of the Library of Congress

James Monroe: Courtesy of the Library of Congress

John Quincy Adams: Courtesy of the Library of Congress; Courtesy of the National Park Service, Adams National Historic Site

Andrew Jackson: Courtesy of the Library of Congress

Martin Van Buren: Courtesy of the Library of Congress; Courtesy of the National Park Service, Martin Van Buren National Historic Site

William Henry Harrison: Courtesy of the Library of Congress

John Tyler: Courtesy of the Library of Congress; Courtesy Sherwood Forest Plantation, John Tyler Griffin, and Tyler Stuart

James K. Polk: Courtesy of the Library of Congress

Zachary Taylor: Courtesy of the Library of Congress

Millard Fillmore: Courtesy of the Library of Congress; Courtesy of the Buffalo and Erie County Historical Society, Millard Fillmore Photograph Collection

Franklin Pierce: Courtesy of the Library of Congress

James Buchanan: Courtesy of the Library of Congress

Abraham Lincoln: Courtesy of the Library of Congress

Andrew Johnson: Courtesy of the Library of Congress

Ulysses S. Grant: Courtesy of the Library of Congress

Rutherford B. Hayes: Courtesy of the Library of Congress; Courtesy of the Rutherford B. Hayes Presidential Center, Fremont, OH

James Garfield: Courtesy of the Library of Congress

PHOTO AND ILLUSTRATION CREDITS

Chester A. Arthur: Courtesy of the Library of Congress

Grover Cleveland: Courtesy of the Library of Congress

Benjamin Harrison: Courtesy of the Library of Congress

William McKinley: Courtesy of the Library of Congress

Theodore Roosevelt: Courtesy of the Library of Congress

William Howard Taft: Courtesy of the Library of Congress

Woodrow Wilson: Courtesy of the Library of Congress

Warren G. Harding: Courtesy of the Library of Congress

Calvin Coolidge: Courtesy of the Library of Congress

Herbert Hoover: Courtesy of the Library of Congress

Franklin D. Roosevelt: Courtesy of the Library of Congress

Harry S. Truman: Courtesy of the Library of Congress; Courtesy of the Harry S. Truman Presidential Library; The White House Collection

Dwight D. Eisenhower: Courtesy of the Library of Congress

John F. Kennedy: Courtesy of the Library of Congress; Courtesy of the John F. Kennedy Library

Lyndon B. Johnson: Courtesy of the Library of Congress; Courtesy of the Lyndon B. Johnson Library Collection

Richard M. Nixon: Courtesy of the Library of Congress; Courtesy of the Richard Nixon Library and Birthplace

Gerald R. Ford: Courtesy of the Library of Congress; Courtesy of the Gerald R. Ford Library

Jimmy Carter: Courtesy of the Library of Congress; Courtesy of the Jimmy Carter Library

Ronald Reagan: Courtesy of the Library of Congress; Courtesy of the Ronald Reagan Library

George H.W. Bush: Courtesy of the Library of Congress; Courtesy of the George Bush Presidential Library; The White House

Bill Clinton: The White House; AP/World Wide Photos

George W. Bush: The White House; George Bush Presidential Library; AP/Wide World Photos.

Barack Obama: The White House.

Glossary

This glossary contains terms used in the entries on the Presidents. It includes descriptions and definitions of political parties, political and historical concepts, wars, and other terms that appear frequently in the entries. Glossary terms are in bold-faced type in the entries.

BILL OF RIGHTS: The Bill of Rights is a document that lists the first ten amendments, or additions, to the **Constitution.** The Bill of Rights guarantees specific freedoms to all Americans. Some of the major rights we enjoy — like freedom of speech and religion — are outlined in the Bill of Rights. The principal author of the Bill of Rights was **James Madison.** It was approved and added to the Constitution in 1791.

BULL MOOSE PARTY: This was a political party formed by **Theodore Roosevelt** in 1912, when he didn't win the **Republican** Presidential nomination. The official name of the party was the National Progressive Party. It became known as the "Bull Moose Party" because Roosevelt told reporters that he felt "as fit as a Bull Moose" running for President again.

CABINET: The Cabinet is a group of advisers who help the President make decisions. The Cabinet is made up of the top officials from different departments in the federal government. Cabinet members give advice to the President on important issues in domestic policy (issues taking place within the United States) and foreign policy (issues relating to other countries).

CIVIL WAR: The Civil War began in 1861 and continued until 1865. The war was between the Northern states, who fought for the preservation of the **Union** and the abolition of **slavery**, and the Southern states, which wanted slavery to continue in the South and extend into the new territories of the U.S. When **Abraham Lincoln** was elected President in 1860, the Southern states began to secede from the Union. They formed a new country, called the **Confederate States of America**. On April 12, 1861, Confederate soldiers fired on Fort Sumter, a fort held by Union (Northern) troops in South Carolina. It was an act of rebellion, and the beginning of the war.

The battles of the Civil War were fought in several states, including Virginia, Mississippi, Pennsylvania, and Tennessee. Some of the fiercest and most decisive battles took place at Bull Run, Antietam, Chancellorsville, Vicksburg, and Gettysburg. All together, more than 300,000 people died in the Civil War. The war ended on April 9, 1865, when the Army of the Confederacy, under General Robert E. Lee, surrendered to General **Ulysses S. Grant**, head of the Union forces.

COLD WAR: After **World War II** (1939-1945), the Soviet Union and the U.S. became the two strongest nations in the world. They represented two very different political systems. The U.S. was a democracy; the Soviet Union was a Communist state. The two "superpowers" also had powerful nuclear weapons. The relationship between the two nations was very important. For more than 40 years, the hostilities between these two nations affected world politics. In 1991, the Soviet Union abandoned Communism and broke up into many independent states. The former Communist nations of Eastern Europe became democracies. This was the end of the "Cold War."

CONFEDERATE STATES OF AMERICA (CONFEDERACY): In 1860, after the election of **Abraham Lincoln**, Southern states began to secede — leave — the United States. They formed their own country, the Confederate States of America, called the Confederacy. The states that joined the Confederacy were Alabama, Arkansas, Florida, Georgia, Louisiana, Mississippi, North Carolina, South Carolina, Tennessee, Texas, and Virginia. The President of the Confederacy was Jefferson Davis. The Confederacy fought against the Northern states — the **Union** — in the **Civil War.** The Confederacy ended when the South lost the Civil War in 1865.

CONGRESS: The Congress is part of the Legislative branch of government. It includes the **Senate** and the **House of Representatives**. People who serve in Congress make the laws. They are elected by the voters in their district. In addition, there is also a Congress in each individual state that makes laws just for that state.

CONSTITUTION OF THE UNITED STATES: The Constitution is a document that contains the plan for the national government. It was written by members of the Constitutional Convention in 1787. One of the most important authors of the Constitution was **James Madison.**

The Constitution divides power between three branches. The Executive branch is made up of the President and the **Cabinet**. The Legislative branch, or **Congress**, is made up of the **House of Representatives** and the **Senate**. They make the laws for the country. The Judicial branch is made up of the U.S. Court system, including the **Supreme Court**.

DECLARATION OF INDEPENDENCE: The Declaration outlined the reasons behind the **Revolutionary War.** It was written mainly by

Thomas Jefferson, with help from **John Adams** and Benjamin Franklin. In simple, powerful language, it describes what the colonists thought about their rights as individuals and as citizens. It states that all men are born equal and free. They have the right to revolt against those who will not give them freedom. On July 4, 1776, the Continental Congress, which was the governing body of the colonies, accepted the Declaration of Independence.

DEMOCRATIC PARTY: The Democratic party was founded by **Thomas Jefferson** as the "Democratic-Republican" Party during the administration of **George Washington.** Washington and **John Adams** were "**Federalists**." That means that they favored a strong central government. Jefferson and the Democratic-Republicans believed that a strong central government was a bad idea because it limited the power of the states. By 1828, the party was known as the Democrats.

It is now one of two major political parties in the U.S., the other being the **Republican Party.**

ELECTORAL COLLEGE (ELECTORAL VOTES): The Electoral College is not a school. Instead, it's part of the process for electing the President and the Vice President.

Americans vote for President and Vice President in a different way than they do for any other elected official. The President and the Vice President are *not* elected by direct vote of the people. Instead, they are elected by "electors"—members of the Electoral College.

Each state chooses its electors for the Electoral College. The state chooses the same number of electors as it has representatives in the **Congress**. On election day, voters within a state cast their votes for the Presidential candidates. But they are really voting for the electors. The candidate who gets the most votes in each state gets all the electoral votes for that state. After voting is completed, the members of the Electoral College cast their ballots for the candidates they are pledged to. The candidate who gets the majority of votes in the Electoral College becomes President.

EMANCIPATION PROCLAMATION: On January 1, 1863, Lincoln issued "The Emancipation Proclamation." It said that all slaves living in Confederate states were free.

FEDERALIST PARTY: The Federalist Party formed during the Presidency of **George Washington.** Washington and **John Adams** were Federalists. That means that they favored a strong central government. They were opposed by the Democratic-Republicans (later called the **Democratic Party),** led by Thomas Jefferson. Jefferson believed that a strong central government was a bad idea. He thought it limited the power of the states.

FREE-SOIL PARTY: The Free-Soil Party came into being in 1847. It was formed by people opposed to the extension of **slavery** into the new territories gained in the Mexican War. In 1848 **Martin Van Buren** ran for President as the Free-Soil candidate. The party lasted until 1854, when most members joined the **Republican Party.**

GREAT DEPRESSION: The Great Depression was a time from 1929 to 1939 when up to one-quarter of Americans were out of work. People who had jobs lost them. Those who wanted jobs couldn't find them. Banks closed all over the country. People who had their life savings in banks lost all their money. Many people were very poor. The Depression began during the Presidency of **Herbert Hoover** and lasted through the Presidency of **Franklin D. Roosevelt.**

GULF WAR: The Gulf War refers to a war that was fought in the Persian Gulf region of the Middle East. In August 1990, Iraq invaded Kuwait. **President George Bush** called the invasion an act of aggression. He demanded that Iraq withdraw its troops from Kuwait. Iraq refused. Bush put together troops from the U.S. and other countries from the United Nations. Together, they challenged Hussein. The allied forces, called "Desert Storm," attacked the Iraqis on land and in bombing raids. The Gulf War lasted only 100 hours. The Iraqis were beaten and withdrew from Kuwait.

HOUSE OF REPRESENTATIVES: The House of Representatives, plus the **Senate**, are the two parts of the U.S. **Congress**. They are part of the legislative branch of government. People who serve in Congress make the laws. They are elected by the voters in their district. In addition, many states also have a House of Representatives that makes laws just for that state.

IMPEACHMENT: The U.S. **Constitution** states that if the U.S. **House of Representatives** thinks that a President has broken a law, it can accuse him of wrongdoing. That is called "impeachment." After a President is impeached, he is put on trial in the **Senate** for breaking the law. The Senate listens to the evidence, then votes to decide if the President should be removed from office.

Andrew Johnson and **Bill Clinton** are the only Presidents ever to be impeached. In 1868, Johnson was accused by the House and tried in the Senate. The Senate found him innocent by one vote. In 1999, Clinton was impeached by the House. The Senate found him not guilty.

In 1974, **Richard Nixon** chose to resign rather than face impeachment in the **Watergate** scandal.

"KNOW-NOTHING" PARTY: The "Know-Nothing" Party was formed in the mid-nineteenth century. The "Know-Nothings" were a conservative group who wanted to stop immigration to America. **Millard Fillmore** ran as the "Know- Nothing" candidate in the Presidential election of 1856.

KOREAN WAR: In 1950, the U.S. got involved in the **Korean War.** This was a war between North and South Korea. North Korea was backed by the Communist nations of China and the Soviet Union. The U.S. was part of a mission that included troops from countries in the United Nations. They fought against the Communist forces to protect the government of South Korea. The conflict lasted until 1953. It began during the term of **Harry S. Truman** and ended during the term of **Dwight D. Eisenhower.**

LOUISIANA PURCHASE: In 1803, **Thomas Jefferson** organized the purchase of a huge amount of territory. The territory ranged from the Mississippi River to the Rocky Mountains, and from the Canadian border to Texas. The territory was owned by France. It cost the U.S. $15 million, about three cents an acre. The Louisiana Purchase doubled the size of the U.S. Jefferson hired Meriwether Lewis and William Clark to explore the land. They led the famous Lewis and Clark expedition.

MEXICAN WAR: In the Mexican War the U.S. fought against Mexico. It started in 1846, after the U.S. had annexed Texas. The war took place during the term of **President James Polk.** The U.S. defeated the Mexicans in 1848. When the war ended, the U.S. gained California and the Utah and New Mexico territories.

MONROE DOCTRINE: The Monroe Doctrine was the major foreign policy principle of **President James Monroe.** It stated that the U.S.

would not allow European countries to develop colonies in North or South America. Its influence lasted into the twentieth century.

NEW DEAL: Franklin D. Roosevelt's economic program designed to end the **Great Depression** was called the New Deal. It was a group of programs that Roosevelt presented to the Congress in 1933. The New Deal contained programs that created jobs, set up building projects, gave financial assistance to poor Americans, and created Social Security. The programs and laws of the New Deal influenced American politics for more than 60 years.

RECONSTRUCTION: Reconstruction was the program that rebuilt the South after the **Civil War**. As part of the program, the federal government was in control of the South. Federal troops were responsible for keeping order. Many Northerners thought that the only way to guarantee rights to newly freed blacks was by using federal authority. But the Southerners resented the troops. The policies and purposes of Reconstruction were hotly debated in the U.S. Congress. Reconstruction ended in 1877, under **President Rutherford B. Hayes.**

REPUBLICAN PARTY: The Republican Party was formed in 1854 by those who did not want **slavery** extended into the new territories of the U.S. The first Republican President was Abraham Lincoln, whose election brought about the **Civil War**. The Republican Party is now one of two major political parties in the U.S., the other being the **Democratic Party.**

REVOLUTIONARY WAR: The Revolutionary War, which is also called the War of Independence, took place between 1775 and 1781. The war was between the American colonists and England. At that time, the colonies were governed by England and King George III.

The American colonists who fought the war believed that the colonies should have their own government, a government that they controlled. The ideas behind the Revolutionary War are outlined in the **Declaration of Independence.** The battles of the Revolutionary War began in 1775 and lasted until 1781. The treaty ending the war was signed in 1783.

SENATE: The Senate, plus the **House of Representatives**, are the two parts of the **Congress**. They are part of the legislative branch of government. People who serve in Congress make the laws. They are elected by the voters in their district. In addition, many states also have a Senate that makes laws just for that state.

SLAVERY: Slavery is when one person is able to hold or own another person against their will. The slave has no rights and is forced to do whatever work the slave master requires.

Slavery in the U.S. began in Virginia in the 1600s. Traders from Europe captured African people who lived on the west coast of Africa. Then the European traders brought the Africans as slaves to settlements along the Atlantic coast. These settlements later became the colonies of the United States.

People in this country disagreed and argued over slavery since the founding of the nation in the 1770s. By the early 1800s the North didn't allow slavery. Some Northerners despised slavery so much that they wanted to "abolish" it, or do away with it. Those were the "abolitionists" (ab-oh-LISH-in-ists).

But in the South, slaves had worked on plantations since the time of the first settlers. Slaves became especially important to raising crops on the plantations. They did much of the work that earned the money for their white owners. The system of slavery was part of life for white Southerners. Despite its inhumane treatment of black people, the South wanted to keep slavery. And they wanted to extend it.

In the 1800s, the nation was growing as new territories were added in the West. Settlers from the North and South moved into these territories. They disagreed over whether there should be slavery in those new areas. In the 1850s the U.S. Congress tried to work out compromises that would satisfy both the North and the South. The compromises didn't work.

Abraham Lincoln was elected President in 1860. He opposed slavery and wanted to abolish it. Eleven Southern states "seceded"—left—the **Union**. They formed their own separate country, called the **Confederate States of America**, or the Confederacy. That led to the **Civil War**, which lasted from 1861 to 1865. In 1863, President Lincoln issued the **Emancipation Proclamation**, which freed the slaves. Two years later, in 1865, the North won the war, and the South surrendered. The Confederate states once again became part of the United States, and all the slaves throughout the country were freed.

SPANISH-AMERICAN WAR: In the late 1890s, Spain controlled Cuba and Puerto Rico as colonies. In 1898, the U.S. battleship *Maine* was destroyed in the harbor of Havana, Cuba. Although no one was sure who sunk the *Maine*, most Americans blamed Spain. At the urging of **President William McKinley,** Congress declared war on Spain in April 1898. The Spanish-American War lasted only four months, and the U.S. won decisively. The fighting took place on Cuba and in the Philippine Islands in the Pacific Ocean, which was also a colony of Spain.

SUPREME COURT: The Supreme Court is part of the judicial branch of government. The Court is made up of nine justices and is headed by the Chief Justice. The Supreme Court hears cases involving the **Constitution**. The justices determine whether laws or decisions made in lower courts—of the states or federal system—are true to the meaning of the Constitution and the rights it guarantees.

TARIFFS: Tariffs are taxes on goods that are imported into the United States. That means that things that are made in other countries cost more than American-made goods. Throughout much of American history there has been a debate over whether high tariffs are good for the economy and for American workers.

TEAPOT DOME: One of the major political scandals of the twentieth century, Teapot Dome took place during the Presidency of **Warren Harding.** Several members of Harding's Cabinet were corrupt men. One of them, Secretary of the Interior Albert Hall, was found guilty of taking a bribe. Hall took money from oil developers to allow them to drill on federal lands in Wyoming, in an area known as "Teapot Dome."

The scandal began to surface in 1923. Harding died that year, and **Calvin Coolidge** became the next President. Coolidge made sure that anyone involved in wrongdoing was charged and tried for their crimes. He was thorough and effective in bringing them to justice.

UNION: The term Union often refers to the United States. During the **Civil War**, the word was also used to mean the North. The terms "Union troops" or "the Union army" refer to those who fought for the North against the South. Preserving the Union—keeping the nation together and united—was a key issue leading up to and during the Civil War.

VIETNAM WAR: The U.S. became involved in the war between North and South Vietnam in the early 1960s. North Vietnam was a Communist nation and South Vietnam was anti-communist. The U.S. supported anti-Communist South Vietnam by sending troops and supplies. **President Lyndon B. Johnson** expanded U.S. involvement in Vietnam, increasing the number of U.S. soldiers to 500,000. Many Americans opposed the war. In the early 1970s, **President Richard Nixon** reduced troops while increasing bombing of North Vietnam. U.S. involvement in the war continued until 1975, when the last American soldiers left.

WAR OF 1812: In 1812 the U.S. declared war on Britain. At that time, British ships stopped U.S. ships and forced American sailors into their Navy. **President James Madison** demanded that the British end this practice. When they refused, the U.S. and Britain went to war. The war lasted for two years. The War of 1812 ended with the signing of the Treaty of Ghent in 1814.

WATERGATE: "Watergate" is the name of the scandal that ended the Presidency of **Richard Nixon**. The Watergate is a building complex in Washington, D.C. where the Democratic headquarters were located in 1972. That year, men working for Nixon's reelection committee broke into the Democratic headquarters. Over the next two years, information came out on other illegal activities that Nixon's aides had engaged in. Members of Nixon's administration were charged with breaking the law. They were found guilty.

Nixon broke the law by "covering up" these activities. He used his powers as President to stop any investigation that could prove he was guilty of ordering illegal acts or covering up what had been done. But tape recordings of conversations in the White House revealed that Nixon had authorized the coverup, and his guilt became obvious.

In August 1974, Nixon resigned rather than face **impeachment** in the Watergate scandal. He always denied any wrongdoing, but accepted the blame for what Watergate had done to damage Americans' trust in the Presidency.

WHIG PARTY: The Whig Party came into being in the early nineteenth century. It was formed to oppose the **Democratic Party**, especially the policies of **Andrew Jackson. William Henry Harrison, John Tyler, Zachary Taylor, and Millard Fillmore** were all Whig Party candidates for President. The party lasted until the early 1850s. The Whig's last Presidential candidate was General Winfield Scott in 1852.

WORLD WAR I: World War I took place between 1914 and 1918 in Europe. In 1914, Great Britain, France, and Russia went to war with Germany and Austria. At first the U.S. remained neutral. In 1917, German ships began to threaten American ships in the Atlantic Ocean. The U.S. declared war on Germany. America's entry into the war gave Britain and France the advantage. Germany surrendered in 1918.

WORLD WAR II: World War II took place between 1939 and 1945 in Europe, Africa, and the Far East. In the war, Germany, Italy, and Japan made up the "Axis" powers. They fought against the "Allies" —England, France, and the Soviet Union. On December 7, 1941, Japanese planes bombed the U.S. naval base at Pearl Harbor, in Honolulu, Hawaii. The U.S. declared war on the Axis powers. From 1941 to 1945, the U.S. and the Allies fought the Germans and Italians in Europe and Africa. In the Pacific, they fought the Japanese. The war ended in 1945, when the Axis powers surrendered.

Appendix

In this section there are three graphs that bring together information on the Presidents in an easy to use format: **The Presidents' Term of Office, The Presidents' Personal Lives**, and **The Presidents in Their Own Times**

- **The Presidents' Term of Office** includes political party, dates of term, age at inauguration, Vice President, electoral vote, popular vote, and runner-up, with electoral and popular vote.

- **The Presidents' Personal Lives** includes date and place of birth, wife (with birth and death dates), children (with birth and death dates), occupation before Presidential term, and date and place of death.

- **The Presidents in Their Own Times** provides a timeline that lists major historical and political events for each President's term, including the births and deaths of other Presidents.

The Presidents' Term of Office

President	Political Party	Dates of term	Age*	Vice President
George Washington	Federalist	1789-1793 1793-1797	57	John Adams John Adams
John Adams	Federalist	1797-1801	61	Thomas Jefferson
Thomas Jefferson	Democratic-Republican	1801-1805 1805-1809	57	Aaron Burr George Clinton
James Madison	Democratic-Republican	1809-1813 1813-1817	57	George Clinton Elbridge Gerry
James Monroe	Democratic-Republican	1817-1821 1821-1825	58	Daniel D. Tompkins Daniel D. Tompkins
John Quincy Adams	Democratic-Republican	1825-1829	57	John C. Calhoun
Andrew Jackson	Democratic	1829-1833 1833-1837	61	John C. Calhoun Martin Van Buren
Martin Van Buren	Democratic	1837-1841	54	Richard M. Johnson
William Henry Harrison	Whig	1841-1841	68	John Tyler
John Tyler	Whig	1841-1845	51	
James K. Polk	Democratic	1845-1849	49	George M. Dallas
Zacharay Taylor	Whig	1849-1850	64	Millard Fillmore
Millard Fillmore	Whig	1850-1853	50	
Franklin Pierce	Democratic	1853-1857	48	Winfield Scott
James Buchanan	Democratic	1857-1861	65	John C. Breckinridge
Abraham Lincoln	Republican	1861-1865 1865-1865	52	Hannibal Hamlin Andrew Johnson
Andrew Johnson	Democratic	1865-1869	56	
Ulysses S. Grant	Republican	1869-1873 1873-1877	46	Schuyler Colfax Henry Wilson
Rutherford B. Hayes	Republican	1877-1881	54	William A. Wheeler
James A. Garfield	Republican	1881-1881	49	Chester A. Arthur
Chester A. Arthur	Republican	1881-1885	51	
Grover Cleveland	Democratic	1885-1889	47	Thomas A. Hendricks
Benjamin Harrison	Republican	1889-1893	55	Levi P. Morton

* Age at inauguration

Total electoral votes	Total popular votes	Runner-up	Total electoral votes	Total popular votes
69	NA	No opposition		NA
132		John Adams	77	
71	NA	Thomas Jefferson	68	NA
73	NA	Aaron Burr	73	NA
162		George Clinton	14	
122	NA	Charles C. Pinckney	47	NA
128		De Witt Clinton	89	
183	NA	Rufus King	34	NA
231		No opposition		
84	NA	Andrew Jackson	99	NA
178	642,553	John Q. Adams	83	500,897
219	701,780	Henry Clay	49	484,205
170	764,176	William H. Harrison	73	550,816
234	1,128,854	Martin Van Buren	60	1,128,854
170	1,339,494	Henry Clay	105	1,300,004
163	1,361,393	Lewis Cass	127	1,223,460
254	1,607,510	Winfield Scott	42	1,386,942
174	1,836,072	John C. Frémont	114	1,342345
180	1,865,908	Stephen A. Douglas	12	1,380,202
212	2,218,388	George B. McCellan	21	1,812,807
214	3,013,650	Horatio Seymour	80	2,708,744
286	3,598,235	Horace Greeley	3	2,834,761
185	4,288,546	Samuel J. Tilden	184	4,034,311
214	4,446,158	Winfield S. Hancock	155	4,444,260
219	4,874,621	James G. Blaine	182	4,848,936
233	5,534,488	Grover Cleveland	168	5,443,892

THE PRESIDENTS' TERM OF OFFICE

President	Political Party	Dates of term	Age*	Vice President
Benjamin Harrison	Republican	1889-1893	55	Levi P. Morton
Grover Cleveland	Democratic	1893-1897	55	Adlai E. Stevenson
William McKinley	Republican	1897-1901 1901-1901	54	Garret A. Hobart Theodore Roosevelt
Theodore Roosevelt	Republican	1901-1905 1905-1909	42	 Charles W. Fairbanks
William Howard Taft	Republican	1909-1913	51	James S. Sherman
Woodrow Wilson	Democratic	1913-1917 1917-1921	56	Thomas R. Marshall Thomas R. Marshall
Warren G. Harding	Republican	1921-1923	55	Calvin Coolidge
Calvin Coolidge	Republican	1923-1925 1925-1929	51	 Charles G. Dawes
Herbert Hoover	Republican	1929-1933	54	Charles Curtis
Franklin D. Roosevelt	Democratic	1933-1937 1937-1941 1941-1945 1945-1945	51	John N. Garner John N. Garner Henry A. Wallace Harry S. Truman
Harry S. Truman	Democratic	1945-1949 1949-1953	60	 Alben W. Barkley
Dwight D. Eisenhower	Republican	1953-1957 1957-1961	62	Richard M. Nixon Richard M. Nixon
John F. Kennedy	Democratic	1961-1963	43	Lyndon B. Johnson
Lyndon B. Johnson	Democratic	1963-1965 1965-1969	55	 Hubert H. Humphrey
Richard M. Nixon	Republican	1969-1973 1974-1974	56	Spiro T. Agnew Spiro T. Agnew Gerald R. Ford
Gerald R. Ford	Republican	1974-1977	61	Nelson A. Rockefeller
Jimmy Carter	Democratic	1977-1981	52	Walter Mondale
Ronald Reagan	Republican	1981-1985 1985-1989	69	George Bush George Bush
George Bush	Republican	1989-1993	64	Dan Quayle
Bill Clinton	Democratic	1993-1997 1997-2001	46	Al Gore Al Gore
George W. Bush	Republican	2001-2005 2005–2009	54	Dick Cheney Dick Cheney
Barack Obama	Democratic	2009-	47	Joe Biden

*

Total electoral votes	Total popular votes	Runner-up	Total electoral votes	Total popular votes
233	5,534,488	Grover Cleveland	168	5,443,892
277	5,551,883	Benjamin Harrison	145	5,179,244
271	7,108,480	William J Bryan	176	6,511,495
292	7,218,039	William J Bryan	155	6,358,345
336	7,626,593	Alton B. Parker	140	5,082,898
321	7,676,258	William J Bryan	162	6,406,801
435	6,293,152	Theodore Roosevelt	88	4,119,207
277	9,126,300	Charles E. Hughes	254	8,546,789
404	16,133,314	James M. Cox	127	9,140,884
382	15,717,553	John W. Davis	136	8,386,169
444	21,411,991	Alfred E. Smith	87	15,000,185
472	22,825,016	Herbert Hoover	59	15,758,397
523	22,747,636	Alfred M. Landon	8	16,679,543
449	27,263,448	Wendell L. Willke	82	22,336,260
432	25,611,936	Thomas E. Dewey	99	22,013,372
303	24,105,587	Thomas E. Dewey	189	21,970,017
442	33,936,137	Adlai E. Stevenson	89	27,314,649
457	35,585,245	Adlai E. Stevenson	73	26,030,172
303	34,221,344	Richard M. Nixon	219	34,106,671
486	43,126,584	Barry Goldwater	52	27,177,838
301	31,785,148	Hubert H. Humphrey	191	31,274,503
520	47,170,179	George S. McGovern	17	29,171,791
297	40,830,763	Gerald R. Ford	240	39,147,793
489	43,904,153	Jimmy Carter	49	35,483,883
525	54,455,075	Walter Mondale	13	37,577,185
426	48,886,097	George Dukakis	111	41,809,074
370	43,860,888	George Bush	168	38,220,427
379	45,628,667	Bob Dole	159	37,869,435
271	50,456,167	Al Gore	266	50,996,064
286	62,040,003	John Kerry	251	59,027,335
365	69,456,897	John McCain	173	59,934,814

The Presidents' Personal Lives

President	Date of birth	Place of birth	Wife
George Washington	Feb. 22, 1732	Westmoreland Co., VA	Martha Dandridge Custis Washington (1731-1802)
John Adams	Oct. 30, 1735	Braintree, MA (now Quincy)	Abigail Smith Adams (1744-1818)
Thomas Jefferson	Apr. 13, 1743	Goochland, VA	Martha Wayles Skelton Jefferson (1748-1782)
James Madison	Mar. 16, 1751	Port Conway, VA	Dolley Payne Todd Madison (1768-1849)
James Monroe	Apr. 28, 1758	Westmoreland Co., VA	Elizabeth Kortright Monroe (1768-1830)
John Quincy Adams	July 11, 1767	Braintree, MA (now Quincy)	Louisa Catherine Johnson Adams (1775-1852)
Andrew Jackson	Mar. 15, 1767	Waxhaw, SC	Rachel Donelson Robards Jackson (1767-1828)
Martin Van Buren	Dec. 5, 1782	Kinderhook, NY	Hannah Hoes Van Buren (1783-1819)
William Henry Harrison	Feb. 9, 1773	Charles City Co., VA	Ann Tuthill Symmes Harrison (1775-1864)
John Tyler	Mar. 29, 1790	Charles City Co., VA	Letitia Christian Tyler (1790-1842) Julia Gardiner Tyler (1820-1889)
James K. Polk	Nov. 2, 1795	Mecklenburg Co., NC	Sarah Childress Polk (1803-1891)
Zachary Taylor	Nov. 24, 1784	Orange County, VA	Margaret Mackall Smith Taylor (1788-1852)

Children	Occupation before presidency	Date of death	Place of death
none	Surveyor, Soldier, Planter	Dec. 17, 1799	Mount Vernon, VA
Abigail (1765-1813), John Quincy (1767-1848) Susanna (1768-1770), Charles (1770-1800) Thomas (1772-1832)	Lawyer, Politician	July 4, 1826	Quincy, MA
Martha (1772-1836), Mary (1778-1804)	Lawyer, Writer Politician	July 4, 1826	Charlottesville, VA
None	Lawyer, Politician	June 28, 1836	Montpelier, VA
Eliza (1786-1835), Maria (1803-1850)	Lawyer, Politician	July 4, 1831	New York, NY
George (1801-1829), John (1803-1834) Charles (1807-1886), Louisa (1811-1812)	Lawyer, Politician	Feb. 23, 1848	Washington, D.C.
None	Soldier, Politician	June 8, 1845	Nashville, TN
Abraham (1807-1873), John (1810-1866) Martin (1812-1855), Smith (1817-1876)	Lawyer, Politician	July 24, 1862	Kinderhook, NY
Elizabeth (1796-1846), John (1798-1830) Lucy (1800-1826), William (1802-1838) John (1804-1878), Benjamin (1806-1840) Mary (1809-1842), Carter (1811-1839) Anna (1813-1845), James (1814-1817)	Soldier	April 4, 1841	Washington, D.C.
Mary (1815-1848), Robert (1816-1877) John (1819-1896), Letitia (1821-1907) Elizabeth (1823-1850), Anne (1825-1825) Alice (1827-1854), Tazewell (1830-1874) David (1846-1927), John (1848-1883) Julia (1849-1871), Lachlan (1851-1902) Lyon (1853-1935), Robert (1856-1927) Pearl (1860-1947)	Lawyer, Politician	Jan. 18, 1862	Richmond, VA
None	Lawyer, Politician	June 15, 1849	Nashville, TN
Anne (1811-1829), Sarah (1814-1835) Octavia (1816-1820), Margaret (1819-1820) Mary (1824-1909), Richard (1826-1879)	Soldier	July 9, 1850	Washington, D.C.

President	Date of birth	Place of birth	Wife
Millard Fillmore	Jan. 7, 1800	Locke Township, NY	Abigail Powers Fillmore (1798-1853) Caroline Carmichael McIntosh
Franklin Pierce	Nov. 23, 1804	Hillsborough, NH	Jane Means Appleton Pierce (1806-1863)
James Buchanan	Apr. 23, 1791	Cove Gap, PA	
Abraham Lincoln	Feb. 12, 1809	Hardin County, KY	Mary Todd Lincoln (1818-1882)
Andrew Johnson	Dec. 29, 1808	Raleigh, NC	Eliza McCardle Johnson (1810-1876)
Ulysses S. Grant	Apr. 27, 1822	Point Pleasant, OH	Julia Boggs Dent Grant (1826-1902)
Rutherford B. Hayes	Oct. 4, 1822	Delaware, OH	Lucy Ware Webb Hayes (1831-1889)
James A. Garfield	Nov. 19, 1831	Orange, OH	Lucretia Rudolph Garfield (1832-1918)
Chester A. Arthur	Oct. 5, 1829	Fairfield, VT	Ellen Lewis Herndon Arthur (1837-1880)
Grover Cleveland	Mar. 18, 1837	Caldwell, NJ	Frances Folsom Cleveland (1864-1947)
Benjamin Harrison	Aug. 20, 1833	North Bend, OH	Caroline Lavinia Scott Harrison (1832-1892) Mary Scott Lord Dimmick Harrison (1858-1948)
William McKinley	Jan. 29, 1843	Niles, Ohio	Ida Saxton McKinley (1847-1907)
Theodore Roosevelt	Oct. 27, 1858	New York, NY	Alice Hathaway Lee Roosevelt (1861-1884) Edith Kermit Carow Roosevelt (1861-1948)

Children	Occupation before presidency	Date of death	Place of death
Millard (1828-1889), Mary (1832-1854) None	Lawyer, Politician	Mar. 8, 1874	Buffalo, NY
Franklin (1836-1836), Frank (1839-1843) Benjamin (1841-1853)	Lawyer, Politician	Oct. 8, 1869	Concord, NH
	Lawyer, Politician	June 1, 1868	Lancaster, PA
Robert (1843-1926), Edward (1846-1850) William (1850-1862), Thomas (1853-1871)	Lawyer, Politician	Apr. 15, 1865	Washington, D.C.
Martha (1828-1901), Charles (1830-1863) Mary (1832-1883), Robert (1834-1869) Andrew (1852-1879)	Tailor, Politician	July 31, 1875	Carter's Station, TN
Frederick (1850-1912), Ulysses (1852-1880) Ellen (1855-1922), Jesse (1858-1934)	Soldier	July 23, 1885	Mount McGregor, NY
Birchard (1853-1929), James (1856-1934) Rutherford (1858-1927), Joseph (1861-1863) George (1864-1866), Fanny (1867-1950) Scott (1871-1923), Manning (1873-1874)	Lawyer, Politician	Jan. 17, 1893	Fremont, OH
Eliza (1860-1863), Harry (1863-1942) James (1865-1950), Mary (1867-1947) Irvin (1870-1951), Abram (1872-1958) Edward (1874-1876)	Teacher, Politician	Sept. 19, 1881	Elberton, NJ
William (1860-1863), Chester (1864-1937) Ellen (1871-1915)	Lawyer, Politician	Nov. 18, 1886	New York, NY
Ruth (1891-1904), Esther (1893-1980) Marion (1895-1977), Richard (1897-1974) Francis (1903-1995)	Lawyer, Sheriff, Politician	June 24, 1908	Princeton, NJ
Russell (1854-1936), Mary (1858-1930) Elizabeth (1897-1955)	Lawyer, Politician	Mar. 13, 1901	Indianapolis, IN
Katherine (1871-1875), Ida (1873-1873)	Lawyer, Politician	Sept. 14, 1901	Buffalo, NY
Alice (1884-1980) Theodore (1887-1944), Kermit (1889-1943) Ethel (1891-1977), Archibald (1894-1979) Quentin (1897-1918)	Writer, Politician	Jan. 6, 1919	Oyster Bay, NY

THE PRESIDENTS' PERSONAL LIVES

President	Date of birth	Place of birth	Wife
William Howard Taft	Sept. 15, 1857	Cincinnati, OH	Helen Herron Taft (1861-1943)
Woodrow Wilson	Dec. 29, 1856	Staunton, VA	Ellen Louise Axson Wilson (1860-1914) Edith Bolling Galt Wilson (1872-1961)
Warren G. Harding	Nov. 2, 1865	Corsica, OH	Florence Kling De Wolf Harding (1860-1924)
Calvin Coolidge	July 4, 1872	Plymouth Notch, VT	Grace Anna Goodhue Coolidge (1879-1957)
Herbert Hoover	Aug. 10, 1874	West Branch, IA	Lou Henry Hoover (1874-1944)
Franklin D. Roosevelt	Jan. 30, 1882	Hyde Park, NY	Eleanor Roosevelt Roosevelt (1884-1962)
Harry S. Truman	May 8, 1884	Lamar, MO	Elizabeth (Bess) Wallace Truman (1885-1982)
Dwight D. Eisenhower	Oct. 14, 1890	Denison, TX	Mamie Geneva Doud Eisenhower (1896-1979)
John F. Kennedy	May 29, 1917	Brookline, MA	Jaqueline Lee Bouvier Kennedy (1929-1994)
Lyndon B. Johnson	Aug. 27, 1908	Stonewall, TX	Lady Bird (Claudia Alta) Taylor Johnson (1912-2007)
Richard M. Nixon	Jan. 9, 1913	Yorba Linda, CA	Thelma Catherine (Pat) Ryan Nixon (1912-1993)
Gerald R. Ford	July 14, 1913	Omaha, NE	Elizabeth (Betty) Bloomer Warren Ford (1918-)
Jimmy Carter	Oct. 1, 1924	Plains, GA	Rosalynn Smith Carter (1927-)
Ronald Reagan	Feb. 6, 1911	Tampico, IL	Jane Wyman (1914-) Nancy Davis Reagan (1921-)
George H.W. Bush	June 12, 1924	Milton, MA	Barbara Pierce Bush (1925-)
Bill Clinton	Aug. 19, 1946	Hope, AR	Hillary Rodham Clinton (1947-)
George W. Bush	July 6, 1946	New Haven, CT	Laura Welch Bush (1946-)
Barack Obama	Aug. 4, 1961	Honolulu, HI	Michelle Robinson Obama (1964-)

Children	Occupation before presidency	Date of death	Place of death
Robert (1889-1953), Helen (1891-1987) Charles (1897-1983)	Lawyer, Politician	Mar. 8, 1930	Washington, D.C.
Margaret (1886-1944), Jessie (1887-1933) Eleanor (1889-1967) none	Teacher, University president, Politician	Feb. 3, 1924	Washington, D.C.
none	Editor, Politician	Aug. 2, 1923	San Francisco, CA
John (1906-2000), Calvin (1908-1924)	Lawyer, Politician	Jan. 5, 1933	Northampton, MA
Herbert (1903-1969), Allan (1907-1993)	Engineer	Oct. 20, 1964	New York, NY
Anna (1906-1975), James (1907-1991) Franklin (1909-1909), Elliot (1910-1990) Franklin D. (1914-1988), John (1916-1981)	Lawyer, Politician	Apr. 12, 1945	Warm Springs, GA
Margaret (1924-2008)	Farmer, Politician	Dec. 26, 1972	Independence, MO
Dwight (1917-1920), John (1923-)	Soldier	Mar. 28, 1969	Washington, D.C.
Caroline (1957-), John (1960-1999) Patrick (1963-1963)	Author, Politician	Nov. 22, 1963	Dallas, TX
Lynda (1944-), Luci (1947-)	Politician	Jan. 22, 1973	Johnson City, TX
Patricia (1946-), Julie (1948-)	Lawyer, Politician	Apr. 22, 1994	New York, NY
Michael (1950-), John (1952-) Steven (1956-), Susan (1957-)	Lawyer, Politician	Dec. 26, 2006	Rancho Mirage, CA
John (1947-), James (1950-) Donnel (1952-), Amy (1967-)	Farmer, Politician		
Maureen (1941-2001), Michael (1945-) Patricia (1952-), Ronald (1958-)	Actor, Politician	June 5, 2004	Los Angeles, CA
George (1946-), Robin (1949-1953) John (1953-), Neil (1955-) Marvin (1956-), Dorothy (1959-)	Businesman, Politician		
Chelsea (1980-)	Professor, Politician		
Barbara (1981-), Jenna (1981-)	Businessman		
Malia (1998-), Sasha (2002-)	Politician		

The Presidents In Their Own Times

*Here is a list of important historical events that occurred during each President's term of office. In some cases, you will notice the same year listed under two Presidents' names. This is because some of these events happened during the final months of one President's term, before the next President was inaugurated, or if a President died in office. Words that appear in **bold-faced type** are explained fully in the "Glossary" section that starts on page 419.*

★ ★ ★ George Washington ★ ★ ★

1789   North Carolina becomes the 12th state
French Revolution ends monarchy in France
First act of **Congress** is passed
Congress establishes Department of Foreign Affairs (later the State Department).

1790   Rhode Island becomes the 13th state
Washington approves plans for a U.S. capital on the Potomac River
Supreme Court holds its first session
First U.S. census shows 3,929,214 people in the United States
John Tyler is born

1791   Vermont becomes the 14th state
Congress establishes the District of Columbia
Washington holds first **Cabinet** meeting
Bill of Rights becomes law
James Buchanan is born

1792 Kentucky becomes the 15th state
Columbus Day observed for the first time
Congress establishes first national mint to print money
Political parties begin to develop

1793 Washington lays cornerstone for the U.S. Capitol building
in Washington, D.C.
Eli Whitney invents the cotton gin. Mass production of
cotton leads to increased slave labor in the south.

1794 U.S. Navy is established

1795 First hard-surfaced toll road is built from Philadelphia to
Lancaster, PA
James K. Polk is born

1796 Tennessee becomes the 16th state

★ ★ ★ John Adams ★ ★ ★

1798 Department of the Navy is created
U.S. Marine Corps is created
Mississippi Territory is organized, which contains the
future states of Alabama and Mississippi

1799 Napoleon becomes dictator of France
George Washington dies

1800 Library of Congress is established
U.S. government moves into new capital at Washington, D.C.
Millard Fillmore is born
The U.S. population is 5,308,483
Indiana Territory is organized

★ ★ ★ Thomas Jefferson ★ ★ ★

1802 U.S. Military Academy is created at West Point, NY

1803 Ohio becomes the 17th state
President Jefferson authorizes the **Louisiana Purchase** from France for $15,000,000

1804 Lewis and Clark begin exploring Louisiana Territory
12th Amendment to the U.S. **Constitution** provides that the President and Vice President be elected separately
Franklin Pierce is born
First steam locomotive is built in Great Britain

1805 Michigan Territory is organized
Louisiana Territory is organized
Lewis and Clark reach the Pacific Ocean

1806 Zebulon M. Pike explores the Rocky Mountains and discovers Pikes Peak
Gas street lights are introduced

1807 Great Britain ends slave trade in their colonies
Robert Fulton launches the *Clermont*, his first successful steamboat
Territory of Orleans is organized

1808 **Congress** prohibits the importation of slaves into the U.S.
Andrew Johnson is born

1809 Illinois Territory is organized
Abraham Lincoln is born

★ ★ ★ James Madison ★ ★ ★

1810 The U.S. population is 7,239,881

1811 William Henry Harrison defeats Indian forces at the Battle
of Tippecanoe

1812 Louisiana becomes the 18th state
U.S. declares war on Great Britain, beginning the **War of
1812**
Napoleon invades Russia, and later retreats in defeat
Missouri Territory is organized

1813 Francis Scott Key writes the words to "The Star-Spangled
Banner"
British forces capture Washington, D.C. and burn the White
House
Oliver Hazard Perry defeats British naval forces at the
Battle of Lake Erie
The Treaty of Ghent ends the **War of 1812**

1814 Andrew Jackson defeats British forces at the Battle of New
Orleans
Napoleon is defeated at Waterloo, Belgium

1815 Indiana becomes the 19th state

1817 Alabama Territory is organized

★ ★ ★ James Monroe ★ ★ ★

1817 Mississippi becomes the 20th state
Construction begins on the Erie Canal

1818 U.S. flag design established by **Congress**
Illinois becomes the 21st state

1819 Alabama becomes the 22nd state
U.S. acquires Florida in treaty with Spain
Arkansas Territory is organized

1820 Maine becomes the 23rd state
Missouri Compromise approved by **Congress**, which tem-
porarily settles disputes about **slavery** in the U.S. terri-
tories.
First football game is played in U.S.
Washington Irving writes "Rip Van Winkle"
First public high school in the U.S. opens in Boston, MA
The U.S. population is 9,638,453

1821 Missouri becomes the 24th state
The Santa Fe Trail opens trade to the Southwest
Napoleon dies
Central American republics declare independence from Spain

1822 Brazil declares independence from Portugal
Clement Moore writes "A Visit from St. Nicholas"
Ulysses S. Grant is born
Rutherford B. Hayes is born
Florida Territory is organized

1823 **Monroe Doctrine** guarantees independence of the
Americas against any European interference

1824 Great Salt Lake is discovered in Utah
Mexico becomes an independent republic

★ ★ ★ John Quincy Adams ★ ★ ★

1825 Erie Canal is completed

1826 John Adams and Thomas Jefferson die on July 4

1828 First railroad in the U.S., the Baltimore & Ohio, begins construction

Noah Webster publishes the first U.S. dictionary

★ ★ ★ Andrew Jackson ★ ★ ★

1829 Chester A. Arthur is born

1830 Under the Indian Removal Act, federal troops drive thousands of Indians west of the Mississippi River, on the "Trail of Tears"

The U.S. population is 12,860,702

1831 Cyrus McCormick invents the reaping machine

William Lloyd Garrison begins publishing his antislavery newspaper, *The Liberator*

James A. Garfield is born

James Monroe dies

1832 The **Democratic Party** holds its first national convention

South Carolina declares federal **tariff** null and void

Jackson issues Proclamation on Nullification, calling disunion treason

Vice President John Calhoun resigns

1833 *The New York Sun*, the first successful penny newspaper, is founded

Benjamin Harrison is born

Slavery is abolished in the British Empire

1836 Arkansas becomes the 25th state

Texas declares independence from Mexico

Samuel Colt makes the first Colt revolver, known as the "six-shooter"

Wisconsin Territory is organized

The first child labor laws in the U.S. are passed in
Massachusetts

Alonzo C. Phillips invents matches

James Madison dies

1837 Michigan becomes the 26th state

Grover Cleveland is born

★ ★ ★ Martin Van Buren ★ ★ ★

1837 The first economic "depression" in the U.S. brings
economic hardship

Victoria becomes Queen of England

Charles Goodyear patents rubber

General Zachary Taylor defeats Seminole Indians at
Okeechobee swamp

1838 Iowa Territory is organized

Morse code is invented

1839 Bicycle is invented

1840 First dental school in U.S. opens in Baltimore

Britain issues the first postage stamp

The U.S. population is 17,063,353

★ ★ ★ William Henry Harrison ★ ★ ★

1841 **Supreme Court** decision frees Africans who seized the
slave ship *Amistad*

William Henry Harrison dies in office

★ ★ ★ John Tyler ★ ★ ★

1842   Henry Clay retires after 36 years in **Congress**

Webster-Ashburton Treaty settles boundary between Maine and Canada

Mt. St. Helens erupts

China opens its ports to world trade

Kit Carson and John C. Frémont begin exploration of the Western U.S.

1843   Mt. Rainier erupts

William McKinley is born

1844   First news dispatch is sent by telegraph

U.S. signs peace and trade treaty with China

1845   Florida becomes the 27th state

Texas is annexed to U.S.

Congress overrides presidential veto for first time

★ ★ ★ James K. Polk ★ ★ ★

1845   Texas becomes the 28th state

U.S. Naval Academy is established at Annapolis, Maryland

Andrew Jackson dies

1846   Iowa becomes the 29th state

The **Mexican War** between the U.S. and Mexico begins

Elias Howe patents the sewing machine

Michigan becomes the first state to abolish the death penalty

Treaty with Great Britain fixes boundary between Oregon and Canada

1847　First U.S. postage stamps are issued

Liberia becomes the first black African republic

1848　Wisconsin becomes the 30th state

Treaty of Guadalupe Hidalgo ends war with Mexico

Gold is discovered in California

Oregon Territory is organized

Women's rights convention meets at Seneca Falls, New York

Karl Marx writes the *Communist Manifesto*

President Polk lays the cornerstone for the Washington
　Memorial

John Quincy Adams dies

1849　Minnesota Territory is organized

★ ★ ★ Zachary Taylor ★ ★ ★

1849　Department of Interior is created

The California Gold Rush begins

U.S. signs treaty with Hawaii

James K. Polk dies

1850　Compromise of 1850 averts civil war over **slavery**

Zachary Taylor dies in office

The U.S. population is 23,191,876

★ ★ ★ Millard Fillmore ★ ★ ★

1850　California becomes the 31st state

Fugitive slave law is passed, making return of runaway
　slaves a federal law

Amelia Bloomer wears pantaloons to draw attention to the
　movement to grant women the right to vote. Her follow-
　ers become known as "Bloomer Girls"

New Mexico Territory is organized
Utah Territory is organized

1852 Direct train service between New York City and Chicago
begins
Harriet Beecher Stowe publishes *Uncle Tom's Cabin*
Commodore Matthew Perry is sent to open trade with
Japan

1853 Washington Territory is organized

★ ★ ★ Franklin Pierce ★ ★ ★

1853 Turkey, Britain, France and Sardinia fight Russia in the
Crimean War
President Pierce opens the Crystal Palace Exposition in
New York City

1854 The **Republican Party** is formed
The Gadsden Purchase is signed, settling the border
between the Southwestern U.S. and Mexico
The Kansas-Nebraska Act is passed, allowing state determi-
nation on **slavery**, and nullifying the Missouri
Compromise
Kansas Territory is organized
Nebraska Territory is organized

1855 The Soo Canal in Sault St. Marie, MI, is opened for shipping

1856 Fighting between pro-slavery and anti-slavery factions in
"Bleeding Kansas" begins
Henry Bessemer patents the Bessemer converter for
making steel
Woodrow Wilson is born

★ ★ ★ James Buchanan ★ ★ ★

1857 U.S. troops are sent to Utah Territory to stop a rebellion by
Brigham Young
Supreme Court, under Chief Justice Taney declares the
Missouri Compromise unconstitutional in the Dred Scott
decision
William Howard Taft is born

1858 Minnesota becomes the 32nd state
First transatlantic cable is laid on the bottom of the
Atlantic Ocean, allowing telegraph communication
between the U.S. and Britain
The Lincoln-Douglas debates in Illinois focus on the
question of **slavery**
Theodore Roosevelt is born

1859 Oregon becomes the 33rd state
Oil is discovered in Pennsylvania
Abolitionist John Brown seizes federal arsenal at Harper's
Ferry
Construction begins on the Suez Canal in Egypt
Darwin publishes his theory of evolution

1860 Pony Express service begins between St. Joseph, MO, and
Sacramento, CA
After the election of Abraham Lincoln, South Carolina
becomes the first state to secede from the union
The U.S. population is 31,443,321

1861 Kansas becomes the 34th state
Colorado Territory is organized
Nevada Territory is organized
Dakota Territory is organized
Confederate States of America are formed, Jefferson Davis
is elected its President

★ ★ ★ Abraham Lincoln ★ ★ ★

1861 **Civil War** begins with Confederate attack on Fort Sumpter, SC, on April 12

First transcontinental telegraph line is completed

French troops invade Mexico

Confederate army wins the First Battle of Bull Run

1862 *Monitor* and *Merrimack* fight first naval battle between iron-clads

Slavery is abolished in Washington, D.C.

Department of Agriculture is created

The Homestead Act is passed, allowing any settler to obtain 160 acres of public land at no charge

John Tyler dies

Martin Van Buren dies

1863 President Lincoln issues the **Emancipation Proclamation,** freeing the slaves in the **Confederacy**

West Virginia becomes the 35th state

The first military draft law in U.S. history is passed

Union army wins the Battle of Gettysburg

Ulysses S. Grant captures Vicksburg, MS

President Lincoln delivers the Gettysburg address

The world's first subway opens in London, England

The Arizona and Idaho Territories are organized

1864 Nevada becomes the 36th state

William T. Sherman captures Atlanta, GA

Montana Territory is organized

1865 General Robert E. Lee surrenders Confederate troops to Ulysses S. Grant at Appomattox Court House on April 9, ending the **Civil War**

President Lincoln is shot by John Wilkes Booth on April 14. He dies the next day.

★ ★ ★ Andrew Johnson ★ ★ ★

1865   The 13th Amendment to the U.S. **Constitution** frees all
remaining slaves in the U.S.
Warren G. Harding is born

1867   Nebraska becomes the 37th state
U.S. purchases Alaska from Russia
Britain creates the Dominion of Canada
Alfred Nobel invents dynamite

1868   Wyoming Territory is organized
Railroad refrigerator car developed
First practical typewriter is patented
President Johnson becomes the first U.S. President to face
impeachment by **Congress**. He is tried in the **Senate** and
is acquitted by one vote. He remains President.
The 14th Amendment to the U.S. **Constitution** grants
citizenship to former slaves

★ ★ ★ Ulysses S. Grant ★ ★ ★

1868   James Buchanan dies

1869   The first transcontinental railroad in the U.S. is completed
at Promontory Point, Utah
The Suez Canal is opened
Franklin Pierce dies

1870   The Department of Justice is created
The Franco-Prussian War begins
The U.S. population is 36,558,371

1872   The first national park is created at Yellowstone
Calvin Coolidge is born

1874   Millard Fillmore dies
         Herbert Hoover is born

1875   Andrew Johnson dies

1876   Colorado becomes the 38th state
         Alexander Graham Bell invents the telephone
         Indians massacre General Custer and his troops at Little
             Big Horn

★ ★ ★ Rutherford B. Hayes ★ ★ ★

1877   Federal troops are withdrawn from the South, ending
         Reconstruction
         Thomas Edison invents the phonograph

1879   Thomas Edison develops the first practical electric light
             bulb
         James and John Ritty invent the cash register

1880   The U.S. population is 50,189,209

★ ★ ★ James A. Garfield ★ ★ ★

1881   American Red Cross is founded
         Czar Alexander II of Russia is assassinated
         President James Garfield is shot on July 2, and dies on
             September 19

★ ★ ★ Chester A. Arthur ★ ★ ★

1882   Franklin D. Roosevelt is born

1883   Standard time zones are adopted by the railroads
         The Brooklyn Bridge is completed

1884   Construction begins on the world's first skyscraper in
Chicago
Harry S. Truman is born

1885   The Washington Monument is dedicated

★ ★ ★ Grover Cleveland ★ ★ ★

1885   Ulysses S. Grant dies
Apache chief Geronimo begins his guerrilla raids in Arizona
and New Mexico

1886   The Statue of Liberty is dedicated in New York City
Chester A. Arthur dies

★ ★ ★ Benjamin Harrison ★ ★ ★

1889   North Dakota becomes the 39th state
South Dakota becomes the 40th state
Montana becomes the 41st state
Washington becomes the 42nd state
Oklahoma Territory is organized
The Eiffel Tower is dedicated in Paris, France

1890   Idaho becomes the 43rd state
Wyoming becomes the 44th state
The Sherman Anti-Trust Act is passed to curb monopolies
Dwight D. Eisenhower is born
The U.S. population is 62,979,766

1891   James A. Naismith invents basketball
The International Copyright Act is passed

★ ★ ★ Grover Cleveland ★ ★ ★

1893   Rutherford B. Hayes dies
President Cleveland opens the Chicago World's Fair

1895 Guglielmo Marconi invents the wireless telegraph
Cuban revolt against Spanish rule begins

1896 Utah becomes the 45th state
Henry Ford builds his first car

★ ★ ★ William McKinley ★ ★ ★

1898 The battleship *Maine* blows up in Havana Harbor on
February 15, beginning the **Spanish-American War**
The Treaty of Paris ends the **Spanish-American War**
December 10. Hawaii, Guam, Puerto Rico, and the
Philippines become U.S. possessions
In France, Pierre and Marie Curie discover radioactivity,
and the element radium

1899 The Boer War between the British and Dutch begins in
South Africa

1900 Walter Reed helps conquer typhoid fever and yellow fever
through experiments he runs in Cuba
The American Baseball league is organized
Sigmund Freud develops psychoanalysis in Austria
The U.S. population is 76,212,168

1901 Benjamin Harrison dies
President McKinley is shot on September 6. He dies on
September 14.

★ ★ ★ Theodore Roosevelt ★ ★ ★

1901 First wireless telegraph message is sent across the Atlantic

1903 The Wright brothers make the first airplane flight at
Kittyhawk, NC
The Department of Commerce and Labor is established

1904   Work on the Panama Canal begins

1905   Albert Einstein publishes his theory of relativity

1906   The Federal Food and Drug Act is passed, creating
            standards for producing safe food and medicine
            The San Francisco Earthquake destroys much of the city
            President Roosevelt wins the Nobel Peace Prize for helping
            to end the Russo-Japanese War

1907   Oklahoma becomes the 46th state

1908   The Federal Bureau of Investigation is established
            Lyndon B. Johnson is born
            Grover Cleveland dies
            The first "Model T" Ford goes on sale

★ ★ ★ William Howard Taft ★ ★ ★

1909   Admiral Robert Peary discovers the North Pole

1910   The Boy Scouts of America is founded
            The Union of South Africa is founded
            The Mexican Revolution begins
            The U.S. population is 92,228,496

1911   Roald Amundsen discovers the South Pole
            Ronald Reagan is born

1912   New Mexico becomes the 47th state
            Arizona becomes the 48th state

1913   Parcel-post service begins
            The 16th Amendment to the U.S. **Constitution** gives the fed-
            eral government the power to collect taxes on income
            Richard M. Nixon is born

★ ★ ★ Woodrow Wilson ★ ★ ★

1913   The Federal Reserve System is created
Gerald R. Ford is born

1914   **World War I** begins in Europe
The Panama Canal is open to shipping

1915   The first transcontinental telephone line linking New York
City and San Francisco begins operating
German submarine sinks the British passenger ship
Lusitania

1916   Jeannette Rankin of Montana is the first woman elected to
the U.S. **Congress**

1917   The U.S. enters **World War I**
The U.S. acquires the Virgin Islands from Denmark
John F. Kennedy is born

1918   Armistice ends fighting in Europe
President Wilson outlines the "Fourteen Points," which
calls for the creation of the League of Nations

1919   The Treaty of Versailles officially ends **World War I**
The 18th Amendment to the U.S. **Constitution** outlaws the
sale and use of alcohol
Theodore Roosevelt dies

1920   The League of Nations holds its first session
President Wilson is awarded the Nobel Peace Prize
The 19th Amendment to the U.S. **Constitution** gives women
the right to vote
The first commercial radio broadcasts begin in Detroit and
Pittsburgh
The U.S. population is 106,021,537

1921   The first transcontinental air mail service between New York City and San Francisco begins

★ ★ ★ Warren G. Harding ★ ★ ★

1921   The Tomb of the Unknown Soldier is dedicated at Arlington Cemetery
West Virginia enacts the first state sales tax

1922   Benito Mussolini becomes dictator of Italy
The Union of Soviet Socialist Republics is formed by the Communist Party
H. A. Berliner flies the first helicopter

1923   Warren Harding dies in office

★ ★ ★ Calvin Coolidge ★ ★ ★

1924   The U.S. Foreign Service is created
Citizenship is granted to American Indians born in the U.S.
The first diesel electric locomotive is put into service
Jimmy Carter is born
George Bush is born
Woodrow Wilson dies

1925   Nellie Tayloe Ross of Wyoming becomes the first woman Governor of a U.S. state

1926   Richard Byrd and Floyd Bennett make the first flight over the North Pole
The first liquid fuel rocket is launched

1927   Charles Lindbergh flies nonstop across the Atlantic
The Jazz Singer, the first "talking" movie, is produced

★ ★ ★ Herbert Hoover ★ ★ ★

1929 Stock Market crash marks the beginning of the **Great Depression**
Richard Byrd makes the first flight over the South Pole

1930 The Veterans Administration is created
Work begins on Boulder (later Hoover) Dam
William Howard Taft dies
The U.S. population is 123,202,624

1931 The "Star-Spangled Banner" is adopted as the national anthem
Construction begins on the *Ranger*, the first aircraft carrier

1932 Adolf Hitler rises to power in Germany

1933 The 20th Amendment to the U.S. **Constitution** changes Presidential inauguration from March 4 to January 20
Calvin Coolidge dies

★ ★ ★ Franklin D. Roosevelt ★ ★ ★

1933 The "Hundred Days" congressional session enacts the **New Deal** recovery programs
The 21st Amendment to the U.S. **Constitution** ends prohibition
The U.S. begins diplomatic relations with the Soviet Union

1935 The Social Security Act is passed

1936 Francisco Franco becomes dictator of Spain during the Spanish Civil War

1939 Nazi Germany invades Poland, beginning **World War II**
New York World's Fair opens

1940   Winston Churchill becomes Prime Minister of Great Britain
President Roosevelt is elected to a third term for the first
and only time in U.S. history
German forces capture France
The U.S. population is 132,164,569

1941   The U.S. declares war on Japan after attack on Pearl
Harbor on December 7
Germany invades the Soviet Union

1942   Japanese forces capture the Philippine Islands
The U.S. Navy sinks a Japanese aircraft carrier fleet at the
Battle of Midway
Allied forces invade North Africa
First nuclear chain reaction is achieved by scientists at the
University of Chicago

1943   Allied forces invade Italy
Soviet troops defeat the German Army at Stalingrad

1944   Allied forces invade France at Normandy on "D-Day"

1945   Roosevelt, Churchill, and Stalin meet at Yalta to determine
post-war policies
President Roosevelt dies in office

★ ★ ★ Harry S. Truman ★ ★ ★

1945   Germany surrenders to Allied forces on May 7, ending the
war in Europe
The United Nations is founded
The U.S. drops atomic bombs on Hiroshima and Nagasaki
Japan
Japan surrenders to Allied forces on August 14, ending the
war in the Pacific

1946   **Congress** creates the Atomic Energy Commission
The **Cold War** begins
George W. Bush is born
Bill Clinton is born

1948   The Marshall Plan provides aid to war-torn countries of
Europe
Israel becomes a republic

1949   The North Atlantic Treaty Organization (NATO) is created
to help protect Western Europe from Soviet expansion

1950   The **Korean War** begins
The U.S. population is 151,325,798

1951   The first nationwide telecast is made

1952   Puerto Rico becomes a U.S. commonwealth
The first U.S. hydrogen bomb is detonated

★ ★ ★ Dwight D. Eisenhower ★ ★ ★

1953   **Korean War** ends

1954   U.S. **Supreme Court** rules that racial segregation in public
schools is unconstitutional
The first nuclear submarine, the *Nautilus*, is launched

1955   Jonas Salk's polio vaccine helps end deadly polio epidemics
President Eisenhower suffers heart attack

1957   The Soviet Union launches *Sputnik I*, beginning the Space
Age
Federal troops are sent to Little Rock, AR, to enforce racial
integration in schools

1958   The first U.S. space satellite, *Explorer I*, is launched
U.S. airlines begin jet passenger service

1959   Alaska becomes the 49th state
Hawaii becomes the 50th state
The St. Lawrence Seaway is completed
Fidel Castro becomes dictator of Cuba

1960   The U.S. severs diplomatic relations with Cuba
The U.S. population is 179,323,175

★ ★ ★ John F. Kennedy ★ ★ ★

1961   President creates the Peace Corps
The 23rd Amendment to the U.S. **Constitution** grants voting
rights to residents of Washington, D.C.
Soviet Cosmonaut Yuri Gagarin becomes the first person to
travel in space
The Communist government in East Berlin builds the Berlin
Wall

1962   John Glenn becomes the first American to orbit the earth
The **Supreme Court** rules that prayer in public schools is
unconstitutional
The U.S. launches *Telstar I*, beginning the age of satellite
communications
The U.S. and Soviet Union narrowly avoid nuclear war over
the Cuban Missile Crisis

1963   The U.S. signs the nuclear test ban treaty
200,000 attend the Freedom March for civil rights in
Washington, D.C.
President Kennedy is assassinated on November 22, in
Dallas, TX, by Lee Harvey Oswald

★ ★ ★ Lyndon B. Johnson ★ ★ ★

1964   President Johnson sends antipoverty program to **Congress**
The Civil Rights Act is signed into law
Herbert Hoover dies

1965   U.S. Marines land in South Vietnam beginning direct U.S.
military involvement in the **Vietnam War**
Medicare bill is signed, providing health care for the elderly
Voting rights bill is signed
Urban riot explodes in the Watts area of Los Angeles, CA

1966   Robert C. Weaver becomes the first African American
Cabinet member

1967   Thurgood Marshall becomes the first African American
Supreme Court Justice
Urban riots break out in Newark, NJ and Detroit, MI
The first successful human heart transplant is performed

1968   President Johnson announces he will not run for reelection
Dr. Martin Luther King is assassinated in Memphis, TN
Senator Robert F. Kennedy is assassinated in Los Angeles
shortly after winning the California presidential primary

★ ★ ★ Richard M. Nixon ★ ★ ★

1969   U.S. astronauts Neil Armstrong and Edwin Aldrin Jr.
become the first people to walk on the moon
Dwight D. Eisenhower dies

1970   Four students are killed by National Guard gunfire during
an anti-war protest at Kent State University in Ohio
The National Railroad Passenger Corp. (Amtrak) is established by **Congress**
The U.S. population is 203,302,031

1971   President Nixon begins to improve diplomatic relations
with Communist China
Communist China becomes a member of the United
Nations

1972   Five men are arrested in burglary of **Democratic Party** head-
quarter at the **Watergate** complex in Washington, D.C.
U.S. combat troops are withdrawn from Vietnam
The U.S. and Soviet Union sign the first strategic arms limi-
tation treaty
Harry S. Truman dies

1973   Vice President Spiro T. Agnew resigns after allegations of
corruption
Gerald R. Ford becomes Vice President
Several members of the Nixon administration are indicted
for crimes related to the **Watergate** break-in
Lyndon B. Johnson dies

1974   Faced with **impeachment** for his involvement in the
Watergate break-in, President Nixon resigns

★ ★ ★ Gerald R. Ford ★ ★ ★

1974   President Ford grants pardon to Richard Nixon

1975   The **Vietnam War** ends when Viet Cong troops capture
Saigon
Cambodian government surrenders to Communist rebels
The first joint U.S. and Soviet space project is launched

1976   *Viking I* lands on Mars

★ ★ ★ Jimmy Carter ★ ★ ★

1977   The Trans-Alaska oil pipeline is opened
The Department of Energy is created

1978 President signs the Panama Canal treaty, returning the
canal zone to Panamanian authority
The Camp David Accords establish peace between Israel
and Egypt
Polish Cardinal Karol Wojtyla is elected Pope John Paul II

1979 U.S. establishes full diplomatic relations with China
Oil producing nations increase oil prices creating fuel
shortages in the U.S.
The Shah of Iran is deposed
Iranian militants take 66 U.S. Embassy employees hostage
in Teheran, Iran
Sandinista rebels take control of Nicaragua
The Department of Education is created

1980 Thirteen percent inflation rate causes a crisis in the U.S.
economy
Soviet-backed rebels take control of the government in
Afghanistan; President Carter announces an economic
embargo against the Soviet Union. The U.S. boycotts the
1980 Moscow Olympic Games in protest over the inva-
sion of Afghanistan
Mount St. Helens erupts
War between Iran and Iraq begins
The U.S. population is 226,542,199

★ ★ ★ Ronald Reagan ★ ★ ★

1981 U.S. hostages are freed in Iran
The U.S. space shuttle *Columbia*, the first reusable space
craft, is launched
Sandra Day O'Connor becomes the first woman **Supreme
Court** Justice

President Reagan proposes a 3-stage tax cut, the largest in
  U.S. history

Egyptian President Anwar Sadat is assassinated by Muslim
  extremists

1982   First artificial heart is successfully implanted

1984   Indian Prime Minister Indira Gandhi is assassinated

China announces plans to adopt free-market economic
  policies

1986   Space shuttle Challenger explodes shortly after take-off;
  the worst accident in NASA history

President Reagan orders air strikes against Libya in retalia-
  tion for terrorist attacks on Americans

1987   The U.S. stock market withstands the largest single-day
  drop in U.S. history

President Reagan and Soviet Premier Gorbachev sign the
  first nuclear arms reduction treaty in history

1988   The eight year war between Iran and Iraq ends

★ ★ ★ George Bush ★ ★ ★

1989   Pro-democracy demonstrations by Chinese students in
  Beijing results in bloody government crack-down

The Berlin Wall is torn down, beginning the reunification of
  Germany

Communist rule ends in Poland, Czechoslovakia, Romania
  and East Germany

1990   Iraq invades Kuwait

The *Exxon Valdez* runs aground off Alaska, causing the
  worst oil spill in U.S. history

The U.S. population is 248,709,873

1991 U.N troops force Iraq out of Kuwait during the Persian **Gulf War**

The Soviet Union is dissolved and Communist rule ends in Russia

★ ★ ★ Bill Clinton ★ ★ ★

1994 Richard M. Nixon dies

Ronald Reagan announces that he has Alzheimer's Disease

1994 Nelson Mandela elected President of South Africa

1995 U.S. normalizes relations with Vietnam

The Dayton Accord is signed, to end conflict in the Balkans

Yitzhak Rabin, Prime Minister of Israel, is assassinated

1998 Terrorists bomb U.S. Embassies in Kenya and Tanzania; 224 killed and thousands injured

President Clinton becomes the second U.S. President to face **impeachment** by **Congress**

1999 President Clinton is tried in the **Senate** and found not guilty

U.S. forces take part in NATO bombing attacks against Yugoslavia

2000 Scientists announce that the human genome, the genetic pattern underlying human development, has been decoded

Results of the Presidential election in dispute for five weeks as lawyers for Al Gore and **George W. Bush** challenge the results of the Florida vote in court. Bush takes his challenge to the U.S. **Supreme Court**, arguing that the votes were not handled equally and fairly. The court rules in his favor on December 12. He is declared President.

The U.S. population is 281,421,906

★ ★ ★ George W. Bush ★ ★ ★

2001 September 11: Terrorists attack the World Trade Center in New York City and the Pentagon in Washington, D.C.; nearly 3,000 people are killed

2003 The United States invades Iraq and Afghanistan as part of an international coalition

2004 Ronald Reagan dies

2006 Gerald R. Ford dies

2008 Worldwide economic downturn causes recession in U.S. economy

Indexes

There are three indexes in this section. There is a **Subject Index, a Places of Birth Index,** and **Birthday Index.**

- The **Subject Index** includes all Presidents, First Ladies, and important historical and political events and topics covered in the entries. Bold-faced type indicates the primary entry on the President.

- The **Places of Birth Index** lists all the birth places of the Presidents, arranged alphabetically by state, and within state by name.

- The **Birthday Index** lists all birthdays, including birth year, of the Presidents.

Subject Index

Places of Birth Index

This Index lists the places of birth of the Presidents. Under the state of birth, the Presidents' names are listed alphabetically, followed by the city of birth.

Arkansas
Clinton, Bill — *Hope*

California
Nixon, Richard M. — *Yorba Linda*

Connecticut
Bush, George W. — *New Haven*

Georgia
Carter, Jimmy — *Plains*

Hawaii
Obama, Barack— *Honolulu*

Illinois
Reagan, Ronald — *Tampico*

Iowa
Hoover, Herbert — *West Branch*

Kentucky
Lincoln, Abraham — *Hardin County*

Massachusetts
Adams, John — *Braintree,* now *Quincy*

Adams, John Quincy — *Braintree,* now *Quincy*
Bush, George — *Milton*
Kennedy, John F. — *Brookline*

Missouri
Truman, Harry S. — *Lamar*

Nebraska
Ford, Gerald R. — *Omaha*

New Hampshire
Pierce, Franklin — *Hillsborough*

New Jersey
Cleveland, Grover — *Caldwell*

New York
Fillmore, Millard — *Locke Township*
Roosevelt, Franklin D. — *Hyde Park*
Roosevelt, Theodore — *New York City*
Van Buren, Martin — *Kinderhook*

North Carolina

Polk, James K. — *Mecklenberg County*

Johnson, Andrew — *Raleigh*

Ohio

Garfield, James A. — *Orange*

Grant, Ulysses S. — *Point Pleasant*

Harding, Warren G. — *Corsica*

Harrison, Benjamin — *North Bend*

Hayes, Rutherford B. — *Delaware*

McKinley, William — *Niles*

Taft, William Howard — *Cincinnati*

Pennsylvania

Buchanan, James — *Cove Gap*

South Carolina

Jackson, Andrew — *Waxhaw*

Texas

Eisenhower, Dwight D. — *Denison*

Johnson, Lyndon B. — *Stonewall*

Vermont

Arthur, Chester A. — *Fairfield*

Coolidge, Calvin — *Plymouth Notch*

Virginia

Harrison, William Henry — *Charles City County*

Jefferson, Thomas — *Goochland*

Madison, James — *Port Conway*

Monroe, James — *Westmoreland County*

Taylor, Zachary — *Orange County*

Tyler, John — *Charles City County*

Washington, George — *Westmoreland County*

Wilson, Woodrow — *Staunton*

Birthday Index

January
7 Millard Fillmore (1800)
9 Richard Nixon (1913)
29 William McKinley (1843)
30 Franklin D. Roosevelt (1882)

February
6 Ronald Reagan (1911)
9 William Henry Harrison (1773)
12 Abraham Lincoln (1809)
22 George Washington (1732)

March
15 Andrew Jackson (1767)
16 James Madison (1751)
18 Grover Cleveland (1837)
29 John Tyler (1790)

April
13 Thomas Jefferson (1743)
23 James Buchanan (1791)
27 Ulysses S. Grant (1822)
28 James Monroe (1758)

May
8 Harry S. Truman (1884)
29 John F. Kennedy (1917)

June
12 George Bush (1924)

July
4 Calvin Coolidge (1872)

6 George W. Bush (1946)
11 John Quincy Adams (1767)
14 Gerald R. Ford (1913)

August
4 Barack Obama (1961)
10 Herbert Hoover (1874)
19 Bill Clinton (1946)
20 Benjamin Harrison (1833)
27 Lyndon B. Johnson (1908)

September
15 William Howard Taft (1857)

October
1 Jimmy Carter (1924)
4 Rutherford B. Hayes (1822)
5 Chester A. Arthur (1829)
14 Dwight D. Eisenhower (1890)
27 Theodore Roosevelt (1858)
30 John Adams (1735)

November
2 James K. Polk (1795)
  Warren G. Harding (1865)
19 James A. Garfield (1831)
23 Franklin Pierce (1804)
24 Zachary Taylor (1784)

December
5 Martin Van Buren (1782)
29 Andrew Johnson (1808)
  Woodrow Wilson (1856)